This LAUGH IS ON ME
The Phil Silvers Story

This LAUGH

by *Phil Silvers* ❧ ❧ *with Robert Saffron* ❧

PRENTICE-HALL, INC. ❧

IS ON ME

The Phil Silvers Story

 Englewood Cliffs, N. J.

This Laugh Is On Me: The Phil Silvers Story
by Phil Silvers with Robert Saffron
Copyright © 1973 by Phil Silvers and Robert Saffron
Copyright under International and Pan American
Copyright Conventions
Printed in the United States of America
Prentice-Hall International, Inc., London
Prentice-Hall of Australia, Pty. Ltd., North Sydney
Prentice-Hall of Canada, Ltd., Toronto
Prentice-Hall of India Private Ltd., New Delhi
Prentice-Hall of Japan, Inc., Tokyo
10 9 8 7 6 5 4 3 2 1

Library of Congress Cataloging in Publication Data

Silvers, Phil
This laugh is on me.

1.   Silvers, Phil   I. Saffron,
Robert, joint author.   II.   Title.
PN2287.S384A326   790'.092'4 [B]   73-11052
ISBN 0-13-919100-3

This book is for my five daughters: Tracey, Nancey, Cathy, Candy and Laury. My deep love for them has been the most enduring, purest fact of my life. I am also grateful to my own

Athos: Freddie Fields

Porthos: Ed Traubner

Aramis: Shep Fields

Contents

Prologue

The place—the New Ed Sullivan Theatre on 53rd and Broadway.

The date—April 23, 1972.

The occasion—the Annual Antoinette Perry Awards (the Tony Award) for outstanding contribution to the live theater.

The precise moment—Gwen Verdon, the mistress of ceremonies, is opening the envelope to announce to the distinguished gathering in the theater and the vast television audience, "And now for the best performance by a male star in a musical, the winner is——" Cut. Let's take it from the top. . . .

CHAPTER 1

"Brownsville's Own Sophie Tucker"

When I was eight I sang at a stag coming-out-of-jail party for a local hoodlum named Little Doggie. In the middle of my number, a man was shot dead at my feet.

The Brownsville section of Brooklyn was a tough neighborhood in the 1920's, so I didn't think that was too strange. My first reaction was, is the program chairman going to pay me my $3?

My specialty number was "Break the News to Mother," a surefire tearjerker. My audience—the pugs in Willie Beecher's gym, where I often sang while they were being rubbed down; the guys in the beer halls; the Murder Inc. enforcers in the hoodlum clubs—always wiped away a furtive tear.

> *Break the news to Mother*
> *She knows how much I love her.*
> *And tell her not to wait for me,*
> *'Cause I'm not coming home.*
>
> *Just say there is no other*
> *Can take the place of Mother,*
> *And tell her not to wait for me*
> *'Cause I'm not coming home.*

It was Little Doggie's special request. He was not a lovable figure in the neighborhood, but he came by his name honestly. A fellow hoodlum had a stranglehold on him in a street brawl, so Doggie raised himself on his hands and bit off the guy's thumb.

Little Doggie's coming-out party followed a routine scenario. Friends paid for the hall and drinks. It was stag, but very proper. No girls, just Prohibition booze and welcome back, buddy. Guns were checked at the door. The guest of honor was responsible for the peace of the evening, and any undue violence was a great affront to him.

> (*Broadway Social Hall: one flight up. Dark, one small pink spotlight on the raised platform. Tables set up for a cabaret.*)
>
> ME (*singing*): ". . . *there is no other, can take the place of Mother . . .*"
>
> (*Two executioners come in through the revolving door, guns drawn. One is named Curly. I don't know the other. They rub out their target. It doesn't seem fair to me because they're the only ones with guns. They back toward the exit.*)
>
> LITTLE DOGGIE (*standing in their way*): "*I thought you was my pals. How can you do this to me at my party?*" (*He pulls a knife.*)
>
> CURLY (*backing away slowly, affectionately*): "*Hey, Doggie, we don't want you. We've been laying for this creep for months.*"
>
> DOGGIE: "*You bastards.*" (*He keeps coming for them, so they wing him. He falls into the revolving door. They push the door against him, to squeeze through. His head is caught there, and I hear the sickening crunch. I grab my $3 and run down the fire escape, puking over my new velveteen short pants.*)

I never told Momma about this. She never asked, "Was a bum shot at the party?" so I never brought it up.

I was two kinds of a kid. I didn't mind being alone but I also flourished in the company of others. I was bored silly at school. I was the youngest in my family, so my five brothers and two sisters didn't have time for me. And since my parents were immigrants, I didn't have much to talk about with them. The only way I could get together with people was by singing. Anywhere. Any time. So I started very early.

I must have been three when I got my new blue sailor suit with a square collar that hung down the back. I stood on a chair while Momma dressed me, tying a bow around my neck. Company was coming to dinner. Momma held a mirror up to my face and pinched my cheek. "What beautiful, rosy cheeks!"

I was cute as hell. Kids know when they're cute, and I was always "on." I'd sing "Yankee Doodle" or "In the Shade of the Old Apple Tree." I sang at family weddings, bar mitzvahs.

What started me singing? I can't remember. There must have been some stimulus, some push that gave me the concept of singing instead of talking—it doesn't come naturally to a kid of three or four. It might have been the phonograph. A neighbor had a longhorn Victrola that produced scratchy Frank Crumit and Caruso songs.

By the time I was ten I had an untrained but glorious high tenor voice. The family was proud of me from the start. I was the cute little boy who sang for everybody. It didn't really take any great guts to stand up in front of an audience when I was four or five; I became nervous when I grew older and realized I could fail. As a kid I just loved singing. If a five-year-old can have an orgasm—that's how I felt.

Still, I got damn tired of hearing my audience exclaim, "Oh, that can't be a boy singing! That's a little girl." All because of my rosy cheeks. I didn't know much then, but I did know there was some difference between boys and girls. And I didn't want to be a girl. I was satisfied just being a boy.

There must have been something in our culture at the time that insisted singing and dancing were only for girls; boys should play violin and become doctors and lawyers. Well, I did a little acting, too.

In kindergarten class, PS 149, Miss Delaney tells us we've got to act out the story of Thanksgiving. It's all about John Alden and Miles Standish and eating turkeys and sweet potatoes. I've never eaten this stuff, and I don't know who these guys are, but I figure if she says John Alden first, he must be the big shot.

"I wanna be John Alden!" I yell.

I am put in the Pilgrim chorus. All we have to do is walk across the stage, carrying a cardboard musket. And Miss Delaney warns us, "If you don't bring your own costume, you're not in the play."

Okay. Pop is a skilled tinsmith. Working from a picture in the Jewish Daily Forward, *he wraps some five-and-dime-store black oilcloth around an old derby to look like a stovepipe, and attaches a belt buckle to the front of the hat with thin iron wire.*

Two days later: As I walk across the stage with the motley Pilgrims, I stop and scream, "Oh! The Indians!" I grab my heart, as if hit by an arrow, and fall down. Hard. Gasps in the auditorium. Then I jump up, smile at the people so they'll know I'm not hurt. And I amble off.

In the hall, teacher grabs my ear, and her huge bosom trembles menacingly over my eyes. "You bad boy! Why couldn't you just walk across like I told you?"

I don't know why. I had to make a production out of it. I had to be "on."

Nobody in our entire lineage had ever been near a stage, except one cousin who was an usher in a Yiddish theater on Second Avenue. Where and from whom did I inherit the consuming, intense desire to get "on"?

My father was eighteen and my mother was seventeen when they ran away from Russia. A very small town near the Polish border, Kamenets Podolsk. Their story, as I heard it later, was a lot like *Fiddler on the Roof*—minus the music, laughter, Chagall-color scenery and friendly Gentiles. The boy Saul, who would become my father, was working in the vegetable garden behind his house when the Cossacks swept into the village. One made a move toward his wife, Sarah. Saul rapped him with his shovel. Maybe he killed him.

The villagers quickly hid Saul and Sarah, forged two passports and got the couple to the next town hidden under a load of hay. From there they made their way to Germany. Forged passports and a Jewish underground were a way of life in Central Europe. To escape the Russian army call-up, you chopped off your trigger finger or you ran away to America.

Momma remembered only one moment of panic in this 5000-mile exodus. When their train stopped in Berlin, she was terrified because she'd never seen so large a city. Pop got off to buy some hot tea, and she was sure he'd never find his way back again.

In the confusion at Ellis Island, when the half-literate Tammany Irish clerks questioned the Yiddish-speaking immigrants, tinsmith somehow came out ironworker. So my father became an ironworker. As soon as he'd settled in a tenement on the Lower East Side—East 12th Street between Avenues A and B—he went to work on the skyscrapers springing up in the city.

The ironworkers were almost 95 percent Irish. My father's conception of the American way of life was learned from Irishmen. An orthodox Jew, my father to his dying day had an Irish brogue overlaying his Yiddish accent. He picked up Irish habits, like chewing tobacco. Newspapers were spread over the kitchen floor because he would start a story with, "Vell, I'll tell ye, bejabbers," and spit on the floor.

From the Lower East Side the family moved to Brooklyn, the edge of Brownsville. Another ghetto, but a couple of steps up socially. We had two more rooms to sleep in.

That's where I was born in 1911. There were now ten of us in the cold-water flat at 417 Pennsylvania Avenue, third floor. A short hall from the entrance door; in the kitchen, an iron bathtub covered by a wood plank on which Momma did her ironing. Toilet in the hall near the kitchen. Next, a windowless little "dining room" we turned into a bedroom. A second bedroom; a third bedroom; a back room for the two girls, Lillian and Pearl; and a little parlor. Four boys in the bedroom: I, Reuben (who turned it into Bob), Mike and Sol. And my father. Harry and Jack had the third bedroom. The males had to sleep tsefeesing—head-to-foot.

Momma slept in the windowless room. And when I was

a baby, I slept in the same bed. I would wake up at night and find Pop in the bed, too. He was doing something noisy with Momma, and the bed would shake. She'd mutter "Ssh, ssh!" as she tried to push him out of bed. Those nights terrified me— I sensed Momma did not want him there. Tiny children are like animals—they can sense a disturbing situation without understanding the words.

But my father would not leave the bed. He was ill most of the years I knew him, but he was lusty. The bed would creak and I'd squeeze my eyes shut and hide under the pillow, quivering in fear.

I didn't know it was "sex." I couldn't ask Momma. Or my brothers. And when I was old enough to pick up the clichés about this classic Oedipal situation, me in bed with the mother and hating the father, I rejected the whole notion. I didn't want to make love to Momma, and I didn't want to kill Pop. He was the most vital, interesting man in the whole family. I had more fun with him than with my five brothers.

Pop was progressive. He enrolled in night school at a settlement house to learn to read and write English. And he joined the Workmen's Circle, which provided insurance and sickness and burial benefits in addition to an education in economics and politics. Pop's hero was Eugene V. Debs, but he was not an activist. Before I was even out of short pants, he would pay me a quarter for each street-corner speech I made protesting Debs' imprisonment. I didn't know exactly what "sedition" was, but it had put Debs in jail; I memorized my speech from editorials in *The Forward,* and I certainly held that audience despite the street noise. Pop even went to visit Debs in prison. I didn't know it then, but Pop was the first true liberal I had contact with.

After Pop's ailments overcame his energy, our doctor ordered him to take things easy. He couldn't. He opened a sheet metal shop, Silver & Son, with one of my brothers. When we moved away, he hung up a shingle on our house, REAL ESTATE BROKER. I think he sold a few houses. Very few.

Nothing defeated his *joie de vivre.* All the guys who hung around the corner loved him. The neighborhood bookie let him bet a four-horse parlay for a dollar, just to give him a little action. When I was in vaudeville and betting in a small way, Momma blamed him for my bad ways. "You encourage it because you're always betting on horses. I *know* you're looking at horses!" she scolded.

He took her at her word. When I came down to breakfast, Pop would hum and sing little songs, new words with familiar tunes, to nobody in particular. "Good morning, cutie-face. Oh boy! You're a cutie-face, with such character! . . ." I didn't get it. And Momma could not understand why he was so cheerful. That night, as I checked the race results in the paper, I noticed two modest winners, Cutie-Face and Character. Each morning Pop put a different horse into a song.

Momma was plump and short. When I was old enough to appreciate women's looks, I realized she was very pretty. She grew up in America, but her vision of life was the one she'd brought over from Kamenets Podolsk. Love your children, keep them warm and well-fed—and never trust a friendly Gentile.

My father persuaded her, somehow, to attend the wedding of an Italian socialist on the Lower East Side. There was a fight, and one of the bridegroom's relatives pulled a knife. For the rest of her years, Momma believed that knife fighting was part of the Italian wedding ceremony.

(Twenty years later, I married Jo-Carroll Dennison, a very Southern girl from Tyler, Texas, and brought her home to Brooklyn to meet my mother. She cried out happily in Yiddish, "Where did you find this beauty?" and threw her arms around my wife. Momma confided, in her broken English, "You know, darling, when my Fischl—Philip—married a Gentile girl, he thought I would be very much upset. He doesn't know his own mother. By me, if it's a nice girl, I don't care if she's *Italian!*")

My parents believed in the old tradition: God wants you to multiply. Momma was continually pregnant. And tired. The only rest she found in the early years was the ten days after a child was born, when the midwife came to take care of the house. The family joke was: Fischl would never have been born if his deceased grandfather hadn't needed a namesake.

My mother never learned to read or write. She was haunted by the dark superstitions of the Russian ghetto. To her, they were the true Hebrew ritual. When my brother Mike came down with double pneumonia, she flew into a withdrawn fury and ran into the kitchen. Her eyes were glazed; I was scared because she didn't really see me. She was smashing every dish in the house.

My older brother Harry pulled me out into the hall. "Leave her alone. She's getting rid of the evil spirit that made Mike sick——the *dybbuk*.

Momma did the best she could. Just as Pop did. And they both loved me.

Lillian, my oldest sister, raised me, because Momma was busy with the rest of the brood. Lillian would take me to the stores for clothes. She never bought the coat at the price they asked–$12.50. There was haggling and oh, no! that's highway robbery, and we'd go on to the shops down the street and around the corner. Later, we'd wander back over the same route, and the first man who came down a dollar got our trade. It embarrassed me–to this day I dislike shopping. I'll buy almost anything that's shown to me, just to get out of the store.

Pearl, the younger one, was always sending me to Red's drugstore for a little box of something. She'd write a note to Red and wrap the money in it. After a while, Red told me they were sanitary napkins, and what they were used for. Why didn't she get this necessary equipment herself? Well, this was in the early 1900's; Women's Lib hadn't made its move.

To escape these female tentacles, I spent more and more time with the boys on the street corner. That wasn't easy, either.

We didn't own bicycles, read comic books or smoke marijuana; the only pills we popped were Smith Bros. licorice flavor. In those days you did two things on the street: you went looking for a fight, or you stole. Sometimes both.

Brownsville was Jewish turf. No anti-Semitism here. A strange face in the neighborhood had to say "bread and butter" in Yiddish fast to keep from being mangled. The Irish kids acquired remarkable Yiddish accents.

The neighborhood was alive with strong, skilled fighters. Dave Rosenberg was a middleweight champ for a while. Joey Glick, Lefty Wallach, Harry Galfund—these were revered names, men who actually made money by fighting. They worked out in Willie Beecher's gym on Livonia Avenue.

The most respected residents were the gangsters. Abie Reles recruited his executioners for Murder Inc. here. They'd kill or maim anybody for a reasonable fixed price. The Amberg boys, Pretty Boy and Hymie, were vicious outlaws—they didn't even respect the code of the underworld. They were crazy. At a restaurant table, using the prongs of his dinner fork, Pretty Boy mangled the face of his friend for accidentally stepping on his newly-shined shoes. And then there was Benny Siegel. Nobody ever called him Bugsy to his face. *Nobody.* I met Benny in Hollywood years later and developed a strange admiration for this gangster.

These were our heroes. They had rolls of bills in their pockets, and nobody dared slug them.

I started my street career modestly enough. The city was building Thomas Jefferson High School across the street from my home, on the vacant lot we used for baseball. They had a hell of a nerve. We climbed the fence at night and pulled out the water pipes; the water would run down and soften the cement. Floors collapsed. Then we'd sell the pipe. We delayed the construction for six months.

We grabbed apples from pushcarts and snatched shoelaces in the dime store. I wasn't eager about it, but it was the thing to do.

As for street fighting, my heart wasn't in it. Gang fights against other neighborhoods were compulsory. I had to be in there swinging, and sometimes I hit somebody. But the blood . . . it upset my stomach.

Here was the difference between me and Abie Reles's boys. Blood turned them on. It must have been a real lust. That's when they'd go to work on a boy, to destroy him. They were very scientific about it.

My best street weapon was my mouth. I could always improvise a way out. I recall an argument with a tough little yegg who was called Chinzo because of his protruding chin. I fractured my thumb on that chin. My roundhouse swing only made him laugh, and I knew I was doomed. I looked up to our apartment window: "Isn't that my mother calling me? Yeah, Mom. I'm coming right up."

At nine I already had a bit of Bilko in me.

Momma signed me up for Hebrew school, to salvage me from "the bad bums on the corner." The gnarled old rabbi, in the prescribed gray beard and black gabardine, gave private lessons in his bleak cellar tenement. He taught Hebrew by rote, and the mumbo jumbo of the rituals made no sense to me. By the second session I hated Hebrew and I hated the old man. He'd slap my palm with a ruler when I refused to recite. One afternoon I pushed him back into his chair as he came at me with the ruler. That was *hutzpah,* to push a *rav!* He unbuckled his strap; I ran out and never came back. For a long time the rabbi said nothing to my mother because he was paid by the week.

The time I saved as a Hebrew dropout was spent at the Supreme Theater, a neighborhood movie house where Gladys, an older woman (she must have been twenty-four), accompanied the silent films on a wheezy organ.

I always sat behind Gladys, fascinated by her impetuous manipulation of the keys and pedals. One night the reel broke in the middle of *Way Down East.* The projectionist flashed a slide:

A MOMENT PLEASE

It took forever to patch that film; the audience hooted and stamped on the floor. I jumped up on my seat and began to sing. Nobody had asked me—it just seemed to be the right thing to do. Gladys, astonished, came in a couple of bars later on "Big Boy," a very peppy number.

There he goes!
Look at the clothes!

On Big Boy, that's Big Boy!
There's a man who certainly can make love! . . .
    They all say that since he kissed old widder
       Johnson
    Now she thinks she's Gloria Swanson! . . .
That's why the women all cry,
They all sigh
For big, Big Boy! *

A smash. They wouldn't let me go, even after the movie began. And so I was launched on a new career. I'd sit there every
night, and whenever a reel broke, I'd leap up on the stage with
"Big Boy" and other novelties. What a glow of power. A big
audience—not family. *Strangers!* And they applauded me.

I wasn't paid a nickel, but I got into the Supreme *free*. I was
the envy of the neighborhood. I was known as the reel-breaker-
down singer.

> *Klinsky Bros. deli: I'm at a table, having my usual—*
> *corned beef on rye, French fried potatoes with lots of*
> *catsup, and a glass of tea and lemon. All for a quarter.*
> *An afternoon snack, before my stint at the Supreme.*
>   *In stroll two kids my age, faces heavily made up in a*
> *greasy orange. And an older man, wrinkled, carrying*
> *roller skates. They order corned beefs, too. But double all*
> *around. Vaudeville performers! They discuss how they*
> *killed 'em at the Bushwick. And the old guy shows a little*
> *soft-shoe dance on skates that he's going to introduce. Oh,*
> *the mystery of it. The hidden world of big-time*
> *vaudeville.* Paid to perform!

It occurred to me later that they couldn't be very big-time
if they hung out in this crummy deli, but . . . I was hooked.
I gave up my petty snitching of apples and shoelaces. I had
something more important on my mind now. I needed to score

fifty cents for the Saturday matinee at the Bushwick Theater. The Bushwick was the Palace Theater of Brooklyn. I had to see that show every week. It was like a fix.

Through my brother Harry, I got a job at Red's drugstore. I helped out in the store, but he paid me nothing. The main advantage was that I called people to the telephone. The tenement people didn't have a phone; calls would come to the drugstore. "Please call Mrs. Feinberg, apartment 4D, 207 Pennsylvania Avenue." I'd run to 4D, and got a nickel for my exertion. If I didn't, I could never find that apartment again.

Red sent me to the bank for ten dollars in change. I brought it back in a paper bag, so it was easy to extract a quarter. I'd time my return to coincide with a customer. Red would dump the bag into the register, wait on the cash customer—and I had the quarter.

If I didn't have fifty cents by Friday night, I'd rattle Harry's jacket. He always hung it neatly on a hanger. I'd shake it casually with the back of my hand, and if I heard a clink of change, I'd reach in for some silver. I suppose Harry eventually caught on, but he never said anything. He probably figured if I was that desperate, he might as well let me have the money. Occasionally I had to go into the hall closet to rattle the jackets of my sisters' boyfriends. To me it wasn't thievery—it was the only way to get into the Bushwick Theater.

I memorized the songs and routines of the headliners there: Belle Baker, Sophie Tucker, Willie and Eugene Howard, John Steele, George Jessel, Ted Healy, Smith and Dale, and others. I learned their special lyrics, their comedy patter, the inflection of every note. Now I was ready to sing for the big money.

Somebody steered me to a dark beer hall on Ocean Parkway. The waiters carried glass steins around like clubs. Once in a while they sang "Roses of Picardy." There was not one pretty girl in a low-cut bodice, like the beer parlors I inhabited for the Fox musicals of the 1940's. This one smelled like Beecher's gym.

The darkness helped: I let it all pour out as if I were onstage at the Supreme. The customers whooped it up, and threw coins at me. The waiters were very friendly, helping me pick up the coins. They skimmed off a few for themselves, but I got out of there around midnight, my pants pockets weighed down with silver.

I'm at the bottom of the stairway to our flat: dark, no lights. It's awfully late for a kid of nine to be coming home in Brownsville. I know in some dark alcove somebody is waiting to grab me. Or my money.

I yell up the stairs, "Pop! Anybody home?" No answer. He is hard of hearing—no help from him. Terrified, I creep up the stairs. Just as I try the door of our flat, it opens. Pop has been waiting up for me.

Tonight he's eighteen feet tall, and he's ready with the razor strap. I try to brazen it out. "I didn't know it was so late, honest." He bawls me out, swinging the strap threateningly over my head. I don't answer. I keep pulling the silver out of my pockets, counting it. It's over twelve dollars. More than Pop makes in a day bucking rivets.

Finally, he sighs heavily. "I don't want ye to do this again, y'unnerstand?" But he doesn't hit me.

From here it was a short step up (or was it down?) to performing at kiddie shows. The movie on Sutter Avenue, which later became the Loew's Premiere, was operated by a man named John Tuttle, one of the few persons in my neighborhood who never changed his name. During the Christmas holidays, when the kids were rampaging out of school, he'd put together an all-day show. Movies, kids and repeat.

The kids lined up to be auditioned in a large ballroom over the theater. The first year Tuttle wouldn't even listen to me. I was outraged. Cripes, I was a *professional.* I wandered into the lavatory—and fixed Tuttle. I plugged up the sink with john paper and turned the spigots on full. I have no idea what this did to the ceiling of the movie auditorium. But next year, when I lined up, he listened to me. I was in.

The kiddie show was literally a riot. The pianist would beat out an introduction. If Tuttle blew his police whistle from backstage, that signaled the kid was not there. Or was sick. Or had peed in his pants. The pianist swiftly segued to the next victim. Performers got $2.50 up to an ultimate $7.50. I got $5 to start.

The third year I was MC of the whole show. My father, now halfway proud of me, waited backstage to pick me up after the final performance. Tuttle handed me the envelope; I carefully counted it outside on the sidewalk. Seventeen dollars and fifty cents! "Let's run, Pop! He must've made a mistake."

"Yer name is on it?"

"Yeh."

My father turned to the stage door and assumed a John L. Sullivan stance. In his Yiddish-Irish, he called, "Let's see ye take it back! I ain't afraid of ye, begorrah!"

The Supreme Theater decided to run kiddie shows, too. The manager was also the bouncer, one of the toughest, craftiest street fighters I ever saw. He was a Turkish Jew who'd picked up the name Jack Elliot. He had been a promising amateur boxer, but he made one big mistake in his first fight. When the referee gave the decision to the other guy, Jack reverted to his street training and kicked the ref in the groin. In full view of the crowd. He was barred from the ring for life. So Jack switched to the movie business. He also moonlighted as an enforcer for the Amberg gang. When Jack said, "I'm putting you in my kiddie show"—you just had to be there.

He teamed me with a song-and-dance team billed as Bud and Buddy Junior. They became Junior because one of them was related to Bud and Buddy, the first two men from our neighborhood who made it big in show business. (Buddy Howe is now head of the New York office of Creative Management Associates, my agents.) Young Bud was the most affluent of our trio. His father was a tailor, so he costumed me in my first pair of long pants. And he even paid for our publicity photographs, taken in one of those storefront studios where the pictures come out purple.

Jack Elliot billed me as "Brownsville's Own Sophie Tucker!"

Sophie Tucker? But I could hardly tell Jack Elliot a boy my age didn't have Sophie Tucker's equipment.

The night of the show I ran a fever. Maybe I didn't want to face that billing; I certainly was sick and shivering. Three men came to the door to ask about me, Momma reported. She was terrified they wanted to rob me. I suddenly lost my fever and went with the three persuaders.

We were a boisterous success. Jack booked us around Brooklyn. He was very active in Turkish-Jewish affairs. Every block, every synagogue, every free burial society had "benefit nights." The procedure was as minutely detailed as a ritual in the Torah. Each group printed 100 or 200 tickets, and all the other groups bought them because they expected the same for their own affairs. In Brownsville, the biggest business, after hospitals, was printing tickets.

Our trio, well-seasoned by now, with long pants and purple photographs, also worked amateur nights, smokers, hoodlum clubs. Then we were picked up—"ready for the big time," we were told—by a promoter from Williamsburg who called himself Captain Schacht. Tall, lanky, with a hook nose and a palpitating Adam's apple, he dressed as a Navy officer in white uniform and cap with lots of gold braid and decorations. The naval flotillas out of Williamsburg were mostly ferry boats and garbage scows. The ferries were his vaudeville circuit. He foisted the kids on the boats to entertain the surly commuters with *Captain Schacht and His Kiddie Revue.* Lucky for us, Jack Elliot did not insist on exclusive booking.

The Captain decided my name was not box office—it had to be changed. It had always been Philip Silver, without the "s." (I changed it a few years later because there were several important people in show business named Silvers—Lou, who conducted for Al Jolson; and Sid, who was the heckler for Phil Baker—and why should I be different? Everybody called me Silvers anyhow.) Captain Schacht ordered me to be billed as Penn Derry.

"Brownsville's Sophie Tucker" made more sense than Penn Derry. At least people didn't get me mixed up with Penn Station. I insisted on my rights: I was Penn Derry only on ferry boats.

Buddy Junior became a close friend, and since I was only

ten, he did his best to further my education. He was very advanced in sex. He offered to introduce me to a cat house which, he assured me, was "perfectly okay because they're all nice Jewish girls, just like your sisters." I wasn't *that* sophisticated. I called him a liar, and my sex education ended. But the trio staggered on.

My education at PS 149 wasn't going anywhere either. My main field of study was hooky. Moonlighting kept me sleepy in class; the only time I had for study was while standing in line, waiting for school to open.

PS 149 was in East New York, right next to Schumer's Turkish Baths. It was there my father tried to teach me how to swim by throwing me into the water. I began to hate the baths. I'd walk around the block, just to avoid Schumer's bathhouse; my phobia soon spread to PS 149 next door. No forced education for me.

My homeroom teacher was no help; I was sure she was a nut. When the kids talked it up a little in class, the old spinster would throw an inkwell out the window, then threaten, "If you don't behave, I'll go out the window after the inkwell."

One day I piped up with the logical question, "What's stopping you?"

Her skinny fingers dug into my arm and dragged me to the principal, Mr. Coleman. She accused me of "attacking" her; all I'd done was try to push her away because her fingers hurt.

I was banished to PS 61—a reform school. Just as I was about to graduate to high school. The shame tarnished the whole family. Momma went into screaming and mourning. Pop didn't wallop me—he just shook his head tiredly. Three of my brothers were going to college and here I was, the youngest, a talented singer with a great future, already the bum of the family.

I was genuinely sorry they felt so sorry about me, because I didn't feel bad about reform school. In Brownsville, reform school was a badge of merit. I met a fascinating bunch of fellows there. They were old—eighteen, nineteen—and they knew the score. I felt I could learn something.

I had broken out of the Jewish ghetto. Here were people I'd

never seen close up: blacks, high-yellow mulattos, Spanish, Irish, Sicilians, guys who were already doing little errands for Murder Inc., malcontents, natural enemies of all law and order except their own. A syndicate controlled the shakedowns in the toilets and lunchroom; they dealt in cigarettes, stolen sweaters and coats, forged report cards. Everybody had a little racket going in PS 61. It was a prep school for Sing Sing.

You started in your homeroom with a clipboard. You'd move on during the day to geography, arithmetic, English, civics. Then back to homeroom for dismissal. Teachers made a note of any demerits for talking or misbehaving on your clipboard. At the end of the day, your homeroom teacher examined your sheet. If a single student got one demerit, the entire class was kept after school for fifteen minutes. You had to be awfully stupid or clumsy to get caught with a demerit, because the other prisoners would beat the hell out of you.

My big mouth produced a steady share of demerits. But no beatings. I had protection from Kid Posy. Harry Pozchynski was nineteen, short, burly, a top enforcer for the reform school syndicate. He had a knack for stomping and twisting vulnerable joints of the body, such as jawbones. I found that Posy had a lot of admirable qualities. On amateur nights I'd add a special chorus to "Big Boy":

> *There he goes!*
> *Look at the clothes!*
> *It's Posy, Posy!* . . .

Posy appreciated public recognition. And he was devoted to his mother. He'd take me to his tenement, where I'd sing "My Yiddische Mama" in the original language for her. She would cry happily, "Such nice boys, you didn't forget your mother tongue."

Loyalty and protection were fundamentals of the Brownsville Code. Jack Elliot, who booked and watched over our trio, left town in a hurry after Pretty Boy and Hymie Amberg were executed by a rival gang. They were found crumpled inside the trunk of a Packard limousine, their penises cut off and stuffed into their mouths, a gangster penalty for talking too much. The car was parked on Elliot Place in Brooklyn. Since Jack Elliot worked for the Ambergs, he took the hint and fled to Turkey.

Somehow, I was rehabilitated; I skipped from 8A to 8B in the reform school and I graduated. I was all set to enter high school in the fall of 1923 when I lost everything. My friends, my neighborhood, my career as a club performer.

My family, in a sudden burst of affluence, moved away to Bensonhurst. My kind of job depended on everyday, eyeball-to-eyeball contact. Nobody from Brownsville was going to come look for me in the wilds of Bensonhurst.

How could the family do this to me?

CHAPTER 2

Momma and the Two Nice Ladies in My Hotel

Easy. Harry was a graduate chemist and contributed to the household, so my father felt it was time to rescue us from the smells and sins of Brownsville. He bought a "house in the country": 66th Street, Bensonhurst.

It was a half block from Bay Parkway, surrounded by open lots, grass lawns and trees. Suburbia. Ours was a two-story brick house that shared a common wall with an identical house. To me it was luxurious. You entered through a glassed-in porch, with a wicker couch and a Philco *radio*. That was another momentous discovery for me; I could hear live singers. WLW, KDKA. Then a living room, which we hardly ever used but it was kept spic and span for unexpected arrivals. Beyond it, a dining room, and behind that was the big kitchen. We ate in the kitchen except when relatives came. Upstairs were three bedrooms and a bath. I shared one bedroom with Harry. My father was again sharing the bed with Momma. The tiny back yard provided a few flowers and radishes and lettuce, protected by a chain-link fence.

Just behind the yard was the open cut of the Sea Beach subway line, where the cars roared through on their way to Coney Island. The noise made me dream: the cars were transcontinental expresses, hurtling off to Chicago, the Grand Canyon, California. I was any kid in a whistle-stop hick town anywhere in America. I wanted to get on one of those classy trains and see the world.

My career heartbreak didn't last long; it was always sunny that summer. There was white sand and cool water at Coney

Island. Just sitting on the stoop with Momma on Sunday was pleasant, as we waited for my married brother and sister to come for their weekly visit.

Harry kept the house and family going; I don't think Pop made enough to pay the mortgage. Harry had built a shack in a vacant lot in Brownsville and set up a chemical laboratory. He wouldn't let me see it. I knew he was working on a bright green dye to camouflage ships, and he hoped to get a contract from the government. The only trouble was, it was highly explosive. My mother lived in terror whenever he'd be late coming home. Once Harry brought a bottle of this stuff into the kitchen, and everything made of wood or plaster turned green. And he didn't even open the bottle.

The government wouldn't touch it.

I liked to talk things over with Harry at night before we went to sleep. He was something of an idol for me. He was successful as a real estate broker and later a customer's man in a large stock market firm. He was the real head of the household. (After the 1929 crash, I remember, he slept in his office for three days and three nights, closing out the accounts, including his own. All he had left was a good wardrobe. He never worked again in his lifetime, except when he worked for me.)

Bensonhurst was another revelation for me. Not only the trees and grass, but the new type of kids I met. Boys with clean white shirts, who got to school on time and actually studied their homework at home. One of them owned a ukelele, which I'd never seen before. He'd strum it along the beach at Coney Island. My hangout was the Brighton Beach Theater, which drew big-time vaudeville acts in summer.

(The beach at Coney Island, near the boardwalk. My new pals are lying around; I'm standing up, facing the sun as if it's a Kleig light, and running through my repertoire. By popular request. "Big Boy," "Harvest Moon," "Yes, Sir, That's My Baby." I do a dialect parody they haven't heard before: "Yes, Sir, That's My Abie," about a mother losing her boy in a department store. It's one of the things

I picked up at the Bushwick. Yiddish and Dutch dialects are very big in vaudeville.

A sporty-looking man stops to hear me on the boardwalk. He waves a come-here finger, like my principal, Mr. Coleman. What's his beef? I walk over to him. A face like a bull, but friendly. In a gray derby, wing collar, gray silk cravat, striped pants and spats. Jeez, it's 90 degrees, and he's not sweating.)

ME: *"Yeah?"*

MAN *(throwing a little card down to me): "Come and see me, son. At the Brighton."*

ME: *"You're Gus Edwards?" (He nods and walks off.)*

UKELELE KID: *"Who's the geezer?"*

ME: *"Gus Edwards, biggest man in vaudeville. He's the star-maker. Discovered George Jessel, Eddie Cantor. Now he wants to audition me!" (They don't believe a word of it. I display Mr. Edwards' card.)*

UKELELE KID *(shrugging): "So what?"*

So what! A possible piece of heaven was handed down to me.

I ran to the Brighton Beach and got in line. A hundred kids jostling for position. As the hours passed, I grew irritable. I'd heard that Edwards held these lineups in every town to pull in publicity and customers. He might hire one out of a thousand —but all the others went to see the show that week.

At last the bored accompanist beckoned to me. It's fifty years since that moment, but that pianist's name leaps to mind instantly: Carl Gray. I sang "Yes, Sir, That's My Baby." Not the parody—straight. And true.

The great man nodded. "You'll hear from me."

Weeks went by. Every time the phone rang, my brothers called out, "It's Gus Edwards." I was confident. He had to call.

One day the phone rang, and it *was* Mr. Edwards. A private audition this time. I went with my father, to show it was okay with my family to work for him. Mr. Edwards listened, eyes half closed. Again, "You'll hear from me."

I went home and now I began to sweat. I was eleven, going on twelve, and already five feet five. How could he use a giant like me in his Newsboy Revue? The kids I knew hustling papers were all runts.

Four days later the call came: Mr. Edwards wanted to rehearse me. For what was not clear. In his office we ran through the lyrics and business of a famous number, which I'd never heard. He had written the music—"If I Was a Millionaire." *

> MR. EDWARDS: *"I heard a newsboy singing at his work. I thought he was so unusual he deserved an opportunity up here. (Flourish) Young Master Philip Silver."*
>
> *(I bow.)*
>
> MR. EDWARDS: *"Philip, you're on the stage of the Palace, the very pinnacle of the entertainment world. Are you going to high-hat these other newsboys?"*
>
> ME: *"High-hat them kids, Uncle Gus? I should say not! Lis-ten . . ."*
>
> *(I hit the "t" hard. My brother had a long talk with me the night before; I better not disgrace the family. "Be a gentleman. Don't mumble like a street bum. Say talk-ing, sing-ing, pronounce your r's and t's." So I figure a gentleman would say lis-ten.)*
>
> ME: *"If I was a millionaire, Gus,*
> *If I was a millionaire?*
> *There wouldn't be nothing too good in this world*
> *For me and my pals to share.*
> *Don't tell me I'm shooting hot air, Gus,*
> *'Cause here's what I'd do on the square—*
> *If I was a real live, honest-to-goodness,*
> *   cross-my-heart millionaire . . ."*
>
> *(Here Mr. Edwards wants me to cross my heart like a Catholic and sing the chorus. But my arm won't move. I'm paralyzed. Talk about superstition: in Brownsville we*

---

*were told that if a Jew blessed himself, all his teeth would
fall out. Mr. Edwards senses something is wrong; he
quickly changes the lyric to "reg-u-lar millionaire" instead
of "cross-my-heart." Now that I can keep my teeth, my
voice comes out full and strong.)*

ME: *"I'd buy up ev'ry schoolhouse in the nation,
I'd write upon the blackboard big and clear:
Instead of one there will be two vacations,
Each vacation six months—twice a year.
There wouldn't be no school when it was raining,
I'd let you stay at home when it was fair.
To the ball games, kids, I'd take you,
To an ice-cream cone I'd stake you,
If I was a millionaire!"*

MR. EDWARDS: *"By now the Newsboy Quartet is on.
They repeat the first six lines behind you. Then—a musical
sting . . ."*

ME: *"Kids, you'd have free soda fountains
And I'd build you ice-cream mountains
If I was a millionaire!"*
(I hit high C and hold it for count of eight.)

Mr. Edwards nodded. He would try me.

Holy Moses! I would make my professional debut at the top
—*The* Palace. At the age of twelve.

I was excited, happy, but not really overwhelmed.

After a second day of rehearsal, Mr. Edwards put me into
the midweek matinee show. My costume was stock, right out of
the trunk. The angelic, tottering wardrobe lady, Mother Elm,
had outfitted hundreds of newsboys. She put together a pair
of knickers, a tattered shirt, a cap, long black stockings. Everything was too tight, but it didn't matter.

I was going to sing from the stage where the foremost performers of the world appeared: Sarah Bernhardt, W. C. Fields,
Will Rogers, Fanny Brice, the Marx Brothers. It was the home
plate of vaudeville.

And sing I did. Four encores before the audience would let

me off. It's quite a few years ago, but I can still remember the joy of stopping the show cold at the Palace.

I was in. At the end of the week I would go with the troupe to Philadelphia, to play the Earle Theater for six weeks in a schoolroom format, *Gus Edwards' Protégés of 1923*. Six weeks solid—$75 every week. I'd been lucky in the timing of my audition. Mr. Edwards needed a boy in a hurry to augment his supply of protégés. I began rehearsing more songs: "Bicycle Built for Two," "Sunbonnet Sue," "School Days."

When Momma heard *Philadelphia*, there was a great weeping and wailing. "My Fischl was never away from home. . . . How do you know what goes on in a train? You've never been on a train."

Crisis. A big family argument around the kitchen table. Harry came to my rescue, as always. "Let him go, Ma. He'll get so homesick he'll come back on the next train."

Pop bought me a fiberboard suitcase, and Momma filled it with little boy's dress-up clothes. Half of it was underwear and handkerchiefs. I had to promise to use a new hanky every day, and send the laundry home every week. Also $50 a week.

The stage manager, Claude Carrington, put me into a respectable traveler's hotel, the Lafayette. If I had to send money home, he told me, "Fill out a money order at the post office, and be sure to keep the receipt."

I did that every week. The rest of my promises fell apart in chaos. I couldn't keep up with the demands of my new life. I didn't open that new suitcase the entire six weeks. I knew how to open it, but what was the use? I didn't know which clothes to wear. My mother always laid out my stuff for me.

I didn't know how to take off the makeup with cold cream —and I sure wasn't going to admit I was a punk amateur by asking. So the makeup irritated my eyes. I was blinking and rubbing; I smeared up all my hankies just working on my eyes. I didn't bathe, either. On Wednesday and Saturday night, Momma would announce it was time to take a bath. Without her prodding, I forgot all about it.

Gus Edwards' wife, a "classy" woman, took me aside one afternoon and recommended the Camac Turkish Baths. For relaxation. "Wonderful place," she added graciously. "Mr. Edwards is a habitué." And she gave me ten dollars.

On the way to Camac's, I met a boy in the company, Sandy Milne, a gifted Scottish comic whom Mr. Edwards had picked up at Ellis Island because nobody had claimed him. Sandy was eighteen now, a natural talent with that magic "presence." When he appeared in an ensemble, the audience had to focus on him. Offstage, unfortunately, he found it hard to focus: he was a drunk.

"What good is a Turkish bath?" he asked me.

I could not answer that. I lent him the ten bucks, and went along to the saloon to watch while he drank it up. Mrs. Edwards, concerned for my health, pressed the same amount into my hand every week. And I turned it over to Sandy. He swore he needed it.

Next to my room in the Lafayette lived two ladies, one blondish, the other red-haired, who were very sweet to me. I first met them in the hall and they invited me in to have tea. Every night when I came home they had cookies and tea for me. They loved the theater.

"How did it go today, Philip?" one would ask.

And I had to admit I'd wowed 'em. Then they'd beg me to sing some songs from the show. They offered to sew buttons for me, and press my clothes; but I didn't think a gentleman should accept such favors from strange ladies. They were real darlings. I enjoyed the chats in their suite, and when midnight came, they would announce, "Bedtime, Philip." I'd shuffle unwillingly back to my room, the makeup still rimming my hair.

The third week, Harry and my mother came down to visit me. Why didn't I send back any laundry? When Momma took a look at me, she began moaning over the strange splotches of color around my face: a sure sign of an evil *dybbuk!* She didn't want to hear about greasepaint.

"And where's the money you promised?" Harry asked.

I showed the receipts for the money orders. He shook his head, resigned. "Kid, you kept the receipt *and* the money order."

Nobody told me I was supposed to send the other part home. I thought the post office had some mysterious system that took my money straight to my mother.

She sat there moaning, "What are they doing to my baby?" To cheer her up, I told her about the nice ladies next door who were taking care of me—they were waiting to meet her right now. A rap on the door. It was Sandy Milne, come for his ten-dollar allotment. We stepped out into the hall. I handed over the money and told him I couldn't go to the saloon today, I was taking my mother to meet the ladies. . . .

He laughed like a maniac. "Jesus, you're a dumbbell! They're whores. I just came up in the elevator with a customer."

I snatched back the ten-spot. "Come on, Momma, Harry —we're going to the theater." I hustled them downstairs and into a taxi. The next three days, whenever Momma wanted to meet the nice ladies (she bought soap for them to wash my hair), I'd exclaim, "Let's take a taxi!" A taxi was my idea of big-time diversion.

Momma's reaction to all this was a migraine headache. Harry dragged me to the Turkish bath, and some of the older kids took pity on me and showed me how to make out a laundry list for the Chinaman. Momma felt she could go home then.

What to do about the two beauties in the hotel? I'd been fascinated by prostitutes ever since that offer by Buddy Junior back in Brownsville. But vaudeville was very proper. Backstage at the Earle, the management had posted a sign:

THIS THEATER CATERS TO LADIES, GENTLEMEN
AND CHILDREN. VULGARITY WILL NOT BE TOL-
ERATED. DO NOT USE THE WORDS HELL, DAMN,
DEVIL, COCKROACH, SPIT, ETC.

If I couldn't even say cockroach, imagine how the Gerry Society would explode if they found one of Gus Edwards' little boys in a hotel room with *two* whores. It was jail, for sure. I played this crisis like a confident man of the world.

I moved to another hotel.

Mr. Edwards gave me some new numbers. Unwittingly, I

began to learn something about comedy: the difference between the real thing and hokum. He put me into a scene with a lovely little girl, Dorothy Forrestal. I'd push her onstage on a tricycle, and we'd sing, "Daisy, Daisy, give me your answer true . . ." The first show, I made the turn too quickly and we both toppled over. I lifted her up, turned to the audience and said calmly, "It's in the act."

It was a roar. Carl Gray, playing in the pit, patted me on the shoulder later. "Good thinking, kid."

If it's good once, it's good twice, I figured. I repeated the bit for the second show. But it was awkward, hokey. "It's in the act" didn't get a titter. But the *look* Carl gave me from the orchestra—utter disdain that said, you fresh punk. I never did it again.

I stayed with Mr. Edwards for the rest of the summer. Since I was approaching thirteen, my father demanded I prepare for *bar mitzvah,* for the sake of Momma. I took a couple of days off and focused on the required lines. Luckily, I had a photographic memory. Father made a donation to the synagogue, and I delivered a perfectly phrased ritual, learned by rote, to the delight of the old men who hung around there because they had no other place to sit. Momma got confused on the time, and she missed the entire ceremony.

At the end of summer the family insisted I must go back to school. I started my first year at New Utrecht High, but I could not concentrate. The excitement of the stage gnawed at me. School was kid stuff. Silly. Harry again interceded for me, and I returned to Uncle Gus. He had a few dates in Philadelphia and Washington.

While he was teaching me a new number, I heard the melody and could not reproduce it vocally. He recognized the symptom instantly. My voice was changing. I would have to take a rest. "If you stop singing," he told me, "your voice may come back in a lower timbre, and stronger."

Shock. I had no control over my own voice. Nothing to look forward to. The special thing inside me that had been propelling me, keeping me tingling, was slipping away. Worst of all, I couldn't go home to my family and admit my big vaudeville career was a freak, a flash in the pan. I was through—a has-been at the age of thirteen.

I begged Mr. Edwards to send me out on the road. Maybe if I kept singing, my vocal chords would grow stronger. I'd take anything, just so I would not have to crawl back to Bensonhurst.

He put me into a presentation act, *Garden of Girls,* that played on the stages of movie houses. It wasn't much of a show: about thirty teenagers, half of them girls. I sang in a quartet. We played the Publix chain, starting at the Rivoli in New York and ending up in Atlanta, Georgia. By then I had no singing voice at all.

It was summer, and I was just another kid on the block. I couldn't even sing on the beach at Coney. I wandered back to the Supreme Theater.

> *(Gladys at the organ. The movie is Chaplin's "The Kid.")*
> ME *(leaning over the railing behind Gladys):* "Surprise!"
> GLADYS: *"Well,* Hello! *How* are *you? You're in the big-time show business now."*
> ME *(agreeably): "That right."*
> GLADYS: *"I've got a break in a few minutes. Let's have a cup of tea."*
> ME: *"Fine. Meet you in the coffeepot."*
> *(As I walk up the aisle, Chaplin, the tramp, is carefully lifting a cigarette butt out of a sardine can. But Gladys is playing for me):*
> *"There he goes!*
> *Look at the clothes!"*
> *On Big Boy, that's Big Boy!"*

Bored and restless, I convinced my family that I needed an operation to remove my infected tonsils. Secretly I hoped this would bring back my voice. It didn't. The sound was as joyless as before. What the operation did was make me grow even faster. That explosive growth also made me tired and weak. Now I was a skinny, awkward kid.

I moped around.

Near the end of World War I, the names MORRIS AND CAMPBELL sparkled on the marquees of the Palace and the Keith-Orpheum circuit all over the country. They were topliners for whom the audience felt a warm glow of affection and recognition. The George Burns and Gracie Allen of the day.

Joe Morris (born Morris Lobel) was about as ugly as a man could be: skeleton face, horn-rimmed glasses, body thin as a jockey's. Yet he had a magic quality that attracted beautiful women. Joe married Flo Campbell when they were in their teens. A gorgeous redhead, with milky translucent skin, Flo had fire and showmanship in her singing. They lived quietly, soberly—a "go-home couple." When the show ended, they'd just go back to their hotel or rooming house. They were deeply in love.

The act prospered from the beginning. Joe was one of the first to develop an act in which he heckled his partner from a stage box. He created a vehement, argumentative character whose strange gaunt face made every line irresistibly funny.

During the war years, everyone was knitting "a sweater for your soldier." Joe knitted his in the box.

> FLO: *"What are you knitting?"*
> JOE: *"Something for my horse."*
> FLO: *"Oh, you have a horse?"*
> JOE: *"Yes, but I lost it."*
> FLO: *"Oh, I'm sorry."*
> JOE: *"It's all right. I found it."*
> FLO: *"How did you find it?"*
> JOE: *"I says to myself, if I was a horse, where would I go? and I went there and there it was." (Big laugh.)*
> FLO: *"What is it you're knitting for the horse?"*
> JOE: *"It's a secret."*

FLO: *"You can tell me."*

JOE: *"Well, if I tell you, then you'll tell somebody else, and by the time it gets back to me, it won't be what I'm making." (Big laugh.)*

The comedy loses a lot in cold type. Like even the best of today's comedy lyrics, it sounds thin and repetitious without its melody. In vaudeville, the melody was character, voice, timing, the magic interplay of performer and audience. Audiences loved it, and they did laugh. Their taste was not the most sophisticated; they came to the theater eager to enjoy themselves. There was no radio or television to tell them—for free—what the wise guys in New York or Hollywood felt were the most sophisticated lines. The same act could be used for years, adjusted and worked over and polished until every line, every gesture brought a laugh.

As Morris and Campbell climbed in money and billing, Joe began to run around with show business studs. Life became a ball with a succession of beautiful women. Then it turned into a ten-twenty-thirty melodrama. The act was the hit of George White's *Scandals* when Joe impregnated a girl in the company. He confessed to Flo, and insisted, "I have to marry her." Flo gave him the divorce, left the act and New York. There was rumor of her "nervous breakdown."

Joe married the showgirl and the baby was born. He was obsessed: was this really his child? And she was fearfully jealous of the man whose ugliness was a love potion to beauties. Joe turned to gambling and drink. He continued the act with a succession of other partners, but it never had the same appeal.

The powers of the Keith circuit saw the obvious solution: Joe would have to take back Flo as his stage partner. Two successful pop writers, Joe Young and Sam Lewis ("I'm Sitting on Top of the World") were recruited to write a new act. It was the story of Joe's life, titled *Any Apartment*.

They could not find a boy to play Joe's son, the catalyst of the whole act. Dozens of kids were auditioned before Joe remembered that kid with the big voice in Gus Edwards' troupe; he'd played on the same bill in Washington.

Joe tracked me down in Bensonhurst, still moping around. He was a little shocked at first by my height.

"Still a cute-looking kid," Joe assured his partners. "And he'll give us a smash finish—he can belt out a song."

I had an outbreak of honesty. "I lost my voice, Joe."

Joe took me anyhow. He saw something in me that I didn't see. I went to work in *Any Apartment.* In short pants.

> *(Scene: a kitchen.)*
> ME *(running on):* "*Mama, Mama, Mama, Mama! I lost Poppa!*
> MAMA: "*Where?*"
> ME: "*The last time I saw him, he was standing in front of the Palace [or whatever theater we were playing then] looking at a picture of a girl in the lobby, and he was saying, 'Oh, Mama, why did I ever leave you?'*"
> MAMA: "*Go do your homework.*"
> *(I go off and Joe enters with a big hello. Mama bawls him out. I come back with my toy train and play with it behind them.)*
> ME: "*Mama! The train won't go! The train won't go!*"
> *(Tremendous laugh.)*

I cannot tell anybody why that was so funny. But half a century later, during the run of *A Funny Thing Happened on the Way to the Forum* in Chicago, a stagehand repeated that line to me exactly as I had said it.

> *(Mama sends me and Joe out to buy groceries. The scene curtain drops. Announcement sign on easel: "Miss Flo Campbell.")*

Flo Campbell now makes her entrance and whatever song she sings becomes a hit. She is the song pluggers' delight. Remember, all this is before the advent of TV and talking pictures.

> *(At the end of Flo's song, Joe and I are discovered in the upper loge box with a basket of groceries.)*

FLO: *"Why, Joe Morris, what a surprise! Is that your boy?"*

JOE: *"That's what I keep asking myself!"*

(This sets me off on a crying jag. Every time I cry, Joe gives me a nickel.)

JOE *(after three nickels, to audience)*: *"Anybody got change for a quarter?"*

(I open my jacket to reveal a motorman's coin dispenser.)

FLO: *"I have a wonderful idea for an act. Why don't we go back together again? Why don't you come down here?"*

(She sings a half chorus of another song, to give us time to reach the stage.)

ME: *"Come on, Pop, let's go. What are you looking for?"*

JOE: *"I lost my taffy."*

ME: *"What's so important about a little piece of taffy?"*

JOE: *"My teeth are in it!"*

(Onstage, Flo explains the new act to us. It involves a dancing, hugging love scene with Joe. In the middle of this, the Other Wife brushes past an usher.)

OTHER WIFE *(screaming)*: *"That's my husband!"*

(Confrontation between the two women. Now Joe has to choose: Which one will he go home with? As Flo sings how much she loves him, and cried waiting for him . . .)

OTHER WIFE: *"Better come home, Joe."*

ME: *"Better come home, Pop."* *(I nudge him with the basket of groceries.)*

The situation had a built-in emotional tug on the audience because most of them knew Joe had actually been torn between two women. How Flo could endure this personal exposure night after night was beyond my young understanding.

(In the end, Joe goes off with the henpecking Other Wife and the fresh kid. Then we do an Afterpiece. The four of us sing "When the Red, Red Robin Comes Bob-

Bob-Bobbin' Along." And Joe skates around the stage
without skates. Joe develops this gag with heel-less shoes
and waxed soles. He glides around like a bird in a mating
flight, a beautiful, happy finish. Ending with a fall and
crash.)

This is a rather bare outline of *Any Apartment*. It ran fifteen to twenty minutes. We rehearsed in a dingy hall on Seventh Avenue. It was the day of Rudolph Valentino's rites at Frank Campbell's funeral parlor. George Jessel was there, ready to deliver the eulogy. George is a great friend, but he never understates and sometimes he isn't sure whom he's burying. He almost buried me.

Joe asked him to stop in to look over our act. George immediately commented, "One thing I can't stand is precocious stage children. That kid does it like an *actor!*"

I was no actor. I'd never spoken lines onstage in my life. That was my problem—I was trying to speak like a juvenile John Barrymore. Joe stuck with me, and let me find my way.

We went on the road, obscure towns I'd never heard of, to make adjustments, build the act. In Providence—disaster. I could not look at Joe without laughing. I must have been tired to the point of hysteria. Joe closed the act. More changes. Then one day, somehow, the act came together. Magic—fifteen minutes of continual laughter, a real blockbuster. And I was playing the Palace again.

The sign outside:

LET'S BAKE A CAKE!
They're together again—
JOE MORRIS and FLO CAMPBELL

It was two years after my debut there. I was fourteen now, taller and a bit wiser. I knew enough to be nervous on the opening matinee.

The Palace audiences loved us, too. We played there six or seven times a year, an unheard-of orgy of mutual admiration. The 1920's were the glory years of vaudeville. The movie chains were building gigantic Egyptian-Chinese-Versailles palaces; eight-act stage shows, with full orchestra, accompanied the movies. All for $1.65. In New York, you had enough theaters to play an act for three months. There were vaudeville and presentation houses in Manhattan, Brooklyn, the Bronx, Yonkers and, of course, the Orpheum circuit could guarantee forty to forty-five weeks. West to Calgary, Canada, and then San Francisco, Los Angeles; south on the Interstate Circuit through Georgia, Texas, Alabama, Tennessee and Louisiana.

Occasionally an act would double from the Palace into another house. Ours was the only one I knew that tripled. It was the end of summer. Many acts hadn't come back from the road; there was an impasse in bookings. Morris and Campbell rode to the rescue. We'd dress at the Palace, carry our hand props (grocery basket, etc.) to the waiting taxi and speed up to the RKO Chester in the Bronx. We'd be third on the bill. A quick washup to cool off, then into the same waiting taxi, same props, down to the RKO 81st Street. Here we'd go on sixth. Back to the Palace in time for coffee and a little relaxation—and we came on strong, next to closing. We played matinee and evening performances in all these houses—six performances a day.

John Charles Thomas, the great American baritone, was the headliner at the Palace, one of his very rare excursions into vaudeville, but I never got to see or hear him onstage due to our tripling. Business was so big at the Palace on Saturday that the management injected a matinee show, and so I was able to stand in the wings and thrill to the magnificence of John Charles Thomas's voice. To this day I am an incurable voice buff. I guess it's part of the frustration of losing my own.

When Mr. Thomas finally came off after many encores, I said to him, "Mr. Thomas, I'd give five years of my life to sing like you."

He answered, "Would you indeed? I gave all of my life to sing like that." What a kick in the groin. And yet, for the remainder of his life, his was the voice I admired most.

Morris and Campbell were making $1,750 a week. They paid me $75. I turned almost all the money over to my family.

When we played in New York, I'd take the subway home to
Bensonhurst every night.

Vaudeville was an exhilarating, great new world for me. It
had its share of deadbeats and egocentric maniacs and joke-
snatchers. But we had warmth and camaraderie and time for
laughs. One comic who shared a dressing room with me was
Jere Delaney (Williams and Delaney). He looked like an Irish
priest. When he was broke, his wife would dole out ten cents
for the subway to Times Square; he enjoyed himself by hanging around "The Beach" in front of the Palace and introducing
strangers to each other. Eighteen people would be shaking
hands, chattering away—and Jere would disappear.

> (Palace Theater, a dressing room: Before the matinee. I
> notice a strange new thing suspended on a wire clothes
> hanger. Looks like giant fabric-covered earphones for a
> radio.)
> JERE: "You never saw one? It's the newest short-wave
> radio. I think Paul Whiteman is on now."
> ME: "Can I try it?"
> (I eagerly put on the earphones. Nothing. Jere fiddles
> with the controls, to turn up the volume. Joe Morris
> wanders in, and breaks into helpless laughter. I am
> wearing Jere's truss.)

I was a sharp street boy, but my range of experience was
very limited. Morris and Campbell broadened it a little. Particularly Joe Morris. I absorbed the thrills of betting horses
from him. Rather innocently, between shows. He didn't ask
me to go to the track . . . he let me come along. He was a
compulsive gambler and he simply needed company.

I'd bet five dollars here and there. When I lost, I fell into the
habit of borrowing, so that I could continue sending the big
payment home. My father urged, "Keep some for yourself," but
I knew he wasn't making much money and I thought that if I
could send enough, he'd stop working and take a rest. But
he was compulsive about working, and he was betting horses,

too. I suffered double guilt: first when I lost and again when I borrowed.

Flo Campbell would lend me twenty-five dollars and make me pay back thirty. I despised her for it—she was making thousands. Years later I understood. She was trying to discipline me, rub my nose in my own irresponsibility by making me pay for it. But I was hooked.

I gambled in anger. I hated what I was doing: five feet ten and playing a kid in short pants. I thought I was better than that. Those short pants caused years of confusion and torment. Today's boys and girls at fifteen are so *knowing* about sex. Boys don't have the answers but they certainly know how to ask the questions. I passed through my adolescence in a state of original ignorance. I knew, of course, that something was happening in my groin. Girls and older women on the same bill would hug me backstage, and I'd have discharges in my short pants. They must have had some clue that I wasn't an infant, yet nobody took me aside to help me understand what I was going through. I couldn't *ask* anybody in the show world for fear of admitting my ignorance. When I talked to my peers in Bensonhurst, they only wanted to hear about sex in the "big time." "Those flappers must be real hot, huh?" I wish I had kept notes of the wild fantasies I invented. They might have made a hit later off-Broadway—*Oh, Bensonhurst!*

Sometimes because of tight hotel bookings, I'd have to double in a room with Flo. Those were nights of torment. I knew she was still in love with Joe Morris, but here I was all alone with her all night. Would she slap me down? After all, she was no virgin. And then the sounds and smells of my father and mother thrashing around in bed overwhelmed me . . . furtive, dark, full of pain . . . and all my eagerness ebbed away. I never touched Flo.

I did attract a female impersonator who put his arms around me one night in the wings. I shivered with nausea and shoved him away. That was never my bag. I didn't really explore women until I was in burlesque and twenty-one. But I certainly played a lot of catch-up ball by the time I was twenty-two.

Flo Campbell was disintegrating. Her deafness embarrassed

the act. She sang offkey, or against the tempo. She hung on doggedly to her love for Joe. His wife bore him a second child, then a third. Occasionally she'd come to visit Joe on the road, and Flo would baby-sit for the children. What wild, desperate fantasies must have propelled Flo to cling to this sick triangle!

She retreated deeper and deeper into Christian Science. She sat alone, reading and meditating. We were playing Loew's State when she closed a window in the dressing room and somehow caught her fingers between the pane and the sill. I pulled her hands loose; she was wearing rings—her fingers were ripped. She refused a doctor in favor of her religious practitioner. The fingers did not heal. She couldn't use her ivory fan, which lent a graciousness to her stage movement.

And suddenly I was twenty and six feet tall, making two hundred dollars a week—and still in short pants. That was tremendous money for a youngster in the bottom of the Depression. Grown men with families were standing on street corners, selling apples for a nickel. But those short pants were castrating me. I hated that kid. I wanted out.

I couldn't bring myself to make the decision. I pressed Joe for a twenty-five-dollar raise, just before we were to go on the road again. That did it. "We'll get another kid," he said. I agreed to stay on until he did.

Joe wanted the same characterization that had taken me six years to develop. He tried a man who was short: Teddy Hart, who later became a very successful comedian. An instinctively funny man, but makeup couldn't mask his heavy beard. And hairy legs. There was a moment in the act when he had to cry. It's very difficult for a grown man to cry convincingly. On his first sob, Flo broke up onstage, and so did Joe in the box. After about six months Joe did find a suitable boy, and I left Morris and Campbell.

By now I'd developed what I thought was a rather exquisite sense of timing. It took me a week to realize that early 1931 was precisely the wrong time to look for another job. Vaudeville was thrashing around in its last desperate gasps.

What killed vaudeville? The movies helped; so did radio. But the real executioner was vaudeville itself. Its complacency.

Acts never changed. The performers thought their successful routines had been handed down from Mount Sinai, on stone tablets.

For a long time, people loved it. When you went on the road, the same people were sitting in the same seats Wednesday night. It was a great big family club. When the orchestra struck up "Some of These Days," you knew Sophie Tucker was coming out. Morris and Campbell were great, but after six years the audience knew every line. To get the full impact of this familiarity, imagine hundreds of television reruns; not a series—just one fifteen-minute sequence—rolling on six days a week, month after month, for six years. The movies came along with new personalities, exciting new stories, bizarre foreign locales. All for fifty cents. And radio—fresh drama, on-the-spot sports, comedy, music, murders—something for everybody. All free!

To make my life more difficult, I had the wrong image. Every booking office was open to me. They knew me, liked my work. To them I was still The Kid in Short Pants. And there wasn't much call for six-foot-tall kids that year.

I lived with the family in Bensonhurst. Most of my friends in the neighborhood had faded away. They were absorbed in business or steady jobs; many were married and wrapped up in wives and children. Brownsville was worse; the old pals who hadn't moved away were dead or in prison.

I was lonely and broke. After all those years in the "big time," I had to borrow from Harry for walking-around money. My salary had slipped away between my family and the horses. It never occurred to me to put money in a bank. I had two good suits left—and lots of short pants, which I donated to the Hebrew Free Loan Society rummage sale.

Before I made the rounds in Times Square, I'd change whatever I had, ten or twelve dollars, into singles and roll them in a loose wad. As I talked, I'd keep my hand on the big bankroll in my pocket, to give myself confidence. I kept punching away, but I couldn't knock out the kid image. Success with Morris and Campbell had ruined me.

CHAPTER 3

My First One-Night Stand, and Other Awakenings

Enter: Mildred Harris Chaplin, billed as
CHARLIE CHAPLIN'S FIRST WIFE
She was a petite woman of classic beauty. In her eyes was nothing but fear and distance, as though she was hiding inside her own body. She had been a minor movie star in the silent days; her divorce created more attention than she ever enjoyed in her film career. As was the custom with champion prize fighters, explorers and attractive lady murderers, a vaudeville act was concocted for her. So that the paying public could inspect the newest sensation close-up, and derive some moral inspiration from her. A freak show.

The Timberg brothers, Herman and Sammy, financed the act and put it together. Miss Harris was a partner in the receipts. She was a beauty all right—all she needed was talent. That was supplied by Herbie Faye, an expert comedian of burlesque and vaudeville. Now they needed another man.

I auditioned and got the usual reaction: nice to see you, but we can't use a kid. I watched their rehearsal and realized they did not have a strong finish. The last few minutes could make or break the act. As I rattled home on the Sea Beach Express, a finish popped into my head, complete with music. A natural.

I caught the express to Times Square early next morning and laid out the idea.

> ME: *"Herbie, Miss Harris and I will impersonate three movie stars, talking to each other as human beings. Without the expected 'I will now do an imitation of Maurice Chevalier.' It's revolutionary—don't ask me why nobody's done it before. Okay, I play the orchestra leader.*

Herbie gets into an argument with me. He tops it with a good line, then he runs off. There's a straw hat on the piano. I pick it up. Now I'm Chevalier: 'Ah, there's only one thing you must do with a straw hat . . .' And I do 'Louise.'

Now Miss Harris comes out in a trench coat, beret, clompy shoes. She's Garbo: 'Aye vant to be alawn.' And then Herbie. He's Jimmy Durante: 'Just a minute! Everybody wants to get into tha act!' He's perfect for it—all he needs is a phony nose. Into a three-way conversation. We end with a strut-off to one of Durante's numbers. It's got to be a smash!"

HERMAN *(after a moment):* "Pretty good, kid. How much do you want for it?"

ME: "Nothing. I want the job."

I got it. And we went into rehearsal. Herbie resisted the entire conception. He was a stand-up, knock-'em-dead comedian, a proud man; this twist embarrassed him because it was outside his accustomed routines. My enthusiasm convinced him halfway.

And poor Mildred—she had to be protected from the audience because she couldn't do anything. No voice, no presence. We had to teach her to walk across the stage. That's all she did. She clomped around in her big shoes and murmured, "Aye vant to be alawn." The drummer helped by accompanying her walk with taps on the wood blocks.

I had some problems, too. I couldn't talk like a man. After all those years of inflecting like a youngster, my conception of an adult was formal, precise. Herbie coached me into some appearance of ease, but I was a stiff for a long time. We tried out the act in Bay Shore, Long Island, at a Saturday matinee. To this day I hate to face a matinee: show business is a night thing. Bay Shore was unpremeditated murder—a kiddies' matinee.

They understood the Chevalier bit because he was very popular in movie musicals. Durante was greeted with puzzled chatter; children weren't going to nightclubs yet. And Garbo was a three-minute wake.

When we came offstage, Herbie was furious. "How could I let a *shmuck* like you talk me into that?"

Fortunately, Harry Savoy, a top vaudeville comedian, was in the audience. He thought it was a great finish. "Give it a chance tonight, Herbie—with older people." That night, all of us got roars of recognition as soon as we came on.

But we still needed a lot of work. We cut and polished in out-of-the-way theaters. CHARLIE CHAPLIN'S FIRST WIFE drew the customers. Then we had to make them forget her. That wasn't easy because we never knew where she'd stand. I could wave my arms, yell at her—no reaction. She was somewhere else.

I'd see peculiar people meeting her outside the stage door, on the sidewalk, in coffee shops. Guys in grubby overcoats, and unshaven lawyer types with peeling briefcases. But everybody in vaudeville was a little offbeat, a little bent. You had to be, otherwise why would you go into this business? I didn't ask questions.

She picked up our mail and drew the money for the act. For weeks, letters from home didn't reach me. They were addressed c/o Mildred Harris Chaplin. "Oh, it's in care of me!" and she'd open them and forget to pass them on to me. After she received the money for the week, I'd hold out my hand and she'd flutter absentmindedly, "Oh! You get some too?"

Some was correct. My salary—as a grown man—was seventy-five dollars a week. Down from two hundred bucks as a kid. That hurt.

I also had to take care of our music "library." As we passed Cleveland, on the train to the Palace Theater in Chicago, I remembered I left the music in New York. I phoned my brother from Chicago, and he put a dozen stamps on the package, so we received it four days after we opened. Luckily, the orchestra leader, Danny Russo, knew me from the Morris and Campbell days. He improvised our music and secured a special permit from the union to let me conduct, since it was part of the act. He even let me conduct the "bow" music for the preceding performers, so I could be on the podium when Herbie started the "argument."

The act cemented overnight. We weren't sure how effective

it was because we'd been playing small-time theaters. The Palace was our first important date. Texas Guinan was headlining, so we came on second or third, a next-to-nothing billing.

After opening night the manager moved us up to next-to-closing. On our third day we received the wire: BOOKED WHOLE ORPHEUM CIRCUIT. We would lay over in Chicago for ten days until the schedule for the circuit could be mapped out, then open in Minneapolis. My loneliness, insecurities, humiliations —all forgotten. I was in the big time again, at twenty. In long pants. A man at last.

I immediately kissed Mildred. Nothing. A blank stare.

Friday I came in to work early, to sit in the theater's Green Room and savor the pleasure of greeting visitors and signing autographs. A well-dressed local congratulated me.

"I hope you enjoy my theater next week."

"Are you from Minneapolis?" I said.

"Chicago. I'm 'the manager of the Star and Garter. I've signed Miss Harris for a week."

This was the grimiest burlesque house in town. He had approached Mildred when she was alone and desperate for money. We were furious, but she had us by the throat—she was the draw. We began to ask questions. Both Herbie and I were so sheltered we couldn't believe what we heard.

Mildred Harris was on cocaine.

We were rather sick, too, as we worked out our week's sentence in the Star and Garter. We laid a quiet, eerie egg. Our family-trade vaudeville routine was slumming on the wrong side of town. The Depression changed burlesque. It had been literally a burlesque, a takeoff on people, events and plays of the day. The comedy was innocent and noisy: mainly in Dutch, Yiddish, Irish dialect. Sex was also burlesqued: the chorus was a Beef Trust, 200-pounders who lumbered around in baggy tights. Good rowdy fun for the whole family. Hard times in the 1930's brought desperate measures. "Blue" double-entendre sketches, and strippers grinding out sex fantasies. The Star and Garter was near the bottom of the garbage heap.

Compounding our indignity, the manager had conned Mildred into spicing up the act with a little strip routine. It was so silly and sad—nobody had taught her to dance.

Variety's front page was appalled: Mildred Harris Peels! The Orpheum circuit canceled our contract by invoking a morality clause. The act was dead. I coaxed my seventy-five dollars out of Mildred, but Herbie wasn't so lucky.

There we were, stranded in Chicago: Herbie, his wife, Bobbie, and I. Like many show-business marriages, they were married young and forever. Bobbie Caputo was seventeen at the time and Italian; he was eighteen and Jewish. She was now as buxom as a Beef Trust girl, and he'd lost most of his hair. I roomed with them in the outside bedroom. When I got the wake-up call, I'd open their door with a gentle "Time to get up . . ." And out of this lavish mountain of alabaster flesh in which Herbie was snuggling came his small bald head. "Okay, Phil."

For some years Herbie had an act that he would play out of town, using his wife, another girl and a straight man. His dream was to bring it into New York. Now was the time. I could play the straight man; all he needed was transportation to New York.

They invited me for one of her lovingly cooked pasta dinners, and Herbie asked to borrow my last week's salary. I turned as green as the *tagliarini verdi.* "I lost it at the horse room," I explained. Bobbie started to cry. I ran to the bathroom and threw up.

We wired friends for money to make it to New York on a bus that broke down ten times. Herbie rounded up a pretty girl and we put the act together. It was based on an early burlesque sketch, *She Won't Take It:*

> Me *(to Herbie):* "*I'll show you how to get a girl. When a girl passes by, you drop your wallet. You say, 'Beg your pardon, miss. You dropped your wallet.' She, being a very honest person, says, 'No thank you, sir.' You pick up the conversation. First thing you know, you take her out to dinner.*"
>
> Herbie: "*How do you know she won't take me to the police station . . .*"
>
> Me: "*Okay, here comes a girl now! Let go of your wallet.*"

> HERBIE: *"I can't let go."*
> ME: *"Why not?"*
> HERBIE: *"I got a Jewish cramp!"*

Ah, those innocent days.

I was as stiff as a scenery brace, and I didn't have a clue to what I was supposed to be. Herbie had no choice: he nursed me along, cajoled me, taught me the fundamentals of stage comedy. I loosened up, became more creative; I improvised instantly on my feet. To this day, Herbie's axiom has stayed with me: Don't move on somebody's line; that hurts his laugh because all eyes go with you.

> *(Twenty years later I am starring in* Top Banana. *Herbie is working with me, developing bits we used in burlesque. After a few months into the run, Herbie is doing new things. I wait for him backstage.)*
> ME: *"Herbie, that joke was always good. You're moving on it. Don't improve it into the ground."*
> HERBIE *(wistfully):* *"I knew this would come back to haunt me someday."*
> *(We both smile.)*

Many nights I wouldn't go home to Brooklyn—I stayed with Herbie and Bobbie. It wasn't a great act, the money wasn't much, but what else could we do? We kept plugging away. We even played a week at the Palace. It was deteriorating now, no longer the pinnacle of the entertainment world. They were booking entire units, put together by an outside producer. The man who hired us specialized in units of "flash" acts; he needed a comedy sequence to break the monotony.

We never admitted to ourselves that the musty odor in the vaudeville houses was formaldehyde. Prosperity was just around the corner. Then one clear day, Herbie and I looked at each other and shook our heads: This was no living. Curtain.

We went our separate ways. I took to the mountains.

The Catskills, the Borscht Circuit, the Derma Road—it was the summer refuge and playground for a million perspiring Jews from New York City. Of course, a few token Gentiles managed to find their way in. I discovered it in the Morris and Campbell years. The act laid off during the summer—no air-conditioning, remember?—and I was in my usual embarrassing condition. Broke.

The office of Beckman & Pransky was the largest slave market for talent shipped to the Catskills. The hotel owners were too thrifty to hire top-name performers for $20,000 a week, as they did later in the 1950's and 1960's. In my day, the hotels based their judgment of your talent on how little you would accept. So they became a showcase for hungry young performers, writers, musicians, directors.

I entered the B & P office just as a hotel owner burst in, looking for a comic to "help out" the MC that week-end. At the Evans Hotel in Loch Sheldrake. Although I was fairly well-known in vaudeville, I'd never done a solo or a monologue. But I qualified as young and hungry. I threw some makeup into a bag and off we flew into the night in the owner's Chevvy, racing through those mountains as if he had to make the eight o'clock show. When I stumbled out at the hotel, I was seasick. And it *was* the eight o'clock show. I slapped on some pancake makeup and walked onstage cold.

The MC called himself Buddy Walker: huge flashy "gold" ring, shiny "silk" suit, and always "on." He made me into his stooge. He lectured me, he berated me. I waited my time. Buddy was down at the footlights, punching over one of his sleazy gags. "Excuse me," I said, pushing him gently away. "Don't stand too close to the lights. I smell ham burning."

Two men in the five-piece orchestra broke up. The violinist, Sammy Cahn; the pianist, Saul Chaplin. And that line started a three-way admiration that continues to this day. Our blood bond was our mutual disdain for Buddy Walker.

The house lights were shut off immediately after the show. I stood there in the dark backstage. Nobody told me if I had a room. Or where I could eat. I wandered around in the night until I heard some happy noises. I opened the door—Cahn and the orchestra were having sandwiches. They found a room for me over the kitchen. That was my debut in the mountains.

Next summer I was the MC. It was a frenetic business. The comedian had to work with the social director as the hotel buffoon, the *tummeler,* the noisemaker who would do anything to keep the guests from checking out. Potato races, "Roll the Peanut," "A Night in Tahiti." The hotel owner gave me strict orders: "I don't want ever a dull moment—dance with the girls." The busboys, the waiters (always college boys) and I, everybody had to dance with the girls. They worked in offices and saved all year for these two weeks, so they could change clothes every hour on the hour. We were ordered to keep the girls happy—"any time, you understand?" I interpreted this to mean: escort the girl back to her hall door and say good night like a gentleman. Anyhow, the work onstage loosened me up. I tried everything. I didn't have time to think of failure—and it didn't really matter.

Next season: Young's Gap Hotel. Here I worked with a surprisingly silent man, a tap dancer named Jack Kraft, whose real name was Albertson. I persuaded him he could talk. We played one-acts, sketches, musicals, and I passed on to him much of the stagecraft that Herbie Faye had taught me.

When I left Herbie Faye, I was ready for the top job in the mountains—social director. At the Evans Hotel, where the salary was now $1,200 a season. Large money again. We were loaded with talent. I recruited Jack Albertson, who promptly fractured a leg playing volleyball. I persuaded Sammy Cahn and Saul Chaplin, who were writing music for movie shorts, to perform some of their songs that were already hits: "Shoeshine Boy," "Rhythm Is My Business," "Please Be Kind." Michael Kanin, Garson's brother, painted scenery, then went on to become an important writer of film and stage comedies. We were very inventive. I announced, "In the casino tonight, the Pulitzer Prize musical, *Of Thee I Sing!*" I got some guests to help me and we did the opening chorus, "Wintergreen for President" . . . "Flugel Street," the burlesque bit . . . "Love Is Sweeping the Country" . . . "Ten Dollars She's Not Here," another burlesque standby . . . and "Of Thee I Sing." The management never knew the difference.

Garson Kanin, down the road in another hotel, sabotaged me by producing Eugene O'Neill plays. And he really did them, word for word. The owner of the Evans, a culture vulture, grumbled to me. "Why don't you do *real* art, like Kanin?" I directed Schnitzler's *Affairs of Anatole,* because I found the tattered script among the props. I didn't understand any of it, but we grayed our temples with cornstarch and the audience thought the play was "class."

The job did help my psyche a little. There was a lot of sex floating around in the mountains, yet my hangups hung heavy on my young shoulders. Men left their wives all week to cool off in the Catskill breezes. The wives turned to the staff for understanding. I was entranced by one of these women on a Thursday; by Sunday, when I saw her husband, I was suffused with guilt because I liked the guy. She boldly paraded her affection . . . what if he found out? I dropped her Monday.

And then the season was over. I came out of the hills with my salary intact for the first time, because nobody would take my bets. At the start of the summer a dignified guest appeared—I'll call her Mrs. Jerry Polan—with her young son. I liked the boy instantly and played table tennis with him. The father, I soon learned, was boss of the betting and slot machines in the Catskills. A five-foot-seven heavy, he was typecast for the role: his left eye had been gouged out in a fight. He had a disarmingly quiet, almost gentle manner. He called me over to his table one night. "I hear you've got a bug—you gamble, don't you?"

I nodded carefully.

"From now on, you don't bet. You tap is shut off."

"Wait a minute," I murmured. "I always pay my debts."

"And you end up with no money. Kid, you belong in a better business than what you're doing. Get smart."

To further my education, Jerry invited me along to watch the Pittsburgh mob, in town to buck his dice game. It was a home-and-home schedule: Jerry's boys would reciprocate.

"You'll see what's only in the movies, kid—twenty thousand a roll." I recall vividly an irrelevant detail: Jerry's thick, crepe-sole sport shoes, as we drove in his car to Monticello's main street. He wanted a cup of coffee in Trachtenberg's, the local Lindy's, before the game.

As we came out, two New York State troopers walked in. Tall, hulking men, they knew Jerry but couldn't touch him because the gambling was protected by their superiors. "Oh, Christ," one of the troopers mumbled, "the Jews are out again."

I froze. No rational hoodlum wants to slug a policeman. Jerry gave the trooper a chance to save face. "You weren't talking to me, were you?"

The trooper grunted, "What's it to you—?"

That was as far as he got. Jerry launched himself at the troopers, kicking, slugging, strangling. This was the job he knew best. The thick crepe soles gave him the speed and leaps of a panther. One trooper pulled his gun. Jerry snatched it away and pistol-whipped the man. A carload of Jerry's men pulled up to join the battle. A moment of stunned silence, as both sides realized what had happened: Nobody looks good when a state cop has been beat up. By one man. Jerry tossed the bullets out of the gun, slipped a hundred-dollar bill into the barrel and tossed it at the inert trooper.

He immediately went into seclusion for a few days—on a cot in our scenery room—while thousands of dollars were spread around to soothe the troopers' bruised egos.

I respected the Jewish musclemen and racketeers. We must have had a soft-focus mutual attraction. They saw in me the gambler who takes his risks and pays his debts; I saw them as the only militant Jews. After thousands of years of racial indignities, the only ones who struck back were the outlaws.

At the end of that season, I talked Jack Albertson into doing an audition with me for the Minskys. Burlesque was about the only steady work in 1932.

We had only two good scenes to present to H. K. and Harold

in their Republic Theater on 42nd Street. They were exuberant, honest men, and refreshingly theater-wise. Billy, H. K.'s brother and Harold's uncle, practically invented modern burlesque. H. K. had a class complex: He dreamed of producing a clean Broadway show. But in laying out a burlesque show, the sequence of chorus, strip, body scene and so on to finale, he had no equal.

The Minskys hired us for a road show. We did our two scenes, and developed a sequence that became part of the finale. I was just learning to noodle around on a clarinet; Jack performed a beautiful soft-shoe dance to my improvisations.

We played six weeks in the Minsky eastern houses: Boston, Philadelphia, Albany, Baltimore and Pittsburgh. The comedians were good friends; it was cozy and fun—one big family. After we came back to New York, H. K. asked us to stay on, to play at the Gaiety, at 46th and Broadway. Jack didn't see any future in it; he thought he'd try to break into serious acting.

(Cut to: the Academy Award ceremonies, Hollywood, 1968. Jack Albertson receives the Oscar as best supporting actor for *The Subject Was Roses*.)

I stayed. And that was the best move I ever made.

Since the 1930's, a great many myths have arisen out of those steamy mists of burlesque. The most popular:

One: Burlesque was a great training ground for comedians. True.

Two: Most burlesque comedians were, therefore, great.

False. Most of them were hokey, rigid and vulgar. That's why they stayed in burlesque. The ones who rose out of it were able to build creatively on the basics they learned. Witness Abbott and Costello, Rags Ragland, Herbie Faye, Ted Healy, Bert Lahr, Red Buttons, Jackie Gleason, Danny Thomas, Bobby Clark, Ed Wynn, Red Skelton, Joe E. Brown, Eddie Cantor. And Fanny Brice.

Abbott and Costello appropriated an old burlesque staple—one of the few clean ones—*Who's on First?* and zoomed to the top of movie clowndom. They were very inventive. And very lucky. They got on first.

It was a rough and tough obstacle course. By the time Minsky hired me, the main attraction was female nudity. The ribald blackout sketches were included only for their redeeming social values. I was pleased to receive $62.50 a week when I started. After three years, I was a top comedian and my pay rose to $250. The big money went to the strippers—Margie Hart, Ann Corio, Georgia Sothern, Gypsy Rose Lee; they got from $700 to $2,000 a week.

To seize the attention of the predominantly male audience, a comedian had to make his presence felt. And fast. The name of the strippers' game was titillation. By stimulating encores and provoking shouts and applause, they scored points that helped raise their salaries. The law called for bras or fringe, but bare breasts somehow managed to poke through. G-strings were mandatory in most states; the clever little beasts would wear fabric under the strings that looked like pubic hair. Sometimes it was the real thing, whereupon the manager would rush backstage, screaming, "Whaddya want to do—close the theater?" The girl, apologetic, would cover up—until the next night that applause was slow.

Among the men, the only weapon was comedy. The management was not interested in how funny you were, just how *often* you were funny. You had to appear in at least three sketches. They were all traditional, in the public domain, handed down by generations of unnamed, underpaid comics. The title gave you the entire routine. When you walked into a theater, the manager asked, "What do you want to do?"

"*Pick Up My Old Hat?*"
"Did it last week."
"*Pullman Scene?*"
"Red is doing that."
"*The Schoolroom?*"
"Did it four weeks ago."
"*Fireman, Save My Wife?*"
"Ecch . . ."
"*The Courtroom?*"
"Maybe."
"*Crazy House?*"
"Now you're talkin'."

I often ran through twenty titles before I got one into the

show. The dialogue was conventional, too. The only chance you had for individuality or freshness was your own improvisation. New facets of character or voice. Bits of business. Costume or style.

I contributed a few modest novelties. All comedians included a catchline, part of their own special bits, in their name. Harry (Hello, Jake) Fields. Peanuts (What the Hay) Bone. I was simply Phil Silvers. Revolutionary. I never used grotesque makeup, which was really a hangover from fifteenth-century clowns. I was a recognizable human being in black horn-rimmed glasses. I instinctively felt the glasses gave a touch of humility to my extremely brash approach to comedy. I still wear them to this day.

And no baggy pants. If I had to be a sailor, I'd jump into a real sailor's suit. When I had to tell a really "blue" single entendre, I'd step to the footlights and add, "That's a little thing I borrowed from the Theater Guild." This meant absolutely nothing to the burlesque audience, but it was my way of telling anybody out front who might be of some theatrical importance, "Listen, I don't want to do it this way, but when in Rome . . ."

Paradoxically, burlesque gave me a lot of freedom. I could improvise anything I wished—a new bit here, a couple of lines there didn't matter to the others in the scene, as long as it got us all to the blackout. The only critic was the audience. If you failed, the show did not close. This was a big, wide-open world for a young comedian. I had a stage, costumes, lights, music, a friendly company and a captive audience. The management gave me all this to play with—and even paid me.

At the Gaiety I began working with Rags Ragland, in a give-and-take relationship that was to last thirty years. I'd met Rags in Chicago in 1930, during our week's incarceration at the Star and Garter. I idolized Rags. What an exhilarating comedian. And what a man. Six feet five, lantern jaw, a loose-boned brawler and lover. He'd been a boxer of no renown in Louisville, but left town to escape a woman demanding a marriage contract.

He used to hang around the burlesque house in Louisville.

Encouraged by one of the comics, Rags joined a touring company on the assumption that the stage was easier than boxing. Or marrying. For him it was, because it gave him steadier opportunities to drink, in higher-toned places. To this day I cannot go into a bar and be at ease because whenever I was in a bar with Rags he was always in a fight. None of which he sought.

I never drank. I'd just stand there while he drank away, and we'd talk. There was always some little man, fired up with booze, who wanted to hit the big guy. Rags tried to shrug him off, or walk away. If cornered, he'd break up the little guy and all his friends—and the bar. Rags was remarkably relaxed, almost languid. Burlesque was just a way to pay for his drinks. And he never hit a saturation point.

Rags left the Gaiety after a few weeks to fulfill a previous contract in Pittsburgh. I was booked into the Oxford in Brooklyn, near the Long Island Rail Road tracks. The Oxford ranked somewhat below the Star and Garter on the social ladder, but far above it in scruffiness. One of my brothers, Jack, who succumbed to the insurance business, talked me into a life and accident policy. The company's investigator took one look at the dungeon in which we dressed and rejected the application. "You'd upset our life-expectancy tables."

It was a small theater, 600 seats, operated by a raging hyperthyroid named Charlie Schwartz. Charlie ran the Oxford like a Prussian general. He'd stomp into the dressing room during the newsreel chaser between shows when the cast was relaxing, and yell *"Ajax! Ajax!"* Meaning *"Energy! Give it to them!"*

Burlesque was a lot less nude and raw than Broadway or Off-Broadway today. It used the *promise* of nudity, suggestion, double meanings. Hypocritical by today's standards, but in the 1930's the audience—and the police who enforced the standards of taste—really believed in surface propriety. We worked within their frame of conventional morality. A sleazy business—but proper.

The Star Theater, in Brooklyn's Italian neighborhood, was

as clean-minded as the Oxford. On Monday nights there was an amateur night before the last show. A small booking office provided the "amateurs"—all obscure performers who had hit the end of the road. I think everybody in the audience knew it was rigged, but they all went along with the game.

> In the lower stage box, from which you can step onto the stage: three Italian truck drivers, who've just finished their night run.
> Onstage: "The Great Resisto." She defies all comers to lift her off the floor. And she actually weighs only ninety pounds. They put their arms around her waist, she grips their upper arms "for balance" and they just can't lift her. Her grip actually neutralizes their strength.
> Two drivers persuade the third man, a giant, to give it a try. He stomps onstage in his oilskin jacket. He strains and strains. Nothing. He looks to see if she's nailed to the floor—a laugh to cover embarrassment. He nods confidently to his buddies. Okay, she can't fool me any more. I'm gonna lift that goddamned broad. . . . He pushes and grunts and the veins bulge on his forehead. Bewildered, he turns to his friends: "Hey, Tony. Thatsa no shit!"

Stunned silence for a moment. Then an explosion. A shock laugh. Because we never used the raw words.

The double meaning is best illustrated by an introduction I gave from the stage for Ann Corio's nostalgia-fest, *This Was Burlesque*, in Los Angeles in 1966. Ann's act itself was a prime example of suggestion and indirection.

She was the first to turn the stage lights down, use magenta and purple gelatins to create a bit of mystery. All acts had gimmicks. Hers was gentility and beauty. She worked with a delicate parasol and some layers of chiffon. "If you want to see more of me," she sang, "clap your hands like this . . ." And then she went into a rather conventional slow strip.

My intro:

> Let me explain what double entendre means. A comic
> walks out in an all-fitting toreador outfit. The straight man
> has convinced him he must fight the bull. He is terrified
> . . . a lot of comedy is built on fright.
>   "It's nothing," the straight man says. "You just go out
> there and take out your machete [knife]."
>   "In front of all those people?"
>   "And you wave it at the queen's box."
>   "What'll the king say?"

That sophisticated audience roared.

Today the stage is more realistic, more "honest" in its attention to sexual details, but I think that hurts comedy. So much of humor is the contrast between real life and the artificial rules we live by. When you destroy those conventions, what can you play satire against?

The code of morality among the performers was strict and monogamous. Strippers usually married straight men. It made sense, it was frugal—they could always be booked together. Casual bedhopping was rare. When a man went with a girl they were considered a couple. Another man in the same show would never infringe. There were no class distinctions, based on salary or billing, in pairing off. The couple would break up only when one partner chose to do so. Pairing off was simple and direct. No games. The man would say to the girl, if she was not tied up, "Would you like to go out for a drink?"

"Sure."

If she went that far, you were paired.

There were occasional brief encounters, of course. I was standing in the wings at the Oxford with my arms around a stripper—just friendly, that's all—watching the Metrotone newsreel. She was married to a straight man I didn't know, so I bent The Code a little. I necked. In two minutes we were

doing the sex bit—standing up. At the climax, Aimee Semple
McPherson on the screen was exhorting her followers, "Oh,
come with me—"

We did.

That was my first real one-night stand. The refined ethics of
the burlesque world freed me from much guilt and repression.
I had been an emotional virgin till I was old enough to vote.
Now I began to *enjoy* sex. On benches, dressing-room tables,
a heap of drapes in the scenery dock. Even in a bed.

CHAPTER 4

The Night Rags
Nailed the
Comic's Shoes to the Stage

I played the Gaiety on and off for two years and the burlesque circuit for five years. I was learning my craft, control, confidence. I knew I was better than burlesque. Why not reach for Broadway? Or the movies? Nothing is impossible when you start at the Palace at twelve.

These years come back in vignettes, scenes, bits. Memory is a kaleidoscope. The patterns are accidental, even though you can shake up the outline of the pieces, and all of it is brightly lit. In memory, the dominant color is rose. Maybe reaching for the goal, the doubtful years, were the best time of all.

> *The horse room on Columbus Circle: crowded and humming. A banging on the door . . . cops' voices. Manny, the boss of this operation, opens the door, and the uniforms fill the room. Somebody has not been paid off.*
>
> *The cops take the names of the bettors; that means I'll lose a day in court. I grab Manny in the toilet. "You've got to protect me. If I miss the show tonight, I'm fired!" (A little exaggerated, but . . .)*
>
> *Manny hides me in a broom closet, where I sweat for three-quarters of an hour. I come out soaked, and run all the way to the Gaiety. Next day: a heavy cold and the shivers. The flu.*

Discovering marijuana.

A new comedian is booked into the Gaiety, Tommy (Moe) Raft. He looks like George Raft and he calls everybody Moe, but he is actually Mexican. He is high all the time.

I am very innocent about that aroma. Whenever I come into his dressing room, I inspect his rack of clothes. I think they are burning.

It's a Sunday matinee, a tough day because we did six shows on Saturday. I'm slightly hung over; I am experimenting with mixed drinks in this period. I finish my first scene, go to my dressing room for more coffee. The stripper goes on, then the chaser music for the next scene. But it keeps repeating, like a broken record. Something is wrong. I run out to the stage. It's empty. I recognize the props for the "Ice Cream" scene. In burlesque, you don't ask questions. I figure Tommy has missed his scene, so I do it.

Every time I come to the blackout, someone else walks on. Tommy has done so many variations, nobody knows where he belongs. I'm going out of my mind—I can't end the scene. By this time, Harold Minsky is in the wings. When I finally come off, I growl, "Where is that sonovabitch Tommy?"

Harold calls his hotel. He's disappeared. I swallow more coffee and go out for my second scene—that's three in a row now. I'm tired and furious. An usher puts his head in the door. "You looking for Tommy Raft? He's up in the mezzanine." This one has got to be a weird scene even for Tommy. I sneak out front to the mezzanine.

And there he is, in the front row, his feet up on the railing. But he's on another planet. His eyes are glassy. I tap his shoulder. It takes about thirty seconds for him to turn and put me into focus.

"What are you doing up here?" I ask.

"Just wanted to see how I look from out front." And he meant it.

Rags comes back from a road tour with a new partner, a young fellow named Bobby. A Yiddish dialect comic. I watch the first performance. Rags, as usual, gives his partner most of the scene. Bobby is the busiest comedian I've ever seen. His tie revolves, and his fake nose lights up. He has a shoe gimmick, too. The soles have a hook which locks into a special screw in the stage floor so he can sway dangerously over the footlights. The Leaning Tower of Pisa bit.

Rags comes into my dressing room afterward. "What do you think?"

"He's very good. But when you have a joke—he's catching flies all over the stage."

Rags is irritated. Just a little. "Oh, he was doin' that?" As he waits to go on for the second scene, Rags tells Bobby quietly, "Don't move on my lines or I'll nail you to the stage."

The boy shrugs that off, because Rags has the reputation of not really caring who gets the laughs. The kid goes into his busy, busy routine. Rags stops the action and calls offstage to Carlo, the carpenter. "Give me the hammer and the spikes." (It's all prearranged.)

Rags nails Bobby's shoes to the stage.

A tremendous howl. The audience assumes it's part of the act. Rags finishes the scene and walks off. I tell my straight man, "Just pretend the kid is not there," and we do our scene. Bobby tries to take his shoes off. They're high tops, reaching up to his knees in order to grip him as he sways, and the heavy laces are tangled. He claws away at the laces.

A stripper is next. As she parades around, the spotlight picks up Bobby, sweating, squirming, pulling his heels to lift the spikes. But, of course, the stage hook still holds. He's trapped. The gag runs through the rest of that show. The cast is watching in the wings. We feel a little sorry for the kid, but Rags is Rags and you just don't interfere with his Thing.

Now there's a feature picture, to cover our dinner hour and a half. The screen comes down, missing Bobby by an inch. Luckily, he's in front of it, blinking in the light. The manager comes out with a crowbar and releases Bobby.

Later, Rags doesn't think this was funny. Or unfunny. He is a man of his word, and he warned the kid.

We usually played four shows a day. On important holidays we had extra performances. It all depended on how much walk-by trade we pulled off the street. One Memorial Day weekend I worked twenty-eight shows.

> *(My dressing room in the Gaiety: Kid Posy is announced by the doorman. Surprise. I haven't seen him since we came out of PS 61. He is smoother now, and wears an expensive wraparound camel's hair. Still a pug.)*
> Posy: *"Phil! What are you doing in a joint like this?"*
> Me: *"Learning the business."*
> Posy: *"You need any money?"*
> Me: *"No. I have a good salary."*
> Posy: *"Take some money, for chrissake!"* *(He throws a wad of tens and twenties on my makeup shelf.)*
> *(I don't even want to see that he has money. If he gets picked up by the police, his friends will start thinking, Now who knew Kid Posy had a bundle?)*
> Me *(stuffing the money back into his coat pocket):* *"Thanks, Posy. I really don't need it."*
> *(He walks to door, disappointed he can't help me.)*
> Posy: *"You always was a dummy, Phil."*

Four weeks later, he was sentenced to Atlanta for passing counterfeit bills.

My first movies.

Warner Brothers made one- and two-reel shorts in a studio on Avenue M, near our house in Bensonhurst. The shorts helped sweeten the double and triple features during the Depression.

Sammy Cahn and Saul Chaplin were very prolific and fast: their first score for a short was turned out in two hours. The producer, a relative of a Warner, said, "Boys, you can't just go into your files and pull out any old crap. I want songs written *specially.*"

Next assignment, they went to the movies, spent the day in New York at Lindy's, took in some ball games. After three days they brought in a score they'd written in thirty-five minutes.

The triumphant producer said, "You see? What a difference!"

The boys got me in on this good thing. Memory has mercifully blocked out the titles and subjects I made. I recall one with Hal LeRoy. And another called *Joe and Asbestos,* based on a popular newspaper cartoon by Ken Kling, who gave predictions for the day's horse races. They needed me for that one.

Cahn and Chaplin and I boosted each other whenever we could. Georgia Sothern, the most violent stripper of them all, was booked into the Gaiety. I don't know how her head stayed on her shoulders—she tore the theater apart. You couldn't hear any music in that uproar.

"My friends have a song, 'Rhythm Is My Business,'" I said, "and you sure have rhythm. Could you use this for your last chorus?"

"Oh, thank you, Phil." She promptly went into Saporta's music store, next door to the theater, to buy the sheet music. She handed it to the orchestra leader: "Play this for my last chorus." Burlesque orchestras could fake Wagner's "Tristan und Isolde" if you gave them five parts. They might not hit every note, but they'd go after it.

That night, her act was the usual smash. Georgia stopped by my dressing room and knocked on my door. Naked, with her clothes over her arm. She bubbled with gratitude: "Phil, that new song was *great* for me!"

The Peerless Hotel, West 45th Street, 1933: a crummy exterior. Inside, the room smells fresh and the curtains are clean. The owner is a burlesque buff. He carries you if you're out of cash. So will the street character who operates the little restaurant. Burlesque people always pay back when they have money.

I'm alone, after the show. I stop off at a Greek place for a moussaka and roast lamb. Then back to my room with two boxes of chocolate marshmallow cookies. I switch on the radio to the Milkman's Matinee, light up a reefer and float through the rest of the night. I hear names of friends requesting musical specials; they hear my requests. We know who's in town by radio.

I chew slowly on the marshmallow cookies . . . they taste like liquid gold. Euphoria. Gray-blue backlights the water tanks on the roofs as I fall asleep. In a couple of hours I have to report for a rehearsal. So what? I'm young. I'm high, man, and I'm beautiful.

Robert Morley, the well-rounded British star, moved in next door to the Gaiety with his internationally acclaimed drama, *Oscar Wilde.* His stage door (at that time, the Fulton) adjoined the wall of our scenery dock. Since we had no air-conditioning, we'd leave the dock door open for a flow of air. When Morley wasn't on stage he would come in and study our routines. It was a new art form for him, and he was fascinated. "Oh, jolly good." He sent mash notes to Margie Hart: "Petroushka, my sleigh is waiting. Let us fly into the night."

He invited me to watch his show from the wings. This was a new horizon for me: straight legit. It was a case of infatuation at first sight. I'd have a drink with Mr. Morley in his dressing room, and we'd talk. We became rather friendly. However, we never went so far as to have lunch together.

Years pass. I'm in *Top Banana.* I have two weeks of vacation, so I fly to London, to do the town with the two top men of my agency at that time, Lew Wasserman and Sonny Werblin. We attend a matinee of a comedy, *Hippo Dancing,* written by and starring Robert Morley. By coincidence, he's also an MCA client. I smugly say nothing about Morley. I want to savor their surprise when they discover this staid Briton is one of my dearest friends. *Hippo* is a rowdy comedy, full of old gags, and I'm surprised to see Morley in a bed scene, projecting his full-moon fanny at the audience. Quite naughty.

I go backstage with my friends, and they introduce me. Morley greets me politely, as if he's seeing me for the first time.

Over tea and cookies, he suggests, "This thing I'm doing— and *Top Banana*—what do you say to an exchange? Mr. Silvers can do *Hippo* in America, and I shall take a crack at *Top Banana.* Might be a rather interesting lend-lease." Still no recognition. I know the British are reticent, but this is excessive. As we leave, I linger behind the others and sidle up to him. "Mr. Morley, don't you remember me?"

"*Remember* you?" he whispers. "Rags and the Gaiety girls? Of course! I just didn't think you wanted these blokes to know."

I used the clarinet more and more in scenes, playing in weird keys. Some of the customers thought I was a wild kind of new jazz artist. I had to play in those crazy keys because I couldn't read music. And I didn't feel like studying.

The Shubert Theater in Philly was a "class" house. The owners ripped out the orchestra pit for steps into the auditorium, and the band sat on the side where the boxes used to be. The house electrician installed a direct line to the bookmaker, so I could hear the results immediately.

One night at the Shubert, there's a heckler, drunk and noisy, in the front row. Sometimes they can be funnier than any gag writer in coming up with fast lines. But this one is spoiling the scenes. As soon as a comic comes to a punchline, the drunk yells, "Ah, bring out the girls!"

I've been away for a week with a little pneumonia, so I'm watching the show from out front and wondering why an usher or manager doesn't shut him up. Rags comes on with Russell Trent, a straight man, for one of the few musical scenes in all burlesque. The straight man scolds the comic, "You ought to be ashamed of yourself, the way you treat the girls!" This leads into a song.

> TRENT: ". . . *and who is to blame*
> *If the child has no name?*
> *It's a man every time,*
> *It's a man!*"

RAGS: *"What did I do?"*
(Another eight bars)
TRENT: *"It's a man, every time,*
It's a man!" *
(He slaps Rags.)
RAGS: *"Hey, I'm a citizen! I didn't—"*

For the second chorus, the comedian sings it, to even the score by slapping the straight man—but he gets slapped anyhow. As Trent starts his swing, Rags stops the action. He steps down to the first row and slaps the heckler. Hard. Rags climbs back onto the stage, sings another eight bars, stops Trent, down again to the heckler, and whap! whap! The first slap puts the heckler away. He lies there, his mouth open, out cold.

I stroll back to my hotel for a shower, marveling at Rags' instant gut answer to any situation. When I stop at the cigarette counter, I overhear two traveling salesmen.

First salesman: "Seen any good shows in town?"

Second salesman: "You'll get a kick outta the burlesque show at the Shubert. Just don't sit in the front row. They got a big comedian that slaps the hell outta you!"

Marvin Harmon, the straight man.

I don't know why or how he gravitated to burlesque all the way from Nova Scotia. The most meticulous, disciplined, organized man in the business. Even in the greasiest, dustiest dressing room, his makeup shelf was immaculate. In his trunk was a list of all the sketches he'd ever worked, carefully typed. He dressed as soberly as an assistant bank manager, and sent exactly three-quarters of his pay every week to his family in New Brunswick.

Marvin was quite precise in his betting, too. In Buffalo we played a morning show at 12:30, a second show at 3:30; from 5 to 7:30 we had dinner, then back to the theater for two more shows. On our way to the theater in the morning, he'd make

* "It's a Man," by Cy Coben. Copyright 1950 by Shapiro, Bernstein & Co., Inc., 10 E. 53rd St., N.Y., N.Y. Used by permission.

exactly the same bet every day—five dollars on a five-horse parlay. My betting was less complicated—twenty dollars on several races but seldom on a parlay. And never a five-horse combination; your chances are merely impossible. On our way to dinner, he and I would check how the morning races came out and size up the horses at the western tracks, about to start their second race.

The betting parlor was a big operation: sheets on the wall listing the races at all tracks, a man up on a platform with a direct phone line who marked up the results as they finished, and two bet windows. Most important, Buffalo was one of the two or three cities that paid full track odds; freelance bookies paid less.

We walk in one evening on our dinner hour, and the room is full of what I call "horse degenerates." They've been there all day—it's a fulltime profession—and they're weary, but now there is an upsurge of energy because the results are coming in from California. I was a gambling degenerate, in my own way, but never *that* bad. I bet, and that was it.

As we circulate, scanning the race results, I can feel an invisible spotlight following us. A stillness, a tension. I've lost my bets, of course. Marvin's first horse has come in at 5–1. (He'd bet it win, in horse lingo.) We consult the second sheet: he's won, 11–1. The third is a winner at 20–1. At the fourth sheet it's pulsating time. And he's won, at 6–1. Now I realize why the regulars are watching us. The last horse in Marvin's parlay, Chance Line at Bay Meadows, California, is the only favorite he's bet! It's now 2½ to 1.

Five minutes to post time, the loudspeaker calls, "Will MH please come to the window." I refuse to go with him, because I know a mind-splitting scene is coming up. Marvin's $5 has pyramided into about $53,000 in the four races; if the last horse wins, he'll have about $185,000. Now the operator of the parlor wants to make a cash settlement before that last race. He'll go all the way with Marvin, of course, but wouldn't it be smarter to quit now?

Marvin returns, perspiring a little; his control is oozing away. "What'll I do, Phil?"

"I don't want to talk to you. Don't put me on the spot."

"I'm not going to do what you tell me anyhow. I just want to bounce it off somebody."

"You won't penalize me for this?"

"Of course not."

"Let it ride. What can you lose—five dollars?"

"All right, that's what I'll do!" And he rushes away.

We wait for the start. I know the Chance Line blood stock are all late finishers. This is a mile and one-sixteenth race, so he is naturally the favorite. But after you win on four long shots, can you realistically expect the favorite to win? I don't, by now. The mathematics may be in Marvin's favor—but the gods of racing are never as precise as he is.

The man on the platform with earphones calls out the race. At the quarter, it's this horse, that horse, another horse.

No mention of Chance Line.

"At the half, it's that one, this one and the other one . . . At the quarter, it's still that one, this one and the other one."

Where in hell is Chance Line?

Finally a call: into the stretch, he's laying third.

And he's first at the finish.

Cheers. Backslapping. All those wild bets of all those desperadoes—hundreds of man-years spent in losing, anger and despair—are now proved worthwhile. You *can* win a five-horse parlay.

The betting window doesn't have enough cash to pay off $185,000, so we come back the next day for the balance. Marvin has decided to buy the family's mortgaged home in New Brunswick. The next morning as usual we start to the horse room, and Marvin Harmon, the fulfillment of the Walter Mitty in every horseplayers' dream, bets his usual five dollar five-horse parlay.

On the train to play New Orleans, our company ran into a Mississippi River rampage. Our Pullman was rerouted as a work train pushed on cautiously ahead of us in the dark night; the laborers laid down sandbags as we went, to hold off the water. The water lapped up within inches of the tracks. We shifted from track to track, to keep ahead of the water, and it seemed to me we were going in circles.

Nobody wanted to go to sleep because it might be the last one. Nothing to do but play poker. When your money ran out, you played for credit. When your credit ran out, you played for matches. After a while the diner ran out of food. All we had to eat was cake that had been loaded in Cleveland. We played cards continuously for two nights and one very grim, drizzling day—stud, seven-card deuces wild, spit-in-the-ocean, you name it. We finally arrived in New Orleans, and the first thing we wanted was a hot meal. We stumbled into a little Italian restaurant, exhausted and groggy, and when the first plate of spaghetti arrived, I lifted the plate to see if I had anything back-to-back.

Boob McManus, the lewdest comic of them all, ruined H. K. Minsky with just one clean line. Boob was an Irish comic, hoarse, loose, whisky voice, red fright wig and all. But funny, by any standard. And the drinkingest. He was never on time for any curtain, even on payday. He actually chose to live next door to the crummy Oxford Theater in Brooklyn.

H. K., in his relentless clutching for class, refurbished a large plush theater in Baltimore. Baroque gold and red, only two shows a day and all seats reserved. It was to be the Palace of burlesque. And, incidentally, a gold mine because this was an old port town, and burlesque had built up a loyal clientele over many years.

H. K. invited the leading Baltimore politicians and other aficionados of culture to the opening. Among them was a local movie censor, a high-busted, pince-nez kind of woman. She took the show as a personal insult and stormed out of the theater. Next day the police raided us. They surrounded the stage and called out the names of all the actors on the program. They were to appear in court. Except me. H. K. had hired me only the day before, to "boost some weak spots," so my name was not in the cast list.

Everybody walked to court, since it was near our hotel. I

followed behind Boob to see the show. Boob veered off here and there, to reinforce himself for the ordeal. The manager had rehearsed everyone on court behavior and where the courthouse stood; but Boob's eyesight dimmed when his blood count reached 86 proof. He entered a large building with a facade of columns and statues, and called out "I demand justice!" It was the public library. I pointed Boob in the correct direction, and then hurried on to catch the courtroom scene. Boob shambled in late, of course.

(Our defense attorney is dueling with the chief witness for the prosecution, a policeman who was thoroughly rehearsed.)

DEFENSE: *"Your complaint specifies that you saw bare breasts on the showgirls. In fact, Your Honor, they were wearing thin mesh nets as brassieres.*

OFFICER: *"I didn't see any mesh nets. Just bare flesh."*

DEFENSE: *"Where were you sitting?"*

OFFICER *(arrogantly)*: *"Fifth row, right on the aisle."*

DEFENSE: *"Then we'd better test your eyesight. You also filed a complaint against the straight man, Russell Trent. Mr. Trent is here in the court. Would you please point him out?"*

(The officer looks around hesitantly. Like the good straight man he is, Russell Trent also looks around the room. The cop is baffled.)

DEFENSE *(triumphantly)*: *"Your Honor, if he can't even recognize a six-foot straight man, how could he recognize a little bare breast?"*

(The officer pokes his face, angry and glaring, at me and even at Boob, who is so fried he can't sit up in his seat. I figure our attorney is ahead in the stretch by half a furlong. Suddenly Boob comes alive. He taps Trent on the shoulder.)

BOOB: *"Russell, he's looking for you!"*

OFFICER *(instantly)*: *"That's him!"*

(Case closed. Theater closed.)

It was the only clean line I ever heard Boob utter.

Waterbury, Connecticut, was a dull town, so I spent my time between performances in the local horse room. When I came back to do the night show at the Jacques Theater, Hap Hyatt was waiting for me with a telegram. A mammoth, fat comedian, he didn't quite know how to tell me; full of sympathy and yet squeamish for fear of saying the wrong thing. I was afraid to read the telegram because it had a star on the envelope.

From my brother Harry: FATHER PASSED AWAY TODAY. COME HOME IMMEDIATELY.

I was shocked, then bitter: Why didn't I know he was dying? Harry had written he was in Bellevue Hospital, getting the best of care, but nothing critical. A doctor friend of Harry's had arranged everything. My brother was a doctor fan—all his friends were doctors. On Thursday night he would go to the Luxor baths with a group of MD's. What went wrong?

Before I left on tour, I'd gone into Pop's bedroom to say goodbye, as I always did. He looked gray and skinny. But cheerful. No pain. We'd hired a professional painter to do the exterior of the house, but Pop insisted on helping him do "a nice job." The cold day and the fumes of the paint left him weak and coughing.

(My father's bedroom: He is propped up in bed, listening to Eddie Cantor on the Atwater Kent. His face is turned away from the door and I hesitate, as always, about making my presence known. He's become almost deaf now. He won't admit it or buy a hearing aid. If his back is turned, I don't want to frighten him with a sudden sound in the dark.)

ME *(carefully)*: "Hello, Pop."

POP *(turning toward me)*: "Hello, Fischl."

ME: *"I'm going out of town for eight weeks."*

POP: *"Take care of yourself."* *(Nods toward the radio.)*

"Ah, that Eddie Cantor . . ." (He rubs his heart with pleasure.)

(I mock-conduct a musical number, and sing along with Cantor. Pop keeps rubbing his chest, nodding and smiling.)

But he must have been dying. Why was I so dumb—or so unfeeling—that I didn't realize it?

Burlesque people rally in an emergency like a loving family. The only way home from Waterbury was a bus at midnight. They bought a ticket for me and packed up everything in my trunk so it would continue with the show until I rejoined them. When and if.

Hap Hyatt said, shyly, "Why don't you do the show anyhow, to keep your mind occupied?" That made sense. I was troubled because I didn't know what I was supposed to do, how to react, what to say. I was twenty-three and I'd never had a death in the family. I was afraid of what I might see at home.

I did my bits onstage well enough, but as soon as I walked into the wings I burst into tears. I cried all the way on that long bus ride.

I walked up our steps, and I remember they squeaked. I let myself in with my key. As I opened the door, the weeping and praying flooded over me. The mirrors were covered over: everything very orthodox. (We never had ham in the house out of respect for my mother. In one of those early years, Pop had taken her out to dinner and ordered up a grand meal. She loved it all. But when she discovered the appetizer was non-kosher fried oysters, she wouldn't talk to him for months.)

The casket was already closed, for which I was thankful. The final diagnosis was leukemia, and my father had withered away in great pain. I always thought he had rheumatism. I'd naively sent him the latest "cures" I picked up on the road: salves, health salts, skin plasters. Somebody told me, if you wore a penny under your sock, the copper would draw out the "acid." I wrote Pop to try that remedy.

Then the orthodox rituals of *shiva*. All the relatives came and sat on wooden boxes, the men mumbling the *kaddish* for the dead man and beating their chests. The moaning and groaning hit me as exaggerated passion, like an Italian opera. Pop wouldn't have wanted it. . . . But I went along with it—this was no time to be a rebel. Momma's older brother was a professional mourner. He arranged everything for the funeral. I begged my brothers not to open the casket for the final look. I wanted to remember my father as a strong, vital man.

I went back on tour. We all needed the money, more than before. I was given instructions in saying *kaddish* (I'd forgotten all the rote Hebrew anyhow) at sunup and sunset. Because of my odd hours, I got a dispensation from a rabbi. I caught up with the show in Union City, New Jersey. My trunk and clothes waited in perfect order, as if I'd never left. I followed the form of the rituals in every town. I sought out the synagogue's sexton, and he'd want a fee before I could pray. I knew he had to make a living, yet the raw commercialism made the whole ceremony feel like a hypocrisy. More so because ritual and rote never meant much to me. One synagogue demanded I have a *minyon* of ten men to pray, and I had to slip a few dollars to several of those who were rounded up. I went back to the dressing room, muttering darkly: Father doesn't need all that mumbo-jumbo, he knows what he means in my heart.

The feature stripper in the show, one of the loveliest in the business, assumed I was deep in mourning. "Let's talk, Phil. Don't keep this in your heart, gnawing away at you, all by yourself." This was the first time she'd ever paid any attention to me. I couldn't tell her that the gnawing in my heart was bitterness over the professional mourners. We talked, and she held my hand to comfort me. We couldn't stop. We coupled right there, on the shaky wooden chair.

That left me with an unbeatable parlay of guilts. I went into moping self-flagellation for the rest of the tour.

On my twenty-eighth birthday I made a rundown of my life to date and where I was going. I'd been a headliner in vaudeville and burlesque for fifteen years. But I couldn't break out of this tight, self-sufficient, self-deluding little world. I had a reputation for an innovative comedy style among the experts. Goodman Ace, one of the most successful and intelligent comedy writers in radio (and later TV)—his "Easy Aces" series is still remembered as a classic—came to see me regularly at the Gaiety. He brought his friends and became my best press agent.

No help.

H. K. Minsky, still theater-climbing, opened another "class" burlesque house, this time on Broadway in the old Warner's theater opposite Lindy's. Opening night, the scenery fell down and the lights didn't come up. The press noted, with appreciation, Phil Silvers and the mishaps—in that order.

Still no help.

I received fascinating, urgent phone calls from the Shuberts, who controlled most of the legitimate theaters in America and manufactured dozens of productions every season. They'd keep me waiting for hours in their reception room. And then they'd promise to call me again.

I received letters from Hy Gardner, the influential Broadway columnist for the Brooklyn *Eagle* (and later for the New York *Herald Tribune*). "You belong in the better show business," he wrote. "You're one of the most inventive young comedians I've seen—and I make the rounds every night. Let me take you by the hand and introduce you to New York show business."

"Let me take you by the hand" froze me. I didn't know Hy Gardner, but in burlesque that line had a homosexual tinge. It was a mistake, of course, but I never answered his letters.

As a first banana in burlesque, I was making $275 a week, on which I could live expansively in 1939. I had my good friends, and I loved New York. It was the big time. It was exhilarating.

To hell with Broadway.

CHAPTER 5

Me, an English Clergyman in Pride and Prejudice?

DeSylva, Brown and Henderson were possibly the most successful team of songwriters in the 1920's and 1930's. One day, Buddy DeSylva left his partners to be a Broadway producer. Lew Brown set out to prove he was just as creative by writing, directing and producing a musical for Broadway, *Yokel Boy*. He must have been the most wildly ingenious, outrageous comedy writer of the time. Also the most undisciplined. He'd needed DeSylva to edit and harness his ideas to make them work. Nobody knew this until *Yokel Boy* went into rehearsal. Least of all, Lew Brown.

He cast Jack Pearl, a popular dialect comedian ("Vass you dere, Sharlie?") as a Lubitsch-like director who discovers an extraordinary young dancer, Buddy Ebsen, while shooting the Battle of Lexington. On location. This was Ebsen's return to the stage. He had left the film business after MGM terminated his contract to play the Tin Man in *The Wizard of Oz*. He suffered from a skin allergy which made the silver makeup painful. Judy Canova, the hillbilly singer, her brother Zeke and sister Ann were also, somehow, laced into the plot. Buddy's girl friend goes to Hollywood, he follows—and becomes a great dancer.

In rehearsal, Brown found he still could not cast the minor part of an assistant to the director. It was a small role, but weird: a two-minute scene in which he tries to seduce a girl. None of the actors called could make anything of it. Hy Gardner suggested the young burlesque comic who never answered letters. Brown ordered Ebsen's agent to send a telegram. I ignored two of them. They weren't going to break my heart again.

The third one I answered.

I walked over to the rehearsal hall in the Edison, almost around the corner from the Gaiety. Brown asked me to read the part. Only three pages. I'm a clumsy sight reader. Some actors are brilliant at this; they give intelligent, smooth performances the first time—and they never improve. I fumble around. I have to keep improvising, building. I understood this character; I had done him many times in burlesque sketches. "Let me wing it," I asked Brown. And Buddy volunteered to do the other part. That was very brave because I never gave him a cue. I tore into the scene, improvising the dialogue all the way.

I understand that this is known today as Method acting. I've been told that Lee Strasberg has described me to his students as "the perfect Method actor but he's not aware of it."

Well, the cast in that rehearsal hall laughed, and Brown immediately offered me $150 a week, a comedown from my usual $275. I would have paid him for the job.

I started rehearsing, and quickly ran headfirst into a stone wall: Jack Pearl. He was a tough man and a very big star. His name means nothing to the under-forty generation today, but someday they'll rave about the great Bob Hope—and their children will ask, Bob *who*? Pearl was that important. He remembered me as the kid with Morris and Campbell; he liked my work but he was not going to let a kid make many points in his show. This wasn't the only problem. Lew Brown ordered up new scenery and costumes, and cancelled them, or forgot to cancel, as the mood hit him.

> *Boston: Opening night. An epic disaster for Pearl.*
> *The audience is bored with Dutch dialect at four*
> *dollars a seat. It's a kind of comedy whose time has gone.*
> *Jack works harder, punching his lines. The louder he*
> *yells, the grimmer his comedy. I breeze on for my fast two*

minutes, and suddenly Pearl is chasing butterflies all over the backdrop. It's worse than Bobby Morris catching flies to upstage Rags. I don't even have a hammer to nail Pearl. He's a star, way up on top—can't he give me an even break for two minutes?

Luckily, burlesque has toughened me up. I stop short, in the middle of a line. Then I march around the stage, mimicking a brass band as it booms out "The Stars and Stripes Forever."

Al Goodman stops the band in the pit. He thinks I've dropped my marbles. Pearl, stunned, mutters: "Vat iss dat?"

"The parade passing you by!" I announce.

When the star comes off, he doesn't berate me. "You're gonna go far, kid." And then, sighing: "This show is not for me."

I'm ashamed of that parade line now. It was cruel. But I'd worked fifteen years for those two minutes, and I had no intention of letting anybody take them away from me.

A few days later, Pearl stepped out of the show. Now came the frantic scramble to replace him. Big names were approached: Milton Berle, Ken Murray. But word of our plague had spread swiftly to New York. No star would touch us. I thought we had some healthy, beautiful assets: a tuneful score by two highly successful writers of the time, Charles Tobias and Sammy Stept ("Comes Love" was a number that became a standard); the audience seemed to like the two stars, Buddy and Judy; they even applauded the scenery.

Suddenly, unpredictable, disorganized Lew Brown had a revelation. "The kid can do it."

I said, "Of course." I was ready.

Fortunately, a second revelation came to the writers: turn the Dutch dialect director into a sharp Hollywood press agent who speaks New Yorkese—Punko Parks. And that's how the role I played for years—the aggressive, smiling, call-a-tall-man-Shorty manipulator—was born. In a caesarean operation.

We had only four days left in Boston. We rewrote at night,

rehearsed and learned new lines in the afternoon, then performed at night. Sleep was for odd moments. I was carrying the comedy now—ninety-five pages of dialogue—so Brown considerately raised me to $200.

Brown's thought processes were bizarre.

> (*Suite in Copley-Plaza Hotel:* 3 A.M. *Two songwriters, Lew Brown and I are looking everywhere for a good, simple story line, which is hard to find in Boston. Our nerve ends are exposed and raw.*)
>
> BROWN (*reading a paper*): "*Hold it.*"
>
> (*Oh, oh, I think. Ken Murray is available now.*)
>
> BROWN: "*What's this about a cigarette tax?*"
>
> CHARLIE TOBIAS (*patiently*): "*Cigarettes are going up to seventeen cents.*"
>
> BROWN: "*Oh, I get it . . .*"
>
> (*We go back to screaming.*)
>
> BROWN: "*Wait a minute.*" (*All action stops. To Charlie*): "*Does that tax go for Boston, too?*"
>
> CHARLIE: "*No, this is Massachusetts. It's only for New York.*"
>
> (*Brown phones the bell captain*): "*Send up nine cartons of Camels.*"
>
> (*After ten minutes, a bellhop enters with nine cartons. Brown gives him a five-dollar tip. He's happy now—he's beat the tax.*)

Buddy Ebsen was a stabilizing influence. He had top billing, but he leaned back, relaxed and told me, "Go get 'em, Phil." I had an open field. A rare magnanimity in show business.

In order to sign Judy Canova, Brown had to take her brother Zeke and sister Annie. He didn't know where to put Zeke, who had minimal talent, so he played the doorman of the Trocadero nightclub, in Hollywood. One matinee I recalled a singing lesson bit I played around with in burlesque. I pulled it without warning on Zeke, and he reacted perfectly because he was bewildered.

"Do you want to be a doorman all your life?" I scolded. "You've got a nice big body. I bet you can sing like a bird!"

"Oh . . . I ah never studied singing . . ."

"Great!" And Punko Parks proceeded to show him how to shape the notes by pinching his cheek, slapping his jaw, compressing his stomach, et cetera. It had a preposterous visual appeal, so Lew Brown ordered me to keep it in.

Now sister Judy, the star, insisted on her rights. She wanted that scene. I was happy to oblige because it was even funnier with the star, who the audience knew could sing. Judy's voice had a phenomenal range, so her high notes built to a strong finish. But she'd spent her entire career doing a hillbilly, and she wouldn't stop now. She'd grimace and make silly faces. I had no important standing in the show, but I suggested that it would not be funny if she mugged. It had to be played straight.

She said, "Sure." And promptly slipped back into the mugging. We never talked about it again. I merely slapped her harder every time she mugged. She knew it and I knew it but we never discussed it. I just slapped her harder.

The Boston critics were invited to come back to review the new material. They could see we were in a state of convulsion, but they were kind to me. Nothing bothered me by now. I was completely nerveless. It all seemed so easy. We got off the train in New York, all set to wow them, and we were met by a stagehands' strike. As I stewed in a room at the Piccadilly Hotel, waiting for our opening, the enormity of what I'd done finally seeped into me. Nobody could develop a new story line and character in four days. I had ninety-five pages of dialogue. I must have been out of my mind.

Sammy Cahn, who shared the room, tried to calm me. "Don't worry, you'll be the greatest!" He worried more than I did. For his ulcer, there was always a bottle of Nujol in the medicine cabinet.

When the show was finally set up at the Majestic, $65,000 worth of scenery was left standing in the alley. Nobody knew what to do with it. On the day of the opening, July 6, 1939, I had the terminal shakes.

I loved Sammy Cahn then and I love him today. But I think Sammy was neurotic when Freud was still an intern. And Sammy was my constant companion this opening day. "Phil, you'll be great. Pull yourself together. You're so nervous. How can you miss? Phil, please, you'll be great."

> ME *(sincere franticness):* "*Sam, Sam, I haven't had a chance to play with the lines, time the jokes."*
> SAMMY: "*Phil, Phil, please pull yourself together. Whoever heard of you? You'll be great."*

He left me to get into his tux for the opening.

I walked over to the Gaiety to say hello to my friends. Rags was there, and Hank Henry. I said, "Rags, let me do your scenes." I did two of them, and the audience never knew I'd left the Gaiety. They never ventured into Broadway shows. The laughter and warmth loosened me up. Relaxed and confident, I strolled back to the Majestic Theater—I couldn't wait to go on. And there was Sammy Cahn in his tuxedo, perspiring, assuring me, "I'm not worried—why should you be?"

I couldn't deprive him of his bit. "I don't know," I muttered. "I don't think I'll get past my opening line."

Sammy kept pepping me up, like Warner Baxter in the early musicals. "Everybody's out there tonight, Phil . . . you'll come back a big star!" From the peephole in the curtain, I saw him take his seat next to Saul Chaplin. On the third note of the overture, Sammy fainted dead away. The ushers carried him out, and he missed the entire first act.

He didn't miss much. The show had not coalesced, the characterizations were not orchestrated. We still had half a dozen subplots rattling around, plus a grotesque Act I finale, dizzy with significance. The United States had not yet entered the war against Hitler, so Brown and the songwriters wrote an "Uncle Sam's Lullaby," to cash in on the public's antiwar mood. Sung by a large blacksmith (Marc Plant), the lyrics telegraphed this message: Uncle Sam's babies can sleep well because America is well-protected from this overseas war.

For the climax, Brown unleashed the most massive military operation since the Battle of Verdun. Starting with a review of the Revolutionary War, through the Civil War and including

World War I—shelling, planes, rockets, machine-gun fire, the entire cast singing and screaming and dying, nurses carrying off bodies of chorus girls dressed as wounded soldiers.

The critics bombarded the show in self-defense. We took the grim news at a small party in a small restaurant. Some critics liked a bit here and there, but nobody recommended the show. Herbert Drake of the *Herald Tribune* noted: "The hero of the evening is Phil Silvers, a burlesque emeritus who carries just enough of the gutter savoir faire of his favorite art to give *Yokel Boy* a little tang. He is all the comedy there is."

It was the thrill you feel only once in a lifetime. I exhaled, took a drink and renewed my interest in a charming girl from the chorus. We adjourned to the Piccadilly to review each other. To warn Sammy away, I set a bottle of Nujol outside the door.

Buddy Ebsen and I wouldn't let the show die. We had vigilante meetings, without informing Lew Brown, and we rewrote again. "Uncle Sam's Lullaby" became the creation of the wild mind of Punko Parks. It was now a satire of Hollywood's bad taste. And hilarious, I thought.

We improved the humor of the show over the summer, but business was pitiful. Only a flaming egocentric like Lew would have kept it running. Buddy DeSylva was bringing in *Dubarry Was a Lady*, with Bert Lahr and Ethel Merman, in December, and it looked like a winner. Brown did not want his ex-partner to have Broadway all to himself. (Next year, DeSylva did just that with three hits: *Dubarry, Louisiana Purchase* and *Panama Hattie*.)

Yokel Boy was losing $8,000 to $9,000 a week. Brown invited me to his house in Scarsdale for a weekend, to play one of his games.

> (*Brown's library, Monday morning: Walls lined with obscure German and Italian classics, in antique leather bindings that have never been opened. A desk as long as the Queen Mary.*)

*Brown calls the box office, then hangs up: "Well, kid,
what do you think we took in today?"*

ME *(playing it straight): "Nineteen thousand?"*

BROWN: *"Nineteen dollars! I just can't go on. This is the
end, Phil." (Reaches into the desk drawer, pulls out a
revolver, slides it into his pocket.) "Well, I have one friend
that'll pull me out of this."*

ME: *"Lew, don't do it! Please! I'll tell your nurse. . . .
You can't do this to me—and all the people in the show.
They all love you!"*

BROWN *(smiling): "No, Phil. You've got me all wrong.
It's for my friend, Waxey Gordon. He needs a gun. . . ."*

*(I know Waxey and other racketeers financed his
previous production,* Strike Me Pink, *and probably* Yokel
Boy. *Maybe Brown doesn't dare close their show? He
puts the gun back in the drawer.)*

ME *(fervently): "Oh, thank God!"*

(There's that Bilko again.)

Lew interpolated one of his big hits, "Beer Barrel Polka,"
into the finale. By September, the show picked up an audience.
The Majestic used a set of curtains to close off the rear of the
orchestra, so the few people huddled down front wouldn't be
frightened by all that dark void behind them. Now the curtains were opened, the theater filled up. We were set for a
long run.

And then good old unpredictable Lew killed the show. He
took full-page ads in every paper. Under a huge black headline

I APOLOGIZE!

he reprinted all the unhappy reviews. As if to tell the theatrical
world: Don't sell me short. Business drifted away.

One night in November, during this wake, I recognized
Louis B. Mayer and a male companion in the audience. The
show had been running eight months; Buddy and I were as
synchronized as the parts in a watch. In the middle of a
scene, in which Punko Parks became human for the first time
in his life, I noticed Mayer turn to his companion and whisper
something. Coming offstage, I told Buddy, "I'm going to be
signed by L. B. Mayer."

"What? The Wizard of Ooze?"

"Himself."

Buddy blinked incredulously. "Give me a drag of that."

Next morning, I received the call from Loew's New York office. I walked in without an agent, and I was given double what I'd set myself as an opener for bargaining. A seven-year contract, with yearly options of renewal, starting at $550 a week and escalating into the stratosphere.

Lew Brown was furious. "They'll break your heart out there. You can't abandon the show."

No? He had abandoned the show long ago.

My mother went into mild hysterics. How could I go away, all alone, 3,000 miles from home? I was twenty-nine years old, I'd knocked around in burlesque for seven years; still, to her, I was little Fischl. Now she came out with her scenario: Harry would go to Hollywood with me. She was sure he would keep me good company and help me in many ways. That was exactly what I did not want. Harry was an intelligent man, a decent, loyal brother, but I felt he would suffocate me. Harry was straight—facts were facts. I didn't think he could survive in the fantasy world of Hollywood.

Enter George Abbott. Another crisis. Milton Berle, starring in the farce *See My Lawyer*, was out for several weeks. Would I take over the role temporarily? Yes, if Mr. Abbott could arrange an extension of my contract with MGM. Phone calls crackled between the two coasts, and in the meantime I began rehearsing. Again it was like Boston, learning a new role in three days. I felt like a fool. Who needed all this tension, merely to be a replacement in a mediocre farce? I was on my way to Dreamville, where the streets were paved with golden girls.

On the fourth day of rehearsal, Mr. Abbott thanked me very much and handed me the telegram from MGM: MUST COME IMMEDIATELY.

Obviously, they had a part waiting for me. I was as twinkle-eyed and naive as any seventeen-year-old bosomy minx discovered in Schwab's Drugstore.

Jack Albertson, now a big hit in Los Angeles in the revue *Meet the People*, had issued an invitation. "Stay with me till you find a place." The MGM office informed me they had

chosen a very prestigious agency to represent me in pictures—
the Orsatti brothers. Great. Frank and Vic were all-powerful
at MGM, the rumor had it, because Mr. Mayer owned a piece
of the agency.

The agency immediately sent me a congratulatory wire.
And an official would welcome me at Pasadena. Great. I'd seen
newsreels. For some reason, important people always got off at
Pasadena and lovely Wampas girls put a floral wreath around
their neck.

I got off the train at Pasadena on December 13, 1939, to be
greeted by nothing. Nobody. I was disappointed but not too
upset. Years of touring had taught me a basic rule: When you
come into a strange town, look over the theater first, before you
go to your hotel. So I hailed a cab: "Metro-Goldwyn-Mayer,
please." The driver squinted at me out of the corner of his
eye. This was the equivalent of driving from Penn Station in
New York to Yonkers. That jaunt put a nice dent in my
first week's salary.

At the gate, I told the guard I had just been signed by Mr.
L. B. Mayer. Where should I report?

What? Who? No one at the gate, no one in personnel or
administration, had heard of Phil Silvers.

I suggested, "Call Mr. Mayer."

He reacted as if I had said, "Call God!"

"You kidding? *Nobody* can call Mr. Mayer."

A little upset now, I phoned Jack Albertson, who immediately drove to the gate to pick me up. Since he was married,
I moved into a small back room. I immediately phoned my
agent, who arranged a pass from MGM "that will get you in
anywhere."

Not to the sound stages. They were closed to me. I did manage to enter the commissary. To eat lunch all by myself. I went
every day, hoping to meet somebody from whom I could learn
what you did when you were in front of the camera. I never
did see how a movie was shot until I was in one.

One day at the commissary, the guard said, "Oh, *you're* Mr.
Silvers? Just a minute. Judy Garland wants . . ." And he
searched around the room.

Judy Garland? What kind of gag was this?

She was sitting with Lana Turner and wanted to say hello.
Judy and Mickey Rooney had seen me in *Yokel Boy* while they
were on a promotion tour. I couldn't eat much that day. Judy
hung onto every word, and stared at me: she was the fan and
I was the star. It took a few months to realize that movie
people looked up to the New York stage as Dreamville. Judy
invited me to her house, and we became affectionate friends.
Mickey Rooney made it a threesome.

After a month, no word from Mr. Mayer, casting, Orsatti,
anybody. I was on the payroll, drawing my $550, but . . .

Judy told me not to worry. Casting must be looking for just
the right role. The wheels were in motion. I would have to be
patient, because L. B. Mayer had to make the decision on
every detail. Mr. Mayer was a complex man, I learned. He
could quote long passages from the Hebrew Talmud on the
philosophy of goodness and justice. And then try to screw the
newest starlet under contract.

I ran into Judy one morning as she came out of Mr.
Mayer's office in the administration building. Her lip was
bleeding and her laugh was on the edge of hysteria. She'd
gone in to complain that it was unfair to raise Mickey Rooney's
salary and not hers.

Mayer, she told me, launched into a lecture, complete with
biblical quotations. She must forever keep the image of America's girl friend . . . in that image was her mystery, said
Mayer. Then he jumped on a couch to sing "Ah, Sweet Mystery of Life." Followed by a recitation of the little joys of life:
"People who have the most money are not the most happy
people." By this time Judy had forgotten all about her raise
to concentrate on biting her lip, so she wouldn't laugh in his
face.

My brother Harry appeared and told me he would take
care of everything. Momma had convinced him it was his
duty to the family—and me—to come west. So I would at least
eat right. Harry moved into the little back room at Jack Al-

bertson's until we could find an apartment. He immediately opened a savings account for me, and tried to interest me in a weekly budget. I'd never had a savings account. But I did appreciate his company because I was lonely.

Another month passed. At last—the call from casting. From Billy Grady, who had the reputation of discovering Clark Gable, Spencer Tracy and many others among MGM's awe-some roster of a hundred box-office names.

> (*In Grady's office: For a minute I think I've made a mistake. The man behind the desk is natty George Murphy.*)
>
> GRADY: "*I have a note on you from Mr. Mayer. Young and intelligent comedian. Where did you have your schooling?*"
>
> ME (*quickly; I can't say reform school*): "*One year of college in New York. Then I had to leave because of a lucrative contract in vaudeville.*"
>
> GRADY: "*That's fine. Now, I've had a lot of trouble casting this part. . . . It could be a feather in your cap.*"
>
> ME (*fervently*): "*Give me a crack at it, Mr. Grady. I'll eat it—I'll drink it—I'll sleep it. Nobody will do it better.*"
>
> GRADY: "*Makeup tomorrow, nine o'clock. On the set at nine-thirty. (Hands me some sheets of dialogue.) Good luck.*"

I hurried back to my apartment at the El Jardin on N. Hayworth Drive, where I was now living with my brother. A quiet, relaxed building, populated by second-level script writers, call girls, people on the way up. I looked over the dialogue and exhaled a sigh of relief. My God, even a busy man like Grady had time for a joke.

He wanted me to portray William Collins, an English vicar in *Pride and Prejudice!* He "offers marriage to Elizabeth, second oldest of the five daughters of Mr. Bennet of Hertford-shire." But what if Grady was not kidding? I boned up on the lines and presented myself promptly at nine in the makeup department.

I was put in the hands of an old-timer called Skipper, cranky, tobacco-chewing and respected as a great wig man. I sat in that chair for four hours and he could not make me look like a nineteenth-century country clergyman. All the while, one of the assistant assistants kept bouncing in, "Are you ready? We're running overtime." Finally Skipper tore up an old wig used by Edward G. Robinson in *Tiger Shark,* glued it on me, and I was ready. As I looked at myself in knee breeches, white stockings and big-buckle shoes, I realized I'd achieved one old dream anyhow. In kindergarten I'd wanted to play that English gentleman, John Alden.

It was lunchtime, and I walked to the set through the swarms of Metro actors hurrying to the commissary.

(Flashback: Minsky occasionally would book into the Gaiety legit dance acts known as "walking towels." They cooled off the heated men between the strip acts. One of them was a tall, engaging, loose-limbed tap and softshoe man, Dan Dailey Jr. His father ran the Biltmore Hotel chain, and Dan had run away from all that for a show business career. Minsky liked him so much he kept Dailey an extra week.)

Striding toward me now was a tall, loose-limbed Nazi. As we passed each other, we did a doubletake. It seemed I'd left burlesque only ten minutes ago, and already Dan Dailey was a Nazi and I was a minister.

The director of my tests, Basil, had a genuine English accent. I warned him there had been a big mistake; this part called for one of his Old Boys. He assured me the cameras would roll, whether I was dead or alive, because "we've spent $4,000 in overtime."

> (*One of the young stock actresses plays Elizabeth. I give my role all the finesse I've picked up in my chats with Robert Morley.*)
>
> Me: "*My dear Dame Elizabeth, your modesty does you no dissoivice—*"
>
> Basil: "*Cut. It's dis-service, Mr. Silvers.*"
>
> Me: "*Okay . . . dis-service in my eyes. You can hardly doubt the poipuss—*"

BASIL: *"Cut. Purr-pose, Mr. Silvers."*
ME: *". . . purr-pose of my discourse. My attentions
have been too marked to be avoided. (On my knees.) Oh!
forgive this passion . . ."*

I saw the test days later. The Bensonhurst-Broadway accent
was as emphatic as a jackhammer. These three minutes were
perhaps the funniest I've ever done.

Mr. Grady agreed it was ridiculous, of course, a huge mistake. "However, I'm sure you've learned a great deal from
this." (The role was finally played by Melville Cooper.)

It was my first lesson in the Hollywood art of conspicuous
waste. My friends Judy and Mickey prevailed on Arthur
Freed, the overseer of Metro's big musicals, to try me in a
scene in their *Babes in Arms.* I played a pitchman, conning
them in a six-minute sequence. It had very little to do with
the story line but it was amusing. Nobody stole a scene from
Mickey and Judy; to help a friend, they stood still and let me
run with it. Mr. Freed, after viewing the rushes, decided he
could not let his two stars play straight to a newcomer. Cut.
Out of picture.

However, I must say I didn't dog it. I kept busy, entertaining at friends' houses—Gene Kelly, Frank Sinatra, Bing Crosby
—at parties and at clubs. I was meeting people at the highest
levels in the business; they applauded me and . . . nothing.

Kelly's house was the corner hangout. Among the raffish
group were Betty Comden and Adolph Green, Johnny Mercer,
Carol Haney. And, of course, Sammy Cahn and Saul Chaplin
—my two friends from the mountains who were now among
the highest-paid songwriters in the movies. We gathered in
Gene's living room to amuse ourselves. We improvised together,
we took ideas from each other; it was a mutual stimulation
society.

George Cukor, Dore Schary, producers and executives
dropped in to see the improvisations. One Sunday, in the
middle of a number, I looked down and there was Greta Garbo,

My father, Saul.

My mother, Sarah.

Me, down through the ages, starting from the worried little boy, upper left, age twenty-one months. Lower left, the bar mitzvah boy.

My brother, Harry, my general factotum.

With Bud and Buddy Junior on the amateur circuit, age ten. Bud on the right; Buddy, left.

At a Catskill Mountain hotel, 1931: three clowns about to
entertain the guests. The one on the right always
carried his noise-maker.

Straight man, almost prim, at Minsky's Oriental. Age twenty-four.

First Broadway musical, *Yokel Boy,* 1939. I'm Punko Parks, the one in the hat.

First screen appearance, *Tom, Dick and Harry,* 1942, with
Burgess Meredith. RKO GENERAL, INC.

Teaching Bing Crosby how to sing on USO tour, 1942.

sitting on the floor clapping her hands delightedly, like a child at her first circus.

Best of all, it was fun. Party fun in formal Hollywood would reach a high point when the butler brought in a rubber hot dog, and all gathered around to watch the patsy try to eat it. Our group preferred our own night-long revues at Gene's. Any one of us, solo or in duet, could go on for one hour.

I developed a satirical sketch here that stayed with me for years. Titled *Old Man River*, it was a confrontation between Jerome Kern and Paul Robeson, in which I played the singer and Saul Chaplin was Kern. The premise was: give a singer a choice and he'll inevitably pick the wrong song. "Old Man River" is one of the greatest dramatic numbers of our time. My assumption: Robeson would rather have sung "Captain Andy," the only song in that great score that never achieved much popularity. (Later, both Robeson and Kern told me I didn't know how close I was to the truth.) I honestly feel this number was the most brilliant piece of material I ever conceived. My so-called liberal friends told me it had anti-Negro overtones. *Nuts.* All I had in mind was that if you give a singer a choice, he'll pick the wrong song. My point was proved many years later when Paramount Pictures produced a huge musical review, using all the stars in their roster; Bing Crosby was their number-one star. He chose to sing the title song, "Star Spangled Something," I forgot what. Johnny Johnson, a contract player, was assigned "That Old Black Magic."

Gene's living room fun opened a door to Ciro's, a plush nightclub where Billy Wilkerson, owner of the *Hollywood Reporter*, ran a series of Sunday night benefits for an orphan's home. Everybody in the film colony who had pretensions of being anybody had to attend.

One Sunday, Darryl Zanuck was in the audience with his entourage. I was doing a number with Ella Logan. It was going over fine, but at one point Ella, in her nervousness, edged onstage blocking Darryl Zanuck's view of me. Instead of going into my next line, which was a lulu, I stopped the orchestra. "Cut!" I yelled, which startled everybody and, with the typical Silvers smile, I said, "Excuse me, dear. Zanuck can't see me." This sounds like nothing to repeat today, but in those days it was unheard of for an unknown to speak of a god so intimately.

On another Sunday I played "Old Man River" at Ciro's. When I retrieved my coat and hat at the checkroom, there was Buddy DeSylva, now the head of Paramount. He knew me from burlesque and *Yokel Boy*.

"Loved that 'Old Man River,'" he said. "I have to tell you, Phil—you're my favorite comedian."

I was feeling unusually frustrated and edgy that night. I exploded. "I'm your favorite comedian? You're the boss of Paramount and I can't even get a job there. Bullshit!"

That burned my bridge to Paramount.

The screenwriters awarded their own prizes for merit in 1940. The first half of the program, the awards, was broadcast from a hotel ballroom; I was MC of the entertainment half.

Charles Lederer, author of many highly acclaimed scripts, was a frustrated drummer. He organized a screenwriters' band and offered his mansion for rehearsal space if he was permitted to play the drums. We rehearsed the show there, between the uproarious music rehearsals. George Antheil, the bad boy of modern music, a serious composer who had scored several films, served as conductor for the "1812 Overture." Since many of the writers were Jewish, and a Jewish boy of that generation always took violin lessons, the string section dominated.

Some ringers were permitted. Willie Wyler, the director, sat in with the violins. Harpo Marx played clarinet; Chico played the piano, of course, and Groucho the guitar. Chico, the ladies' man, brought in two buxom, blonde high school girls from Pasadena, and each played a double-bass. Antheil was a stern conductor; when the string section went a half-tone off, I could see them cringe. Somehow, before the finish, they all sneaked back on key. They rehearsed for weeks, and it was hilarious because they all took their musicianship so seriously.

Lucille Ball's film career up to this time had been spent in straight pretty-girl roles. Now she did a rowdy sketch with me, a takeoff on the preposterous thank-yous of the Academy Awards, in which she played a sexpot who is named Best Actress. Lucy grew apprehensive at rehearsals after the first two run-throughs, because the boys in the band naturally stopped laughing. On the night of the show, everything worked beautifully—except for Charlie Lederer, who fouled up his one and only cymbal crash. The award sketch was the birth of Lucy as a bust-out comedienne, and it opened up a lot of new roles for her.

Not for me. I had the admiration of the writers. What I needed was the casting directors.

Toward the end of my first year, I learned I did not need Mr. Grady. My option was about to come up for renewal and I had not one screen credit. I met a gifted and prolific film writer, Harry Kurnitz, who remembered with happy nostalgia my burlesque days in Philadelphia. He'd been a music critic for one of the newspapers, and the Academy of Music was a few steps from the Shubert. Harry had just written a comedy, directed by Clarence Brown, so he instantly proposed me for a role. Brown asked Metro for anything they had of me on film, and Grady sent the Reverend Collins test. This burned my bridges to Clarence Brown. I learned more. About half a dozen producers and directors had asked Grady about me—and received the same test. Not once did he send out the *Babes in Arms* scene that showed me as a comedian.

It had to be more than coincidence. Some of my friends insisted that Grady actually wanted me to fall on my prat. He resented me because I had been discovered by Mr. Mayer, and he wanted to show the boss that one of his discoveries was useless.

I found that hard to believe. Yet, in the shifty politics of Hollywood, it was possible. It was also possible that Grady disliked me as a brash young man who needed to be put down. But movie business had been invented by brash young men. And yet, why would he have tested me for an obviously impossible part if he was the casting genius so many non-admirers admitted he was? I was bewildered and angry.

As the weeks slipped by, I became a little paranoiac. Why didn't Mr. Mayer, who had "discovered" me, even inquire where or when I was to be employed? Was Grady determined to destroy me, for some reason I couldn't even guess? Or was it someone else? . . .

One day I saw Mr. Mayer at the commissary. Everyone congealed when he entered. I walked right up to him to say hello.

"How are you, my boy?" He smiled genially.

"Fine, Mr. Mayer. But I can't get in to see them make a picture."

He turned to his publicity man, Howard Strickling. "Howard, take care of that. Phil, have you seen our racetrack here?"

"No, sir."

"Ah! Well, come with me." All eyes followed me as I climbed into his custom Rolls. Who is this Silvers and what has he got on Mr. Mayer? . . . As soon as His Highness settled into the deep leather, he lowered a small rosewood desk behind the front seat and concentrated on a scratch sheet. He ignored me all the way; I had to hang close to him to get past the entrance.

The invitation was part of the game: the benevolent king mingling with his peasants. Next day I was granted a dressing room. But no hint of a role to dress for.

I saw Mr. Mayer and Mr. Grady some months later. Sunday lunch at Mr. Mayer's beach house was like an audience at the Vatican. Of course, it wasn't His Highness's ring you kissed. I went there with Judy to see Red Skelton perform for an hour. The monarch greeted me with, "How are you, my boy?" and turned away before I could say I was growing old in his service.

I soon received my second call from Mr. Grady. Mr. Mayer was planning a dinner meeting with his department heads, and would like to turn it into a social evening, too. Have some of the new talent entertain, so that everyone could become acquainted. Dinner, catered in the executive dining room, would be served at eight, Mr. Grady said.

"Am I invited to dinner? I asked warily.

"Of course." Very crisp.

"Now, I have a friend who plays piano for me—"

"Bring him along."

Saul Chaplin and I reported at eight. A mob scene in the hallway, where the new talent was milling around. New talent was anyone who had never worked for Metro: Gracie Fields, Tony Martin, Kathryn Grayson, Igor Gorin of the Metropolitan Opera.

In the dining room, dessert was being served. Billy Grady had thrown me another curve.

Howard Strickling was ready to introduce the performers. He waved me in. I told him we hadn't eaten.

"But, Phil—we're starting now."

I said I'd run down to the commissary, I couldn't perform without some food.

"Come in, come in," he urged. He walked us to the kitchen and ordered places set for Mr. Silvers and his guest.

I could not repress my anger. "We will not eat in the kitchen. I don't mind for myself, but Mr. Chaplin is a top songwriter."

Strickling, without blinking, directed a waitress to seat us in the dining room. Since she was the caterer's employee, innocent of protocol, she seated us at the only two empty places— the table of Louis B. God.

He rose to the occasion warmly. He smiled. "Phil! How are you? . . . Try our chicken soup—my own recipe." Around the room, eyes focused on us and, I'm sure, the minds behind them wondered again, What the hell kind of hold does this guy have on Mr. Mayer?

I was *ready*. In all those months of waiting, I'd polished up new material, immediately topical and directed to movie insiders. The other performers entered from the hall. I made my entrance from God's table. I worked each table as if it were a nightclub, with impressions and interpretations of Metro stars and pictures. I held them for twenty minutes. After the applause, I walked off into the hall, to go home. I couldn't suppress a feeling of humiliation. The evening had been an affront to performers; we were professionals, we had a reputation. Yet we'd been herded in the hall like an animal act, then unleashed in the arena to provide free amusement for the emperor and his sycophants.

Suddenly, Mr. Mayer stood up. "You all seem to be thrilled by this young man. I signed him personally, after seeing him in *Yokel Boy*, but I didn't know he was so versatile. Now, all of you had notification about him, but somehow none of you have seen fit to use him. Aren't you ashamed?"

I turned my face away and eased out into the hall. Saul and I slapped each other's back. At last! At last! This was worth all those months of wandering in the desert. God had spoken.

That was Friday night.

Monday morning, Metro dropped my option.

I think Mr. Mayer simply forgot about me. Nobody told the appropriate underling to renew my contract. I was finished at Metro, but I had to kill Grady's *Pride and Prejudice* test before it destroyed me.

> GRADY (*looking up at me tolerantly*): "*Phil, this is not the place for you. We're jammed up to the ceiling with talent.*"
>
> ME: "*The only thing that bothers me, Mr. Grady, is this terrible habit of mine. I repeat things I shouldn't.*"
>
> GRADY (*puzzled*):"*What's that got to do with——?*"
>
> ME: "*Remember the Sunday at Mr. Mayer's beach house? You were talking with another gentleman under an umbrella. Something about Mr. Mayer . . . quite nasty.*"
>
> GRADY: "*Oh, really? What did I say?*"
>
> ME: "*Sounded like kike to me.*"
>
> (*He blanches, and stares at me.*)
>
> ME (*slowly*): "*I want that test destroyed, Mr. Grady. Right now. It's extension 483.*"
>
> (*He lifts the phone and asks for Lefty, extension 483. The vault where the tests are kept.*)

Years later, when I told this to Gene Kelly, he tried to track down the test at Metro. It was not in the vault. I never heard of it again. It had killed a year for me.

Republic Pictures bought the film rights to *Yokel Boy* and began searching for a Phil Silvers type. I suggested the original. They chose Eddie Foy Jr.

CHAPTER 6

Under the
Table at Mocambo

I was pleased for Eddie's sake, because the Foy family and I had been embracing each other for years. Soon Charlie Foy and I became entwined in his latest project, a supper club.

The family was one of the most beloved headliners in vaudeville: Eddie Foy and the Seven Little Foys. The one who held your eye when they all lined up onstage, by height, was Eddie Jr. He was a superb performer and the one closest to me in age and temperament.

Father ran a wild, loving family. I'd visit at their big house in New Rochelle and find the little ones sawing off the piano legs. Father explained, out of the side of his mouth, "Let the kids have fun." Eddie Jr. was the inventive one. On a hot summer night, he suggested a swim in their pool to Ted Healy and me. We stumbled around in the dark for half an hour; I was surprised their estate was so large. Since I couldn't swim very well, I floated around hunting the safe shallow part. I couldn't touch bottom. Suddenly, police whistles and flashlights; we were in the New Rochelle reservoir.

When their father died, Charlie kept the family together as Charlie Foy and the Five Foys. Byron, the tallest, went into films and became King of the B's, so adept was he at paring costs. Charlie was not the most talented one in the act, but he had a precious sense of organization. In fact, when I was growing up in vaudeville, I worked at intervals for Charlie. I wrote part of the act, *The Nuthouse Revue,* and he put me in as one of their stooges.

Eddie was not accustomed to money. After he'd signed

with the Ziegfeld Follies for an astronomical $750 a week, he decided to splurge on a hotel in Boston during the break-in. Charlie invited me up for the opening, so we both went to see Eddie at the Copley-Plaza.

Eddie was shaving in a tiny lavatory, next to a midget room with daybed. For this he was happily paying a huge twenty dollars a day. Charlie insisted he was being robbed. When he looked around for a closet to hang up his coat, Eddie pointed to a door: "I guess that's the closet." Charlie opened it—into a lavish, beautiful suite. Eddie had been living for a week in the servant's room.

For a while Charlie and his wife operated the Grace Hays Lodge outside Los Angeles, a famous little place into which Charlie lured Joe Frisco out of retirement. Charlie and his wife divorced and remarried several times until she gave him a final dispossess notice. Charlie scrounged around for money to open a rowdy booze club. He found the ideal spot at Ventura Boulevard where it meets Coldwater Canyon: a pretty little house in which two spinster ladies operated a lending library and lived over the shop. He converted the downstairs to Charlie Foy's Supper Club, and persuaded me to entertain on a percentage basis. "You're giving it away," he said. "Why not gamble on yourself?" He had to borrow a cash register for opening night.

It was an instant Leon & Eddie's, with the frantic tempo, rowdy heckling, uninterested waiters and mediocre food that transplanted New Yorkers missed. Rags Ragland came in every night to drink. Metro had enlisted him from *Dubarry Was a Lady*.

Charlie told Rags, "You're throwing your money away here every night. Let me pay you to work with Phil." I went off to Murietta Springs with Sammy Cahn to write material for the act. Rags stayed home; he didn't care. He'd perform anything that was handed to him. Our hit act, which I eventually created with Rags, was a living testimonial to what killed vaudeville. *Love That Boy* squeezed all the monotony, banality and phony sentiment of fifty years of Keith-Orpheum into fifteen minutes. I was the debonair half of a song team and Rags was the ruggedly attractive one.

We opened with a robust "Hello, everybody, we're going to entertain you! . . ." Then Rags laughed uproariously, for no reason except to get the ball rolling. Sometimes he switched to bitter scorn: "How can you make such a fool of yourself!" It was a flexible opening. Then both into a soft patter song, à la Van and Schenck.

> ME: "*. . . I'm going home,*
> *What's the matter with you, pal?*"
> RAGS: "*No more to roam,*
> *You miss your old gal . . .*"
> ME: (*stepping downstage, collar open, very serious*):
> "*I think about you, all through the day,*
> *My buddy, my buddy . . .*"
> RAGS (*sings*):
> "*Nights are long, since you went away . . .*" *
> (*Rags sings this song, over and over, in the same*
> *monotonously quince-shaped tones for about ten minutes.*
> *My exuberant chatter is heard over it. My affection for*
> *Rags is never homosexual; it's the enthusiasm of a good,*
> *clean young comedian for his straight man.*)
> ME: "*Yes, ladies and gentlemen, this is my buddy. I*
> *love this boy. We have been partners ever since I found*
> *him on the doorstep in Louisville. I am not ashamed. I*
> *will say it to the whole world. I love this boy!*"
> (*Rags give me a sickly look: What's happened to my*
> *pal? He's a little too enthusiastic . . .*)
> RAGS: "*Nights are long . . .*"
> ME: "*This boy is working with a 104 fever, to keep this*
> *act on the boards. (Slight cough). How can I help loving*
> *this boy?*"
> (*I give him a whopper, a real kiss right on the cheek.*
> *Rags has a wistful look: What's happened? Has he*
> *switched?*)
> RAGS: "*. . . nights are long . . .*"

* "My Buddy," by Gus Kahn and Walter Donaldson, copyright 1922 by Jerome H. Remick & Co. Copyright renewed. All rights reserved. Used by permission of Warner Bros. Music.

ME *(rolling on and on):* ". . . *and there's nothing un-clean about my love for this boy . . . (Another kiss on the cheek. Rags tries to pull away, but I have my arm around him. As Rags blushes, I stare at him with a big, happy smile. Rags pantomimes: he's okay, just carried away with our great friendship. . . . Then he waits for the kiss. It doesn't come. Now his face says: Oh, well, it's nothing really. . . . He smiles and turns to me. I kiss him full on the lips. He goes wild with surprise, and wants to run away. I hang on to him.)*

RAGS: ". . . *nights are long . . ." (He knows the kiss will never come again. What the hell, it's just a great friendship. He smiles at me—and hesitantly kisses me.)*

ME *(triumphantly):* "*I think this boy loves me, too. . . . . That's why I say—*"

(Rags and I sing "Auld Lang Syne" and strut off waving the American flag. We come back for a bow with musical instruments, an old vaudeville trick to stimulate applause: You want more?—we play too, you know.)

We were forced to cut one section of our routine after a while because it seemed to be too real. I played straight for Rags in the burlesque bit—how to get a girl.

ME: "*You just have to learn, Rags. Suppose a girl was passing by. What would you say to her?" (I pantomime a girl crossing in front of him.)*

RAGS *(coming out of character):* "*Hey, you did that very good.*"

ME: "*Come on, Rags. Let's do the bit, huh?" (Walk across again.)*

RAGS: "*You did that too good.*"

ME: "*Look, do you want to do the bit or do you want to forget it?*"

(Apprehensive hush in the audience.)

RAGS: "*I like to have a little ad lib, too. Are you so big. . . ?*"

ME: *"You shouldn't be talking this way in front of the audience. Let's get the goddamn bit over with." (Walk across again, furious. Then I quit. To conductor:) "Give me Miss Whiting's introduction, please."*
(Charlie Foy runs out.)
CHARLIE: *"Fellows, what are you doing?"*
ME: *"Charlie, please, I have a headache. I don't think you should show your temper in front of an audience."*
CHARLIE: *"Come on, Rags. Play with him."*
ME *(apologizing): "Let's do it." (I walk across again.)*
RAGS: *"I'll be goddamned if you don't look like one!"*
(And now the audience knows for certain it's a joke.)

This was, essentially, a Pirandello concept, although Rags and I had never read him. Mike Nichols and Elaine May did a somewhat similar—and brilliant—quarrel in their nightclub act twenty-five years later. Our improvisation was so realistic that Joan Davis one night ran out to the ladies' room and retched. We eliminated the scene.

Rags could not understand why I fumed and rumbled, just because I could not break into a movie. He was always cool and unflappable.

We sat at a table at Mocambo waiting to perform in a Bundles for Britain benefit. The girl Rags had brought for the occasion succumbed to the heat, and fell over in a faint under the table. Both of us dropped to the floor to revive her with napkins and cold water. Someone told us there was a fire escape balcony off the hallway. We couldn't carry her because the scene would create a commotion and interrupt the show. So, crouching behind the tables, we dragged the limp girl toward the door. Out of one ear I heard ". . . and now, those two young men who are the talk of the . . ."

"Rags! *That's us!*"

"That's right," he muttered. He stood up, called "Waiter!" pointed to the body on the floor—and we ran onstage.

Nothing could bother Rags as long as he had a drink and a

woman in hand. And they both came easily to him. I had to do everything the hard way. I did not consider myself attractive to the opposite sex. The Judy Garland syndrome. So I would extend myself to amuse women: I was always "on." I felt I had to pay my way, by taking them to elegant restaurants.

I lived alone now at the El Jardin. Rags lived in an apartment at the Wilshire Palms Hotel, off Wilshire Boulevard. On the ground floor, surrounded by shrubbery, and you didn't have to pass by a room clerk. When Rags went away for weekends, I borrowed his key. I found his secluded apartment more stimulating for amorous adventures. It was a wall-to-wall aphrodisiac.

I wish I had been able to drink along with Rags. It might have given me a less expensive outlet for my exasperation. I forgot my problems while gambling, but it was never relaxing. It grew more intensive and obsessive. I felt pressed to do something BIG. Win big. Lose big. I was an impatient man—I wanted instant results. I bet bigger and lost bigger on horses because I did not want to bet against individuals. That was too personal. I wanted to beat the house, the Establishment, *Them*—the anonymous, faceless people who wouldn't give me a job in films. My percentage from Foy's, plus my fee for a little job with Rags, warming up the audience for Bing Crosby's *Kraft Music Hall* show, added up to $400 to $600 a week. I bet more than I made, and on Tuesday I'd have to ask for an advance from Charlie Foy.

I was in Rags' apartment when he finally lost his cool. It was Saturday morning. I'd spent half the night at Foy's. I was with a girl and now all I wanted to do was sleep. The doorbell awoke me. The outlines of a soldier's uniform swam around in my clouded eyes.

"Does John Ragland live here?" it asked.

As soon as I heard John, I came awake. Nobody knew that was his name. "He's away for the weekend," I said. "Want me to give him your name?"

"Well, I have to report back to the base tomorrow. I'm his son."

He was shorter than Rags, but he had the face, the lantern jaw. When Rags returned, I greeted him with, "How are you, *Daddy?*"

"What the hell are you talking about?"

"Your son was here. In uniform. He'll be back in a couple weeks."

Rags clenched his fists. "I have no son. This is a frame-up. I never had a son."

When the boy appeared again, Rags was embarrassed. Since he was a soldier, Rags played host. He wouldn't take the boy to his usual hangouts or the Crosby show. "Whaddya want to do?"

"Well, is there a pool hall?"

Rags escorted him there under protest. He kept away from pool halls because, among his other accomplishments in Louisville, Rags had been a pool hustler. The boy picked up a stick and ran twenty-five balls. Rags' eyes opened a bit. "Where do you want to go now?"

"I hear there's a beautiful stag line at the Palladium ballroom."

The boy picked a pretty girl out of the hundreds waiting to dance with the GI's, and sequed into a wild jitterbug routine.

That convinced Rags. He brought the soldier to the Crosby show and asked Bing, "You ever meet my boy?"

Garson Kanin was the man who got me involved with Olivia deHavilland. I'd met Garson in New York, where he was George Abbott's assistant. He made *The Great Man Votes*, starring John Barrymore, for RKO, a critic's and box-office success, and Garson immediately became a hot property. We palled around together, a peculiar sight because the Hollywood caste system frowned on a top director even nodding to an unemployed actor. Yet Garson refused to give me a job "until I find something that fits you. I'm sorry you're not doing well in pictures, but stay with it. I think you're great. You've got to make it eventually."

Garson had a rapport with me because I came from the stage. He was stagestruck. He still is. He and his wife, Ruth

Gordon, never miss a show in New York. We played our own little game—no bets—in the RKO projection room. I challenged him to find obscure films such as *Variety* with Emil Jannings, and he could always arrange it. That was power in those days. I saw a lot of Warner pictures, too, and Olivia deHavilland was in them.

She figured in my dreams. In the projection room, I'd put my feet up on the red plush seat in front of me. I could adjust the opening between my heels and my toes to frame the screen, and I'd just follow Olivia. She was the beautiful, warm, sexy epitome of my kind of woman. Of course, I had never met her.

Gar scolded me for my self-denial. "She's probably sitting home right now, because men like you think she is unapproachable. Call her."

"She'll think I'm a nut."

Gar arranged for me to meet her at a party. She didn't flip into somersaults at the party, but I took her to ball games and the fights at the American Legion (a "must" social event). It was a world she didn't know, and she loved it. When I drove her home one evening, she remarked, "You know, you are rather conceited. You never take off your glasses, and you're not the least bit concerned about them."

To this day I cannot understand what she meant. Of course I didn't take them off—I have the vision of a myopic mole. Next time I set out to meet her, I met a neighbor on the elevator with a large police dog. I borrowed the animal and presented myself at her house, on the George Cukor estate, without my glasses. "Where do you want to go? I've got my seeing-eye dog." She thought it was mildly funny.

I mentioned this gag while I was sitting around the apartment pool with Herbie Stein, who wrote a gossip column for the *Hollywood Reporter*. He promptly used it. It did not sit well with Miss deHavilland; she evidently felt I'd planted the item to exploit her prominence. I did not see her after that even with my glasses on. Yet that item has been kicking around the media for thirty years. It breaks on the UPI or AP wire, it appears in movie magazines, and I heard a TV comedian use it last year. It's always about two other people.

*Dear Olivia: When you read this, after all those years,
you will know that I did not mean to take advantage of
your name. But tell me—what did you have against
glasses?*

Artie Shaw and Benny Goodman were the supreme jazz
clarinetists of the world. But Artie had a quality that gave
women palpitations and hot flashes. We'd met in New York
when I was in *Yokel Boy*. I worshiped him and hated him,
because he played that clarinet so masterfully. He read
omnivorously and spouted theories of Friedrich Nietzsche:
The strong man is morally superior to the common mass
of slaves; he is not bound by any laws in fighting for his
individuality against the petty restraints of rigid society. This
was the German philosophy that encouraged Hitler, but that
didn't bother Artie Arshawsky. It worked wonderfully for him.
The superman's arrogant disdain combined with his sensual
clarinet brought the most beautiful women of Hollywood to
his feet. I went through a lot of *sturm und drang* for Artie and
Nietzsche.

When I met him, his love was Betty Grable, who had been
given her release by Paramount and was playing the second
lead in *Dubarry Was a Lady* on Broadway. She was lovely
and great in the show. She was in essence doing what she
was to do over and over again in her later 20th Century-Fox
musicals. When he went out on tour, he'd asked me to keep
her company, squire her around New York. We went to
movies mostly. I adored Betty, yet I could hardly wait to take
her home right after the movie. This amused her. "Listen,
you cross-eyed sonovabitch, I'm the toast of the town and
you can't wait to get rid of me."

"If I hurry," I said, "I'll be in time to pick up my stripper at
the Gaiety."

Somehow, this came to be my role in Hollywood, too; in
films and in real life. Brother confessor.

I looked up Artie soon after I arrived in Hollywood. He lived
on Summit Ridge Drive, at the top of Coldwater Canyon, on a
treacherous road that separated his friends from casual ac-

quaintances. I drove up in my little Dodge, the first proud
possession bought with Mr. L. B. Mayer's money. It was red
and had a rumble seat: I was ready for adventure. I flunked
the driver's test three times because I couldn't shift gears fast
enough. Driving up to Artie's was a wrenching series of stops
and stalls, a real act of devotion.

We'd make home records, do impressions or characters
and musical styles. But mostly, I loved to hear Artie talk. Once
he complained that he was sick of being separated from Betty.
"What does she *really* want? The gold pants? The tinsel? Or
me? I make enough to take care of her."

"Did you ever tell her that?" I asked.

He thought a minute. "No."

I suggested he write a letter telling her exactly where he
stood. And he did.

I drove down with him one day to Metro for a recording
session. He was not on their roster, but he had made one picture there with Lana Turner in a minor role. They didn't
get along at all—he considered her a pain in the butt. On
the way, he told me about a raw talent at Metro just going to
waste, a young girl who did everything wrong musically—but
emotionally, she was great. Judy Garland, who was then less
than seventeen. "A moonstruck little girl," he called her, and
she had a crush on him.

We walked on the set of *Two Girls on Broadway*, starring
George Murphy, Joan Blondell and Lana. And zoom! Like a
bee making for the honey, Lana veered right to Artie. She'd
seen him playing at the Palladium, and the clarinet had enchanted her, too. Artie's disdain was monumental, but they
made a date for that night. He insisted I come along, "because
she might bring me down."

As soon as we got into his car I knew he needed help. Lana
wanted to visit a place called Victor Hugo's, which featured
Guy Lombardo.

Artie Shaw grooving on Guy Lombardo?

He did it for her. Lombardo's musicians, in awe of Artie,
tootled as if their fingers were stuck on flypaper. On the way
home, Artie ran through the routine I'd heard so often:

"I want a girl that will be satisfied with me alone on a desert island. . . ." The girl would agree, "Yes, just two people who need each other." And then they would roll into bed for a pleasant jam session. Next day, all the philosophic rationalization would be forgotten. Artie was always brutally honest: He really did mean what he said. Every time.

Lana crossed him up. "That's exactly what I want. A man who has the brains to be satisfied with me only."

He was vehement. "Look, I'm sick of this Hollywood crap. I want to break out."

"Me too. Anywhere you say."

Artie couldn't back out. He turned around, drove out to Paul Mantz's plane rental service and chartered a plane to Las Vegas. To get married. I felt this was reaching too far for a joke, but Artie was flying against the petty restraints of slave society. Superman. He gave me the keys to drive his car home.

Driving up the canyon in his new car, with an unfamiliar gearshift that congealed in new combinations, was madness. I nearly went over a cliff. And as soon as I reached his house, I saw a special-delivery letter under his door. From Betty. I managed to fall asleep on his sofa.

Artie called me from his agent's house at 5 A.M. "We're back. We did it!"

"Artie," I whispered. "There's a letter here from Betty."

"Oh, God!" he said. "Read it to me."

It went right to the point. "Darling, this is what I've been waiting for. I've just handed in my notice to the show. Let's get married tomorrow."

I didn't even want to think of the hot vibrations that would zing through Betty's mind when she saw the newspapers. She was an earthy woman. And she had walked out of a hit show. I jumped into my Dodge to get away from all this—and remembered Judy. The little girl who had confided to her best friend, Lana, that she loved Artie. The classic triangle of a B picture, but it was real.

I speeded away to pick up Jack Albertson for a day on the golf course. I had to get away from all this heartbreak. A caddy found me on the eighth hole: "Miss Garland is in the clubhouse."

Judy used to have freckles; now they stood out like black

polka dots. She had been crying, her eyes were red, and she was in humiliating pain. "How *could* they? I confided in her!" To add to her wretchedness, she had to drive to school at Metro this morning. By state law, she was still a child.

I rode to school with her, again the brother confessor, and my words came burbling out—anything to comfort her. "You're the luckiest girl in the world. . . . It was just hero worship. Nobody can live with a Nietzsche superman. . . ."

Her eyes were blinded by tears, and we were speeding through red lights up Sunset Boulevard. I'd seen movies in which a hysterical woman is slapped back into good sense. But I'd never hit a woman. Goading myself, I delivered a soft-edged rap on the cheek.

It worked. Instantly she became Judy Garland, movie star. Slapped by a bit player. . . . She really told me off. We reached Metro safely, and they were waiting—her mother and the others who had pushed her into stardom: "Judy, you're too fat . . . Judy, you're too thin."

Emotional setbacks hit children with a one-two punch. First, because they have no defenses, and second, they believe life is just and fair. Judy felt she'd been betrayed by a man she loved and a woman she trusted. Betty Grable recovered from her shock because she had a great inner strength: She knew she was beautiful. Judy never considered herself attractive to men, and her emotional resources were thin. Artie and Lana split after only five months, but that was no help to Judy. I believe this hurt was the start of the emotional torment that troubled the rest of her life.

Metro liked me to work with Mickey at the Hollywood Canteen, because if he went alone he'd sing songs that he had written. They were less than sensational; who wanted to hear America's boyfriend singing "and then I wrote . . ."?

I spent a lot of my very free time with Mickey. He was nineteen; he'd drive around in his new Cadillac and pick up girls on the street. This was a perfectly normal hobby for any boy that age. But Mickey was a first-rank box-office personality, immediately recognizable. Picking up strange girls could have led to blackmail, or at least scandal damaging to the Andy Hardy image. Part of Mickey's problem: He lived far out in the San Fernando Valley with his mother, who'd married a tall, strapping young man about Mickey's age. Either he didn't think of renting an apartment—or his mother wouldn't let him.

"Mickey," I said, "use my apartment for a meeting place." It had two bedrooms and a back entrance, up some stairs. I was sitting at home one afternoon, brooding over my future, when the phone rang. It was Mickey with two cronies, Sidney and Billy. They had connected with a girl who would give all three pleasure for thirty bucks. Sidney had been dispatched to meet her at a corner drugstore near my apartment.

Mickey and Billy arrived first. Then we heard Sidney coming up the back stairs, singing "Lady Be Good." That was the code signal meaning she's good-looking. If he whistled "I Got Rhythm," she was a dog. Why Mickey had to have this advance knowledge, I never figured out. She would have been in the apartment in another two minutes. Star system?

A very attractive young lady entered. I guessed she had tried to make it in films, and now had to make her rent wherever she could. I served her a drink, and Cokes for the boys. With all their bravado, not one made a move.

"Gentlemen," I said, "this young lady is a professional woman whose time is valuable. Who's first?"

Mickey nodded to Sidney; he followed the girl into the bedroom. He came out, embarrassed and dejected, three minutes later. As Big Brother, I consoled him—this kind of pro was skilled in quickie turnovers; if you were in love with a girl, it was certainly different.

Next, Mickey gave the nod to Billy, a vital, voluble boy. He came out five minutes later, exulting. "Boy, I never saw anything like that. She's in *love* with me!"

"She told you that?" Mickey laughed.

"All the while, she was saying, 'Oh, Daddy, do it—I love it!' "

Mickey told him, "That's the girl's business, for cripes sakes."

And now it was Andy Hardy Goes to a Party. We sat in the living room, watching my little white electric Westclox. Mickey stayed in that bedroom over an hour. I thought Sidney's heart would break. He moaned, "Even in bed that guy's a star!"

Mickey and the girl came out. Sidney paid her and the three gallants immediately left. The girl thought my hospitality was very decent, "because they could get into trouble." Then she asked if I would be her guest. I declined gracefully with a question: "The two boys were so jealous of Mickey. Is he really that good a stud?"

The girl laughed. "He's just as quick as his pals. Only he didn't want them to know it. So he sang songs, told jokes, did his imitations. You know, he's a very talented boy."

Garson Kanin lived with his parents, but that didn't stop him from swinging. We were rounding out a tour of the late spots with Burgess Meredith, and ran out of bars. Gar and Buzz had to have just one more, for the road. I was neutral: liquor never did much for me. Gar led us to his house. "My father worries about my drinking—he locks it up in a cabinet." Nobody is more ingenious than two men who need a drink. Sly as safecrackers, they unscrewed the door of the cabinet with a nail file. They had a couple more jolly drinks for the road, until Buzz had to sleep in the guest room.

Months passed. Kanin moved his entire family to a grander house. Meredith came to town late at night and remembered Kanin's hospitable after-hours bar. Finding the door of the house open and everyone asleep, he opened the cabinet with the handy nail file. Buzz enjoyed the selection of whiskey, and toddled off to the guest room. Next morning, the occupants of the house found a strange man in bed. Fortunately, Angelenos did not stock as many guns in the house as they do today. Buzz was able to convince them he was Burgess Meredith, the actor, and they invited him to breakfast.

Orson Welles allowed me on the set to watch the shooting of *Citizen Kane*. He had barred the head of his studio. It was assumed, of course, that I was blackmailing Welles. He was only twenty-five, a brilliant conversationalist and an authentic genius.

Orson knew me from the Gaiety. I think he always wished he had been a straight man in burlesque. He realized a bit of that ambition in the party scene of the picture, when Kane throws a rowdy party with a line of girls, singing and dancing with them. At the end of shooting, he organized an elaborate party in a huge restaurant, where he really indulged his nostalgia for burlesque. With a small stage and orchestra, he dredged up a lowdown "blue" sketch, *I Got a Whiz and a Wham.* Orson was straight man at last. The comedian was Gus Schilling, a second or third banana at the Gaiety, whom Orson had cast in a straight role in *Kane.* The whiz was an aphrodisiac that Orson waved in front of a girl; it made her fall on him with a mad passion. It did not work for the comic. For the tagline, Gus reached into the baggy pants and pulled out a salami: "You got a whiz—I got a wham!"

That low down.

The rest of the entertainment laid a dozen eggs. Disgruntled noises from the audience. Orson stepped down from the stage and looked them all in the eyes. Particularly the RKO studio chief in the first row. With utter disdain: "Any suggestions?"

The studio chief promptly jumped up and whispered ideas into the director's ear. Awesome Orson drew himself up to his full majesty and roared, "*Sit down!*"

The boss persisted. "You don't understand—"

"SIT DOWN!"

Embarrassed lull in the audience. I waved at Orson.

"Yes, Phil?"

"Get the hell off." I borrowed a clarinet and closed out the show with some original bits.

Orson, the genius, bombed. I, a virtual unknown, was a smash.

Garson, now signed by RKO to direct a script by Paul Jarrico, was going to Palm Springs with him for preproduction work. Since I was working only Sundays at Ciro's, Gar invited me along. Jarrico wrote at night, and they would go over the script together next day. It was a comedy, *Tom, Dick and Harry*, to star Ginger Rogers, George Murphy and Buzz Meredith.

One night Garson had a date, so I stayed in the hotel and read a good book. A knock on the door. Paul Jarrico: "Phil, I have a scene with a wisecracking ice cream salesman who interrupts a petting party. A New York type. . . . What would the fellow talk like?"

I suggested a few lines in choice New Yorkese and fell asleep.

> *(Garson and Paul revising script: next morning.)*
> GARSON *(seeing me)*: *"Why don't you stay out of production?"*
> ME: *"Paul just asked me for some New Yorkese . . ."*
> GARSON: *"You want to play the vendor?"*
> ME: *"Garson, you've been a real friend. Now don't you turn into a bastard, too. Of course I want to do it!"*
> GARSON: *"I think you're much better than this bit. But if you want to do it—it's yours. I'm not going to say it twice."*
> *(I got the message. When the studio calls me in, ask for twice the money I expected.)*

> *(RKO casting office: several days later. The head of casting surveys me doubtfully.)*
> CASTING: *"We have no established price for you. What's your salary?"*
> ME *(focusing on his eyes, casually)*: *"A thousand a week. And I want a four-week guarantee."*
> CASTING *(laughs lightly)*: *"Thank you very much for coming in."*
> *(Well, I blew it.)*

> *(On the set: an hour later.)*
> CASTING *(chuckling to Garson)*: *"I've got a laugh for*

*you. That guy Silvers wanted a thousand and a four-
week guarantee. Why, I can get Allen Jenkins or Walter
Catlett for $250 a day."*

GARSON: *"You really can get them?"*
CASTING: *"Sure."*
GARSON: *"Then you get them and get a new director."*

I received my thousand a week. Every morning I reported
on the set as an ice cream vendor, with my bicycle cart and
white uniform. "Not now," said Garson. I turned my cart and
pedaled away. My job: to sell at a petting park and interrupt
the spooning of Buzz Meredith and Ginger Rogers in a parked
car. And I was brash: "Don't raise your voice to me. Just because I'm obnoxious . . ." I'm sure I could have done the
scene in one day; it became a six-week job. Ginger, I found,
was very movie-wise, a painstaking professional—and very
kind. She and Buzz went along with the game, even though it
inconvenienced them. In the final takes, they both laid the
scene into my lap. Except for Mickey and Judy, I don't know
any stars who would have stood still for an unknown. Those
were the halcyon days of Hollywood.

Garson Kanin was one of the first men in Hollywood to receive a draft call. He worked like a demon to edit the picture
before he left the studio. Sammy Cahn and I ate with him
almost every night at Lucey's, a little restaurant across the
street from RKO, which served a delectable chicken hash.
Sunday night after dinner—I had three hours before I was due
for my stint at Ciro's—Sammy bugged Kanin to let us see the
scene.

Garson refused. "I have a rule against that. Actors don't
know how to look at rough cuts. It's a very good scene, believe
me."

We hammered away at him until he let us into the projection room. I was appalled at what I saw. Could that smartass
be me? I recalled that Tyrone Power often puked after his
rushes. Garson stopped the film, brought up the lights and
beamed at me.

I was overcome by a severe attack of nausea. That idiot was

me? That voice was mine? I begged Garson, "Do me one more favor. I see now I'm not for movies. Please cut that scene."

He took a deep breath. "I should cut it out—that's what you deserve, you ungrateful sonovabitch. But I need that scene." And to Sammy: "I never want to see you again."

We crept out. It was now a year since Metro dropped me. I was all for driving right back to New York. Sammy drove me instead to Ciro's and deposited me with the maître d'.

Three months later I saw *Tom, Dick and Harry* at the Pantages after it was released, and I laughed louder than anybody. Garson was right, of course. Actors are too self-conscious to judge their performance in unfinished form. The critics embraced *Tom* as a bright, witty comedy. More important, Zanuck saw the film at his home and grunted, "Oh, Christ! That's the guy from Ciro's I meant to sign." He signed me for a contract that ran almost nine years.

I would never have bet on it.

CHAPTER 7

My Nine Years
With Blinky—
and How They Grew

As soon as I signed onto the 20th Century-Fox roster, Metro found it needed me for *Lady Be Good*. Metro used Dan Dailey as a dancer this time, in the musical based on the 1924 Gershwin hit. Mine was a tiny part. Since it had nothing to do with the story, I managed to work in my singing lesson bit; my partner was Virginia O'Brien, the deadpan vocalist. This scene soon joined my bit from *Babes in Arms* as scrap in the Metro cutting room. It would be nine years before I made a scene for Metro that stayed in.

Unlike Mayer, Zanuck actually had plans for me. He rented me to Warner Bros. for *You're in the Army Now*, a real half-mast comedy. America had entered the war in Europe and the Pacific, and the movies volunteered for battle with any comedy, melodrama or musical they could splice together. I was teamed with Jimmy Durante for what Jack Warner envisioned as another Abbott and Costello team. We played a vaudeville duo drafted into the Army. Jimmy and I worked well together because we respected each other's abilities, but the chemistry was all wrong. And the sight gags were something no one should have to face. They still haunt me on the late-late TV.

Mr. Warner wanted the people in his pictures to be attractive. So he insisted on toupees for me and Jimmy. Jimmy loved the notion because he always wore a hat to cover his open space. This was my first toupee; I felt stiff and ridiculous. Losing my hair had created something of a trauma: I was only thirty, and in films the bald pate was standard for a hick, a cuckold or the A&P manager. After a few years of hiding under a rug, I said to hell with it. This is not me. The bare dome and the glasses were my signature. My daughters have seen my early films on TV, and made it clear they didn't approve of my full head of hair. "You look so *bushy.*"

I pulled some naughty pranks on Jimmy. He was full of gusto and affection, but his memory for names and places was leaky. Hal Wallis came on the set the first day of shooting to wish us good luck. Hal was married for many years to a beloved comedienne of the silent era, Louise Fazenda. As Jimmy thanked him profusely, I saw that he couldn't recall who this man was. I whispered, "Hal Wallis, head of production."

"Ah, Mr. Wallis!" Jimmy enthused. "It's nice of you to come down here. Just saw your wife—threw me a kiss when our car drove off the lot. A great actress!"

I couldn't resist it. "What's her name, Jimmy?"

"Trixie Friganza."

Jimmy and I had a table reserved every day at the Green Room in the Warner commissary. Raymond Massey had been called in by Warner for a movie, and Jimmy knew him because he'd starred in *Red, Hot and Blue,* right next to the theater where Massey played *Abe Lincoln in Illinois.* One morning I asked Jimmy would he mind if Johnny Mercer joined us for lunch.

"Great guy, Johnny!" Jimmy said. "Nobody can beat his lyrics."

Johnny was a few minutes late. Massey entered, scanned the room and spotted his old friend from New York, Durante. I waited until Mr. Lincoln's hand was about to clamp onto Jimmy's back for a greeting. I looked past Jimmy's head. "Johnny! How are you?" I said.

Jimmy jumped up to shake Massey's hand. "Johnny Mercer! I love your songs!"

Zanuck finally put me to work for his own company in *Roxie Hart* (1942). This picture did a lot for me: It introduced me to Dr. Harry W. (Docky) Martin, medical director for Fox and husband to Louella Parsons, whose column in those days could make and break movie careers.

Ginger Rogers was Roxie, a good-hearted Chicago murderess. William Wellman (called Wild Bill for his ferocious temper) directed the comedy-drama, set in the 1920's. I played a news photographer in knickers and a turned-around cap, who photographs Roxie in jail. The flash shots of the period used a metal container of exploding powder. I held it close to my eye, to line up the shot, and—foof!—I was blinded. Wellman ordered me to the infirmary. Doc Martin put some drops in my eyes and assured me the powder was harmless.

"You don't want to go back right away, do you?"

"I can't see anything with these drops . . ."

"Well, let's play a little gin rummy." He fortified me, and himself, with drinks as we played the afternoon away. Inevitably, I lost a few dollars. After that, I met Docky (also known as Lolly's Pop) at parties, and we'd hoist a toast to his restoration of my vision. He constantly mistook me for a drinking man.

Some time later I was asked to MC the Panhandle Dinner, a night when the publicity slaves of the studios, who had to cater to every whim of Louella, Hedda and Florabel Muir, found an opportunity to get even. I slipped a few well-placed stilettos into Louella. "When she hears two young stars are dating, she's the only one who bothers to check the girl's blood test to find out if she's pregnant." She smiled gamely, but her shoes left bloody tracks. After the show she sidled up to me to murmur: "I could crucify you. But Doc says you're a wonderful guy." And she and I lived happily at peace ever after. She was always helpful.

The last time I saw Doc and Louella was at a party where the only thing that saved them from collapse was intravenous feeding of alcohol. "I've got to take you home," she told Doc as they headed down the stairs. They missed the last two and slid flat on the floor. "Gotta get the doc home," she insisted, struggling to her feet. "He's operating in the morning."

Fox put me into *Tales of Manhattan*, produced by Borris Morros and S. P. Eagle, who became much more successful under his real name, Sam Spiegel. *Tales* was an interesting idea that didn't come off: a series of episodes following the deterioration of an elegant tailcoat as it passed from owner to owner, till it ended as a scarecrow on a plantation. The producers, determined to make a "quality" film, used Charles Laughton, Rita Hayworth, Charles Boyer, Edward G. Robinson, W. C. Fields. Director of the Fields episode, in which I appeared, was the Frenchman noted for his finesse, Julien Duvivier.

Marcel Dalio, who'd made an international reputation in Jean Renoir's *Grand Illusion*, played my partner in a second-hand clothes shop. The scene was intended to be a piece of whimsy or irony, preferably both. We placed wallets, stuffed with paper, in a pocket of the shabby coats; the customers, feeling a wallet, would quickly buy the coat just to get the wallet. The store had a trick mirror that transformed the tawdry tailcoat on Fields into a new costume. To film this illusion, the movement of Fields, savoring the new tails in the mirror, had to exactly match the movement of Fields seeing himself in the old coat, so that it could be superimposed. But Fields, who was in his dotage, never made the same gesture twice; he was always improving. This was a very difficult bit of business, even if you were cold sober. Fields' valet encouraged him every day with a thermos bottle of lemonade.

And every day the producers appeared on the set to plead with Fields: "Please don't drink while we're shooting—we're way behind schedule. . . . After this is over, we'll take you out on the biggest binge of your life—you can drink *all* week."

Fields merely raised an eyebrow. "Gentlemen, that is only lemonade. For a little acid condition afflicting me." He leaned on me. "Would you be kind enough to taste this, sir?"

I took a careful sip—pure gin. I have always been a friend of the drinking man; I respect him for his courage to withdraw from the world of the thinking man. I answered the producers a little scornfully, "It's lemonade."

My reward? The scene was snipped out of the picture.

The war years found Zanuck and the Fox factory well prepared for the escape from reality. Month after month, year after year, they confected those period musicals with lush songs and hummable tunes that cheered up the home front and the boys overseas. *Footlight Serenade, My Gal Sal, Coney Island, Diamond Horseshoe, Where Do We Go From Here?* among others. They symbolized a whole decade: beautiful women, healthy men, clean love and just enough sex to make it look real (a "touch of the muff," they called it). The villains and heroes were clearly identified, so their problems could be easily, quickly solved. All in blazing color beyond your wildest dreams. It was so wonderfully naive and innocent. And so profitable. Fox used the same beer-dancehall-café set for every one.

Every picture made money. With block booking, the studios could force the exhibitor to take three dogs for every hit. All you had to do was open the theater doors and customers streamed in. It was like the boom of the early 1920's, when geniuses like Mr. Mayer made only one decision—to get into the picture business. Other geniuses were discovered in their fathers' offices. Everybody was a genius.

For nine years I played the same character: Blinky, the good-humored, bespectacled confidant of Betty Grable or John Payne. In the middle of the picture, for some reason that escapes me, I came rushing up to Rita Hayworth or George Montgomery and yelled, "I've got the stuff in the car!" I never knew what *the stuff* actually was. I know now: It was a plot complication. Ten minutes before the end of the last reel, I told Betty she wasn't really in love with Cesar Romero; it was George she *truly* wanted. Or vice versa. You could be damn sure of one thing: It was never Phil Silvers.

Rita and Betty and Alice Faye dominated this era. They were fabricated into pinups, sex goddesses, symbols of soldiers' puppy love. They were all things to all men because they were actually human beings. Real women.

In *My Gal Sal* I was the pal of Victor Mature, playing Paul Dresser, the writer of those old four-part harmony favorites "My Gal Sal," "By the Banks of the Wabash," etc. The plot demanded Vic and Rita have a falling-out, and I tried to patch it up by demonstrating "My Gal Sal" to Rita—without telling

her who wrote it, of course. (In those musicals there was always a point, about five minutes after the opening, where a
simple yes or no answer would have ended the entire story.)
No matter, it was a cute little scene and Zanuck liked it.

Because films were doing so well at the box office, there was
very little tension on the set. Irving Cummings, a former
leading man, directed in the grand tradition: jodhpur boots,
a riding crop and ascot. A kind man with great taste. His favorite line, after a take: "That's a *peach* for me!"

I began to discover that after all the time and energy I had
expended to break into films, making movies for fun and profit
could be a drag. It was like the Army: hurry up and wait. It's
not natural for human beings to be funny at nine in the morning. Makeup at eight, on the set at nine . . . and then you
sat around until the camera, lighting, sound and a hundred
other technicians were good and ready. In playing scenes with
the big names, I found they could blow a line over and over,
while mine could be perfect. By the time they reached the
final take, my energy was shot. I learned to save my energy:
Wait until the scene was perfected, then go all out.

All performers have neuroses. I'm a normal neurotic: I don't
want to die; I'm afraid of high, open places; and I hate anything that moves on my line. *My Gal Sal* had one scene that
brought all my phobias together in the same moment. When
Cummings invited me to work in the finale, I accepted eagerly
because my small part didn't entitle me to that. The finale, I
discovered, was on a giant Ferris wheel. Everyone in the cabs
swaying to a reprise of the title song. The camera was on a
platform sixty feet high; as the wheel turned, you sang your
line into the camera. They put me in with a gay would-be
starlet who rocked the cab to build up her part. And when
anyone sang a line, something on the Ferris wheel was moving.
Or the cab moved before you finished. Cummings had to take
the shots again and again. And there I was, whirling up in the
air. Then they called lunch, and the crew left me sitting up
there. Acrophobia took over—I tensed up. I eased myself out
of the cab to climb down. But that was ridiculous. I was not
prepared to do a Harold Lloyd scene sixty feet in the air.

One of the crew, a kind grandfather, revolved the wheel to

bring me down. After lunch, Mr. Cummings said he needed one more shot of me. I went home that night and broke into welts.

Zanuck personally produced "important" films, such as *Wilson*, but he saw every rush of every film that Fox made. He became a fan: "Any Silvers rushes today?"

Footlight Serenade (1942) starred Vic Mature again portraying a character like Max Baer, the heavyweight champ. Mature, a virile womanizer and very intelligent, was surprisingly gentle for a muscleman. He abhorred violence, couldn't stand anyone hitting him with a glove or even touching him.

Plot: Mature was producing a musical and Betty Grable wanted a job in the chorus for herself and roommate Jane Wyman. John Payne was a college football stud in love with Betty. I was stage manager, and so I repeated the opening night peptalk Sammy Cahn gave me before *Yokel Boy*. I gave it to Betty Grable, because she had got the lead through an accident and she was excited and scared. I was pretty manic myself.

> ME (*rapping on dressing room door*): "Good luck tonight!"
> BETTY: "I'm so frightened . . ."
> ME (*arm around her*): "No, no, not tonight. This show belongs to you. The cream of society, they're all out there, waiting. It's the magical moment that comes only once in your career. (Excitement building.) The overture will strike up and—suddenly, there you are all alone onstage—in that spotlight—all eyes on you—"
> (*I get sick, and run out of the room, hand over my mouth.*)

I did that scene about twenty years later when Freddie Fields brought Judy Garland back from "retirement" (depression and near bankruptcy) to be rehabilitated as a star at Carnegie Hall.

> *(Judy's dressing room. She hugs me affectionately; I'm keyed up as if it's my own opening.)*
>
> ME *(enthusiasm and tension mounting):* "Judy, you're going to be great tonight. I've never felt such excitement, such sheer joy in an audience. God, they love you! I'll be out there rooting for you—fantastic! They're waiting for you. Don't be nervous—you'll be great!"
>
> JUDY *(laughing, to her dresser):* "Listen, we better get the doctor for Phil—I don't think he can make this opening."

Gregory Ratoff, our director, was one of the few who never did his homework. While the cameras, crew, extras and principals waited, the assistant director would ask, "What sequence do you want to do today?"

Ratoff would scream, "Kveyet! Vyy kent I heff kveyet on thees set?" Then, *sotto voce,* "Vattahell eess dee next shott?"

Ratoff's thick Transylvanian-Gypsy accent added to the delirium. His distortions of the language were explosive and colorful. And Betty, a real scamp, helped him along. The scene: Betty had to play up to Mature, to get that precious job. Ratoff explaining: "You arrr chorruss girrl and he ees beeg star from price fighting, but now in show, you want to make heem think he's terrific. You want to play up to heem. You want to suck heem." (I guess he meant flatter him, suck up to him.) The set rattled with belly laughs, work suspended for five minutes. Ratoff, bewildered, "What did I sayed?"

Betty never let him forget. In subsequent scenes before the camera rolled, she leaned toward Mature's belt and asked: "I do it now?"

Jean Arthur was a neighbor of Ira Gershwin's. I met her there several times with her husband, Frank Ross, a man of wit and intellect, a serious writer who turned into a producer. I could not understand why he went into the movie business.

When we worked together in *A Lady Takes a Chance* (1943), my offscreen role as Big Brother expanded to include Jean.

She had a quality that was rare in films. A flip surface, a throaty little voice, and underneath it all, a wistfulness, a sense of impending loss that told the audience she really *cared* for Jimmy Stewart or Joel McCrea. Offscreen she was a reticent, very private person with her share of the performer's problems. Her hair was thinning out and she feared she'd lose it all. Somehow, this was magnified into an intense need to withdraw from the public and even from her old friends. Garson Kanin picked her for the uncultivated chorine who smartens up in his play *Born Yesterday* (1946). During its troubled tryout period on the road, Jean's insecurities convinced her she was not right for the part, so she withdrew. It made an instant star out of Judy Holliday.

Soon after *Lady* began filming, Frank Ross asked me for a small favor. "Drop in to see Jean, even when you're not shooting." She was pleasant, yet she had no friends on the set. I was the only person, aside from her maid, permitted into her dressing room. As a top-billed star she was granted a portable dressing room on the set, furnished to her own taste, with a refrigerator, bar, all home conveniences. All this in addition to the studio's regular star dressing room.

We were worlds apart in background and interests, and I suppose that's why I amused her. She was not the swinging kind. I'd come every day to tell her the gossip of the day before—who slugged whom, who was under the table at Ciro's, who was at a benefit dinner he couldn't afford. . . . The blonde girl I came to pick up for dinner and found her hair was green—she'd picked up the wrong dye. Details of the boxing at the Legion Hall, the racing at Santa Anita. I invented and embroidered situations to make her smile. I was Cyrano de Bergerac, dramatizing his daily journal for Roxanne in the nunnery. Except that I was not as nosy, and not secretly in love with her.

Some years later, I had a night on the town with Jean. She came to New York to take ballet lessons. Frank Ross called me again, asked me to escort her around. I took her to supper at the Barberry Room. We changed tables three times to find privacy for Jean. Well, she was a familiar star face, and the tourists did stare and whisper. Halfway through supper, she exploded at them. "You enjoy looking at the monkey?" she cried out. "Do you want me to hang from a chandelier by my toes?"

That was the end of my night on the town with a big star.

Then 1944: a vintage year. I appeared in four films released that year: three for Fox and one for Columbia. *Four Jills in a Jeep* was memorable for the ironic difference between the "family entertainment" on film and the sharper reality off-camera. Kay Francis, Mitzi Mayfair, Martha Raye and Carole Landis had gone overseas to entertain the troops. Mitzi wrote a book about it, and for once the producer was able to cast the movies with the original faces. Except me. I was Special Services Sgt. Blinky, who accompanied the girls and handled the tour details. The trouble with using the four girls was— each had her own version of what actually happened, and wanted the script changed to fit her "truth." Director William Seiter had to explain over and over that this was entertainment. Who cared about reality?

Kay Francis was shown falling in love with an officer. This was a tribute to her acting skill, because she had very little interest in men.

Carole Landis, the glamour girl in the film, was the opposite of Kay. Carole oozed sex appeal, yet she was utterly vulnerable. After a series of unhappy affairs, she committed suicide. I found it hard to understand why, in the middle of all the cynical, endless make-believe of Hollywood, people would still kill themselves for love.

Cover Girl, a joyous musical that I consider a classic, was created at Columbia. Here I also had the pleasure of meeting the dictator of Columbia, Harry Cohn, also known as His Crudeness. (Before the war, an autographed photo of Mussolini hung in his office.) He did not want me, even though it was another Blinky role, this time named Genius. Gene Kelly wore him down eventually; it was like sculpting Mount Rushmore with a screwdriver. Some men, blessed with talent and great determination, become known as the doctor's doctor; Cohn was the bastard's bastard. But an honest one. You always knew where you stood. When Harry discovered I had a bit of special knowledge he could use for his own peculiar needs, he practically adopted me. All the while he needled me that Fox loaned me to him for three times the salary I was paid by Fox.

We started shooting *Cover Girl* in 1943. The nominal producer of the musical was Arthur Schwartz and the director was Charles Vidor, but the genius on this film was Gene Kelly. Naturally there was friction, and "sonovabitch" was like saying "good morning." Vidor, a skilled director, was Hungarian, and in Hollywood Hungarians had the reputation of entering a revolving door behind you and coming out ahead. Gene would slam his cap to the floor and Vidor would stalk off, never to return. Cohn immediately came barreling onto the set and knocked heads together. Cohn had spies everywhere; he even knew which horses I bet.

Gene choreographed that buoyant "Make Way for Tomorrow" sequence, in which he and I and Rita Hayworth danced up and down a New York street. The number, as conceived, called for an expert dancer. Gene, who helped many people with his enthusiasm, felt it would strengthen the story if I, the comic, danced it. There would be an extra fillip of surprise. He assigned his assistant, Stanley Donen (who later became a director-producer), to teach me the dance. That was not easy. Rita had been a professional dancer since the age of six as Margarita Cansino, and she needed four weeks to learn it. I worked on the edge of embarrassment and anger; dancing does require a special physical skill and Gene forced me to keep up with him and Rita. The sequence ran for eight minutes, up and down steps, leaping onto boxes, kicking trashcans, parading. I couldn't fake it. In the end I had a great feeling of accomplishment: I felt I could do anything.

During this, Rita had become involved with Orson Welles. Passionately. They had to see each other; like Romeo and Juliet, nothing would stop them. *Citizen Kane* had closed a lot of doors to Orson Welles because William Randolph Hearst felt that Orson had shafted him by using him as a model for Kane. Harry Cohn barred Orson from the lot, but Gene and I would let Orson in through a back door, to see Rita.

> *(On the set: a run-through of "Make Way." Gene, Rita and myself. We dance with our backs to the camera.)*
> GENE: *"She sees a lot of Orson, doesn't she?"*
> ME: *"Yes, she sees him all the time."*
> *(Rita smiles. We continue dancing.)*
> GENE: *"What does she see in him?"*
> ME: *"Well, I guess he's attractive."*
> GENE: *"Does he do something to her?"*
> ME: *"Well, he's doing to her what he did to Hearst."*
> *(Rita collapses in laughter.)*

Rita and Orson were married in 1943 and divorced four years later. I understand it was a reasonably happy marriage —and creative. They had a beautiful child, Rebecca.

Because of my eyes, the draft board classified me 4F. Before I signed for *Cover Girl*, Harry Cohn made very sure of that. If he lost an actor in the middle of shooting, those scenes would have to be remade. Suddenly, in the middle of shooting, I received an order for reexamination of my physical condition. Cohn lashed me up and down—he swore I had tricked him. I was the one being tricked.

The Air Force was casting for its big benefit Broadway musical, Moss Hart's *Winged Victory*. Irving Lazar, a wheeler-dealer agent, and Ben Landis, later of the California Supreme Court—both good friends of mine—told Moss to get me for the show. They, with someone in the Air Force, I guess, were influential enough to have me reconsidered. So I could be sent into the Air Force to play their show! I expected this kind of sly string-pulling in the movies and Broadway, but what a way to run an army.

I dutifully took all the prescribed tests. On the urine exam, the fellow next to me tensed up. I said, "He's my guest," and filled his cup, too. This may have had something to do with keeping me in my original classification—4F. I did what I could for the war effort by playing in USO shows.

The Air Force found a good man to fill my spot. Edmond O'Brien.

I was receiving frequent calls on the *Cover Girl* set: "Mr. Cohn wants to see you in his office right away." I received quizzical looks from actors and crew; they must have assumed I was one of the boss's stool pigeons.

All the studios supplied a night of entertainment for servicemen at the Hollywood Canteen. For the 20th Century-Fox night, Zanuck simply ordered his head of casting to call Betty Grable, Harry James's orchestra and several other performers under contract, and put together an exciting show. Not Cohn. He had to prove that he knew show business, that he knew talent and how to combine it in a live show. "I started out as a song plugger," he bragged, "and I know more about stage shows than all these half-ass producers put together."

After I came into his office and the door was closed, he'd ask casually, "What kind of act does this Chester Morris do?"

"He does magic with hankies and cards."

"How many minutes?"

I made a quick guess, and Cohn added him to his list for Columbia's night at the canteen. To fill his bill, I offered an hour of hints in the form of questions—"Don't you think, Mr. Cohn, this act could . . .?" Production on *Cover Girl* was held up, Kelly was stamping on his cap in exasperation; costs ran up $10,000 an hour. That didn't bother Cohn. He was playing Show Business.

After a while he invited me to view rough cuts of new films, and he'd grunt, "What do you say, Blinky?" I contributed a few lines and a finale to *A Thousand and One Nights,* and got acquainted with Cohn's unpredictable, crude affection. Cornel Wilde was Aladdin. I played Abdullah the Thief, a Middle East Blinky in pantaloons and pointy-toe sandals. Beautiful Evelyn Keyes was the genie. A lovely notion to make the genie a woman—and it may have been Cohn's. She wanted to do something to reward me at the end of the story. She raised her hand, a puff of smoke, and there I was, in jewels and silks, surrounded by the lovely harem girls. (Among them: Shelley Winters; Dusty Anderson, who married director Jean Negulesco; and Erle Galbraith, who married Al Jolson.) The script called for me to look straight into the camera and say, "I must have had a heart attack!"

It's a wonderful feeling of power to have the fadeout of a picture all to yourself. But I had to tell Cohn it was not a funny line. "People sometimes have heart attacks while watching a movie."

"You got anything better, Blinky?"

I just happened to have a concept for the finale—and, more important, I could deliver the star to make it work. A wave of the genie's hand, smoke puff, I disappear. The courtyard of the Oriental palace comes into focus. The harem girls are sitting around, entranced, as they hear Frank Sinatra's voice singing "All or Nothing at All." Where's the voice coming from? Camera pans to the girls' feet—they're wearing bobby sox. Then up to me, on a balcony. I'm wearing a Sinatra wig, and it is *my* voice. The genie sits on the rail of the balcony, enjoying the view of the girls squealing at this sex symbol she has created. I turn to her, singing . . . and she faints dead away.

It was an engaging bit of fantasy, certainly an improvement over the original. Frank, as a friendly gesture, spent half a day recording the song and teaching me the lip movements so I could synchronize with his sound. Cohn liked it.

Later, I hinted to him that I would not refuse a token payment for the idea.

"You ungrateful, blind sonovabitch!" he shouted, his lower jaw quivering. "Look at all the opportunities I gave you! Get out of my office!" In a few days, my brother Harry, now my business manager, received a check from Cohn for $10,000. That was really subtle consideration; if it had been made out to me, I would have been obligated to turn it over to Fox, since all income from my services on loan went to them.

Later, Cohn said to me, "You know, that was a goddamn fine thing for that guinea bastard to do."

I knew Frank would not accept money. I suggested, "Why don't you present him with one of the grand pianos from your studio? For a top singer, he has a lousy piano in his living room."

Cohn thought that was a great idea.

He not only sent nothing to Frank—when he discovered that Frank's wife, Nancy, had her clothes designed by Jean Louis, who was then under contract to Columbia, Cohn barred her from visiting him on the lot. That was his thanks.

There was no explaining Cohn. He could send a generous check, yet if I wanted one of the cheap hard candies he kept on his desk, I had to ask first. His crudity and mental whippings drove many distinguished talents away from Columbia. He resented anyone with a formal education because he had so little, and he was determined to prove he was smarter.

> *(Cohn's office: He presses all the buttons on his desk call box at the same time. All department heads hurry in, each with his script of* Thousand and One Nights.*)*
>
> COHN *(to the assembly):* "*When would you say the Arabian Nights took place?*"
>
> SCRIPT DEPT.: "*About 2000 years ago.*"
>
> COHN *(his scorn building up):* "*Oh, really? Would you turn to page 48, scene one. (All find the page.) Now, will somebody tell me why the fuck you got all this modern language crap in here! Yessiree this, yessiree that!*"
>
> *(I look at the line. It reads "Grand Vizier: 'Yes, sire.'" Nobody wants to be first to tell Cohn he's wrong.)*

I was in the projection room when he ran the rough cut of *The Jolson Story*, by Sidney Buchman, an experienced, conscientious writer whom even Cohn respected. As the film ran, Cohn dozed off for a minute. It was a habit that kept him refreshed and shrewd all day.

> *(After the lights come up):*
>
> COHN: "*Sidney, when are you going to learn that you can't pull any bullshit on me?*"

BUCHMAN: *"What are you talking about?"*

COHN: *"I told you I want that kitchen scene in. It's important to the story. You don't have it."*

BUCHMAN: *"Of course it's in there!"*

COHN: *"You sonovabitch! You tryin' to make a shmuck out of me? I just saw the picture!"*

(The argument rages. I know the scene is in—it ran when his eyes closed.)

ME: *"Harry, I saw it."*

COHN: *"What the hell . . . I must have been reaching for a candy or something."*

He could only communicate by swearing. So you had to listen to the *tone* of it to decide whether it was friendly or angry. He knew he was coarse, but he wore it as a badge of sincerity. He thought he was Columbia's goodwill ambassador at the Hollywood Canteen. Ann Miller danced one night for a group of soldiers back from Europe. Some of them sprawled on the floor down front, and one of them propped his feet up on the edge of the little stage. Cohn bounded across the hall and kicked the soldier's feet off. "What the hell are you doing?" he shouted. "Looking up the girls' dresses?" This was one of his many goodwill gestures.

I did my clarinet bit with Saul Chaplin at the Canteen. The fun of it is my trying to get a simple introduction from Saul, who goes off into elaborate flourishes of his own and won't let me play. Cohn came in late and heard me pleading with Saul, "Please, let me squeeze in a few notes, will you?"

Cohn did not know Saul, who was assistant musical director at his own studio. He walked up behind Saul and chopped the back of his neck. "Let him play!" he roared.

End of that bit.

When you worked for Cohn, he owned you. He had to have your private number, and he'd phone at four or five in the morning, to Jerry Wald, to anybody on his payroll. He phoned me late one night, laughing hysterically. "Did you read this?" It was an article in *Confidential* magazine, titled THE MOST HATED MAN IN HOLLYWOOD. He thought that was the funniest thing he'd ever read. As if it wasn't Cohn in that article but Louis B. Mayer.

He may not have been the most hated man in town, but he was probably the man who hated most. He hated to be wrong in anything. He played gin with Sammy Cahn, shuffled the cards twenty times—and still lost regularly. All the while cursing Sammy, who wore glasses, as a "blind Jew sonovabitch." Cohn would never pay his twenty-five dollar or forty-eight dollar debt at the table. No, he made Sammy work for it by giving him chits. Sammy had to make a trip to Cohn's secretary at the studio to pick up his money.

Cohn hated sentiment or displays of affection. After his wife, Joan, delivered a healthy boy, Cohn assembled his department heads and poured drinks of fifty-year-old brandy. "What do you think of this? An old sonovabitch like me knocking out a kid!"

One of the underlings, a starchy milquetoast, rose to the occasion with a toast. "May he be as fine a man as his father."

Cohn reached over the desk and knocked the glass out of his hand. "You know everybody in Hollywood hates me. What have you got against a little kid, you sonovabitch?" And he threw the man out of his office.

I was on the back lawn of his mansion when he told me someone was coming to see him on a business deal. "Wait in the house—I'll get rid of this jerk." I couldn't help looking back as I turned into the door. His visitor was a pretty little girl with glasses, a handicapped orphan he'd adopted. She threw her arms around his neck and they hugged each other. I suppose he did not want me to witness this, because he considered it weakness.

Still, he was a good family man. In the fictional tradition of the Mafia dons, he loved his wife and children. When he died, services were held on the biggest stage at Columbia. It was mobbed. This prompted one wag to say, "Well, you give the public what they want—you'll sell out."

I felt a loss. With all his bluster and drive, he made a lot of memorable pictures. He was fair to me. And nowadays it's hard to find an honest bastard.

The third picture released in 1944 came from Fox in July. It was titled *Take It or Leave It.*

I can leave it.

The fourth, *Something for the Boys,* meant something else important for me. A wife. Many of the fateful steps in my life, I realize, have not been conscious decisions where I considered the alternatives and made a rational choice. They were the result of sheer chance. Meeting Gus Edwards on the Coney Island boardwalk . . . taking over a role in *Yokel Boy* because the star was incapable . . . making my first screen test in a part for which I had absolutely no qualifications. My life has been a 1940's musical: full of unbelievable twists, irrelevant farce scenes, boy-girl misunderstandings, confused opportunities—with singing! dancing! hilarity!

I was on the set of *Something* one day when I noticed two girls about to cross the stage. One of them was the most beautiful girl I'd ever seen. Now the situation became as confused as the "Who's on First?" bit.

> ME *(to Assistant Director):* "Say, who's that beautiful girl?"
>
> ASSISTANT: *"Oh, that's Martha Montgomery."*
>
> ME *(as she crosses over):* "How do you do, Miss Montgomery?"
>
> FIRST GIRL *(looks blank, then snaps):* "When you have more time, my name is Dennison."
>
> ME *(grabbing Assistant):* "Kenny, didn't I just ask you who was that beautiful girl over there?"
>
> *(Kenny nods vaguely.)*
>
> ME *(to first girl):* "He said that was Martha Montgomery. I assumed that was you because there was only one beautiful girl—and it had to be you."
>
> *(She gives me the loveliest smile—and, more important, she believes me.*

I persuaded her to have dinner with me. And she *was* the most beautiful woman in the country—Jo-Carroll Dennison had been chosen Miss America of 1942. She had a bit part in *Something.*

From here we progressed to misunderstanding. Our backgrounds, our goals, drives, even eating habits were a continent apart. Jo-Carroll came from the heart of Texas—Tyler,
population 40,000. Her mother was a widow. Jo-Carroll at
sixteen was helping out by working in a bank. Her beauty
attracted the interest of an elderly state senator, who felt she
could bring fame and possibly some fortune to herself, to
Tyler and to Texas. In those days, Miss America candidates
had to display some performing talent. The senator bought costumes, secured a pianist and arrangements, and she became
Miss Citizen's National Bank, Miss East Texas and, in time,
Miss America. She was seventeen then, just a little less than
the required eighteen. She received a stock contract from Fox,
then a small part as Al Jolson's first sweetheart in *The Jolson
Story*. Her only important film role came in *Winged Victory* as one of the wives. She made it clear that a career in
movies was not her life's ambition; it was a way of making the
most of her abilities to earn a living and support her mother.
I had no feelings about marriage, pro or con. I just didn't
think about it.

I took her to parties, to my friends' houses, the home entertainment circle. And, of course, the American Legion fights.
This became an exciting world for her. Her mother, a sweet,
unworldly, church-going lady, would wait up till I brought
Jo-Carroll home in my little Dodge. When we stayed out in
the car too long, mother flashed the lights in the house. If this
sounds like a high school romance—that's about the emotional
level. I'd never gone to high school. I was catching up, and I
loved it.

After about six months of this, Jo-Carroll went away with two
other couples for a weekend of active sports: fishing, swimming, hiking. They went off to a cabin in the wilderness. When
she did not come back by Monday, I phoned her house every
hour. Not home yet, her mother reported. I began patrolling
the house. I went into a jealous fantasy . . . all sorts of horrible
possibilities. I assumed she was doing what I would have
done.

When she came home, her answer was simple: She had picked
up a tick in her skin and after one of the woodsmen tried to

burn it out with a hot knife, they had to find a doctor. I believed her. Then, in my anger, the peculiar logic of love and possession overwhelmed me.

"Let's get married," I said.

"Okay," she said.

That intention immediately broke into the gossip columns. The senator offered to set up an annuity of $100,000 for Jo-Carroll if she didn't marry "that Jew." And this dear silly girl turned him down.

I asked Rags to be my best man. He waited for us in the judge's chambers, but when we were held up by the medical tests, he had to rush back to a picture he was shooting. My brother Harry stepped in, and I phoned Rags on the set so he could hear the ceremony. Afterward, we had a small lunch at the Brown Derby, and we both returned to work on *Something for the Boys*.

We came back to my one-bedroom, tiny terrace apartment on the edge of Beverly Hills for the honeymoon. And then . . . into the back of my head popped—hey! it's Friday night, the Legion fights, and I've got my usual two seats . . .

I asked Jo-Carroll, "Do you want to go see the fights?"

She laughed. Fortunately, she thought I was kidding. I laughed, too, and Jo-Carroll won out. For our wedding breakfast we walked to a hamburger joint.

After the picture was wrapped up, we flew to New York for a delayed honeymoon at the Sherry-Netherland. I wanted her to meet my mother, and all the way out to Bensonhurst I briefed her on the pitfalls of a Jewish celebration: the horseradish, the stuffed derma. As we walked into the house my mother leaped up and hugged her. Momma laid out a mammoth spread of Jewish delicacies, and my bride from Tyler ate it bravely. My mother sat there, staring at her and muttering: "I love her, I love her." And then, for some reason we were never able to understand, turned to my sister Lillian and said, "*Better* than you!"

I took Jo-Carroll around town, showing her off to my friends. To Toots Shor's, where we sat around with Joe DiMaggio, Barney Ross, my gang. It never occurred to me that my wife was a romantic. She would have preferred to walk hand-in-hand through Central Park.

She threw a surprise party for me in the hotel. This took a lot of effort, to learn my friends' addresses and phone numbers in secret. It was a complete surprise. I was puzzled and a little irritated: Why did she have to go to all this trouble for me? Did she expect to gain something—a mink coat? I could not accept the simple fact that this beautiful woman loved me and my bald head.

Jo-Carroll awoke late that night with a stabbing pain in her stomach. I called the hotel for a doctor, who turned out to be a jolly guy from Atlanta. Appendicitis, he said. He called the hospital and ordered an operation.

I didn't want this lovely woman cut up. And I felt her mother should have some say in this matter. The doctor agreed —the operation was not immediately urgent. I phoned Goodman Ace, one of the great hypochondriacs of the day; he would know a good doctor. He sent an elderly gentleman, a brilliant doctor who did not make house calls but came as a favor to Goody. Jo-Carroll was unsettled by the old-fashioned way he pressed his fingers into her stomach and asked, "Show me where your belly hurts."

This doctor said it was not appendicitis. It was the result of tension. Whirling around New York on a honeymoon with a husband who was still a bachelor at heart. I'd been one for thirty-four years; I just couldn't break the habit. Except now, I found, I had a date *every* night.

While Jo-Carroll and I were discovering all those little details we never knew about each other, I was asked to join Frank Sinatra on a USO tour of Europe. Frank was in a bit of trouble.

The four Crosby sons, juvenile Marx Brothers, at Bing's
Rancho Santa Fe, 1943.

My favorite comic, Rags Ragland, just before the warmup for
Bing's Kraft Music Hall radio show, 1943.

Wife-to-be, Jo-Carroll
Dennison, Miss America of
1942.

That classic dance on a
New York street in *Cover Girl*,
"Make Way for Tomorrow,"
with Gene Kelly and Rita
Hayworth.

Frank Sinatra, at my Copa
opening, in the finale of
"Love That Boy." A takeoff on
the kind of act that killed
vaudeville, we waved the
American flag as we went off.

Peddling curative snake oil in
High Button Shoes. Joey Faye
is my shill at left, 1947.

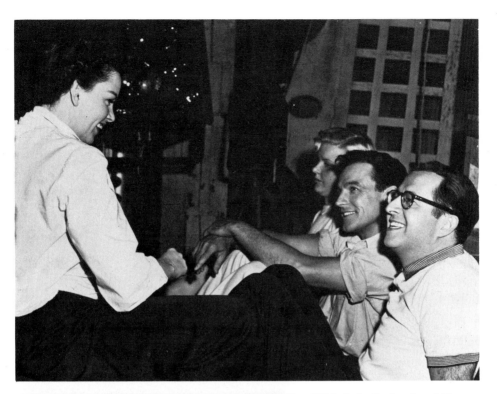

With Judy Garland and Gene
Kelly during a break in the
filming of *Summer Stock*, 1950.

Judy's daughter, Liza Minnelli,
age five, visiting set of
Summer Stock, in a hip-
swinging "Darktown Strutters
Ball."

Martin and Lewis, backstage at
the television studio, before
our Colgate Comedy Hour
special, 1950.

Top Banana: Scene with Jack
Albertson, who started with me
as softshoe dancer in Catskills
and became Academy Award
winner for straight role in *The
Subject Was Roses.*

CHAPTER 8

Bing Crosby and
Frank Sinatra in:
"The Road to the Vatican"

Sinatra was the singing sensation of the nation. The bobby-soxers squealed and swooned over him, older women merely adored him. But the men in the service saw him as a virile guy making millions—and why wasn't he in uniform? Frank was a legitimate 4F: punctured eardrums. There is a scar on his face, a reminder of the forceps a doctor used to pull him out of the womb. Frank told me he was a gigantic twelve pounds at birth, and the forceps punctured his eardrum. He wanted to contribute to the war effort by entertaining overseas.

Frank and I were very close. Like Gene Kelly, he ran an open house of good fellowship. Just before my marriage, he celebrated his baby Nancy's birthday party. My present was "Nancy With the Laughing Face."

A few weeks before, I'd been sitting around the pool at Johnny Burke's house with Jimmy Van Heusen. Bessie, Johnny's wife, laughed at one of my jokes, and I remarked, "Oh, Bessie with the laughing face."

"Good title for a song," Van Heusen said.

Burke, who'd won Oscars for his lyrics, answered, "It's my day off. You two guys do it."

I did the lyrics in about twenty minutes. For the birthday party, I changed the words to fit Nancy. Frank liked the song, and presented it on his Old Gold radio show. I forgot all about it.

When Frank's manager, Al Levy, asked me to put together

a show to tour Europe with Frank for six weeks, I was torn apart. Here I was, still on my honeymoon with Jo-Carroll, yet Frank was a pal—if he needed me, I had to help. Jo-Carroll lost out to the tour. Frank left the details of the show in my hands because of my stage and USO experience. Saul Chaplin agreed to come along as accompanist. And we picked two girls—Fay Mackenzie and Betty Yeaton. Betty was a lithe, lovely, amazingly acrobatic dancer. Fay was primarily an actress, blessed with a first-rate singing voice.

I knew Frank had to be presented in a very special way. I couldn't give him the usual buildup—"And here he is, the idol of America's youth!"—because those youths in uniform might have thrown C-ration cans. (They didn't resent me, I suppose, because my gleaming pate and thick lenses were obvious disabilities. Maybe they resented Frank as a sex image who made their girls swoon at home, while they were unavailable overseas. Wartime provides an excuse for strange, irrational emotions.)

I suggested to Frank that he be presented as the underdog of the show. I would open with a few well-aimed Army jokes —food, the draft, civilian clothes. Then Frank wanders on, casually. Jokes about Frank: "I know there's a food shortage, but this is ridiculous. . . . He weighed twelve pounds when he was born, and he's been losing weight ever since." Frank asks if he can sing. We go into my singing lesson bit. I shape his tones, slap his cheeks, browbeat him, convince him he can't sing at all. Then my clarinet bit, for which Frank goes into the audience and heckles me. By this time, I figured the men would be demanding, *"Let Sinatra sing!"* The soldiers had been underdogs so long, I was sure they would love this under- dog.

We rehearsed two days, and that was it. The military wanted to put us all into uniforms, but Frank, the rebel, said, "The hell with that—the GIs are tired of looking at uniforms." We wore our own clothes, and Frank kept his immaculate, no matter what mud field we played (a knack picked up in his years of touring with bands, which somehow had eluded me). He shined shoes with a positive fervor; he shined all our shoes. He actually went out and bought a shoeshine kit.

We flew in an Air Transport Command C-54, with Air Force generals, and we were told to watch our language. First stop: Gander, Newfoundland. I'd never flown in a plane, and frankly, I was petrified. I have flown thousands of miles since then, but I've never enjoyed it. Some people just don't like ice cream—I just don't like planes. As we passed the edge of Maine, approaching Newfoundland, I recalled the old burlesque joke:

"I got a girl in Maine."

"Bangor?"

"I just met her."

This relaxed me. Saul Chaplin, a very gentle, proper man, was scrunched down in his seat, not quite green. To cheer him up I dropped the line:

"I got a girl in Maine."

Anxious to prove he was hip, he blurted out: "Did you give her a bang?"

That kept us alive all the way to Gander.

The weather socked us in; we stayed for two days. We toured the show around the base . . . and it played like a dream. No allowances for young troops; we played it as if we were at Ciro's. When the Special Services officer learned that Frank planned to walk out into the audience to heckle me, he wanted to send two MPs with him! Frank would have no part of that. He had those audiences in the palm of his skinny hand. When he asked for requests, the first scream from 2,000 men was "Nancy With the Laughing Face." The song had been picked up by the Armed Forces Radio network from the Old Gold show. (It became the number-one request among the soldiers on the Continent, and in England. I was flabbergasted; it's the only lyric I ever wrote. When we came back to the States, Frank made a formal record, from which I still receive royalty checks. It's one of his perennial hits.)

At a stop in the Azores, we learned that wounded men were being flown back to the States. We asked the base operations officer to call us at any hour before a plane took off so we could talk to the men. There wasn't much we could say to cheer them up. The important thing was to let them know somebody from the States cared enough to be there. The opening to conversation was, "Where are you from, buddy?"

I discovered one amputee came from Brooklyn. I called Frank over, but the man had a grim look on his face. "I don't want to see him."

Well, I felt Frank didn't deserve that. "What do you mean?" I said gruffly. "Why the hell don't you want to see him?"

"I used to hack a cab around Lindy's," the man said. "Once in a while he got into my cab. And those goddamn bobby-soxers kicked in my fenders!" Now he laughed. He'd been saving that joke a long time.

In one show Frank joked, "Gee, we never get any souvenirs." A hundred captured revolvers were tossed up on the platform. Frank then went on a buying binge. Enemy grenades, mortar tripods, machine guns, flags, Portuguese lace. Since I held the money to pay expenses and the salaries of the two girls, Frank kept borrowing fifties and hundreds from me. I was the only head of a USO troupe who came back $5,000 short. Frank's obsession infected me. I heard there was a shortage of pipe cleaners in the States, so I started buying them up in PXs wherever we stopped. They cost something like twenty for a dime, and I accumulated a barracks-bagful. I didn't smoke a pipe—I thought they'd make a great gift for Bing Crosby.

When we returned to LaGuardia airport, all of Frank's souvenirs were confiscated.

Every commanding officer invited us for dinners, parties. And Frank, always the rebel, said, "Screw that—we'll stick with the GIs." Well, there were hundreds of GI offers. One sergeant kept pestering Frank to come to his billet for dinner. Frank put him off for three days. Then, on the last night of our stay, he said to me, "Come on, let's get it over with." When I saw that billet, I could have rapped Frank with my pipe cleaners—it was the grandest layout in Italy.

The sergeant was a combat hero who'd been taken off the line and given a job chauffeuring the American ambassador. His billet was a castle that Hermann Goering had once requisitioned. Goering ran off with most of the treasures but left behind a rare Bechstein grand piano, whose tone drove Saul Chaplin into ecstasies. The dinner began with several pastas and ran the full gamut through fish, steaks, chops, dessert, champagne. With that piano we had to have a concert. The Italian cooks and servants lined up outside the long music gallery to hear that great Italian singer from America—Signor Sinatra.

As Frank went through his new hits and old favorites, I noticed frowns of incredulity, then disgust, creep over the Italians. They expected a great baritone to do "Rigoletto."

In Rome we had been booked into a three-floor walk-up hotel. Frank said, "We'll stay at the Excelsior." It was the most luxe hotel in town, and booked up to the ceiling. Frank muscled us in. Then he began to feel his strength. "We ought to have an audience with the Pope."

"Come on, Frank," I said. "What've you been smoking?"

"For a USO leader, you're very conservative." He got in touch with the office of Myron Taylor, President Roosevelt's envoy to the Vatican, and an appointment was made for an audience with the Pope: 3:30 P.M., at a certain side door in the Vatican.

Frank, of course, was in beautiful shape; but by now I looked like a displaced person. The girls couldn't wear their sexy stuff. What were the most formal *clean* clothes we could wear? The USO uniforms! We'd been carrying them all around Italy and never worn them. The girls ran out to buy mantillas, to cover their heads.

I thought of Bing Crosby, a devout Catholic, and decided to ask the Pope to bless rosary beads for him. I had saved a Prince Albert tobacco can, stuffed with pipe cleaners. I dumped them, cleaned the can and took it along to protect the beads, which I bought from an old lady outside the Vatican entrance. Frank primed himself to tell Pius XII a few things he didn't know about. "Like that bigot Father Coughlin in Detroit. This priest is doing a lot of damage to the church."

We were ushered into a private room and briefed by a Cardinal on the protocol. It was to be a private audience. The Cardinal instructed us to kneel and kiss the ring of St. Peter. He took a look at me and added, "This is not compulsory." For some reason, he knew I wasn't a Catholic.

Pius XII entered. I was never much of a believer in religious ritual, but his deep-set eyes, the dignity and inner fire made me know I was in the presence of a great holy man.

> THE POPE *(to Frank): "*. . . *And you, my son, are a tenor?"*
>
> FRANK: *"No, Your Holiness, I'm a baritone."*
>
> THE POPE: *"Ah. And what operas do you sing?"*
>
> *(I bite my lip. This is no place for a laugh.)*
>
> FRANK: *"I—eh, don't sing opera, Your Holiness."*
>
> THE POPE: *"And where did you study?"*
>
> FRANK: *"I—eh, never studied . . ."*
>
> *(The Pope looks him over quizzically: What are you doing here? Frank shrugs humbly. I wait for him to explain the errors of the Catholic Church in Detroit. The Pope blesses Frank and turns to me. After all our travel, I'm weary, and a little hung over. I look like Lazarus before he was warmed up.)*
>
> THE POPE: *"*. . . *And you, my son?"*
>
> ME: *"I am a comedian."*
>
> *(He turns to the Cardinal for a quick translation.)*
>
> THE POPE: *"It is a blessed thing in these sad times to bring laughter." (He blesses me.)*
>
> ME: *"I had the honor of seeing Your Holiness in Chicago, when you were Papal Secretary, at the Eucharistic Convention. I was playing a theater there . . ."*
>
> THE POPE: *"Yes, I have fond memories of America."*
>
> ME: *"Does Your Holiness know of Bing Crosby?"*
>
> THE POPE: *"Ah, yes!"*
>
> *(Going My Way didn't hurt Bing in the Vatican.)*
>
> ME: *"He has four sons and I would like to take these rosary beads to him." (I bring out the beads.)*
>
> THE POPE: *"You have three beads. Is there a Mrs. Crosby?"*

ME: *"Yes."*
(The Pope turns to the Cardinal, who adds three
mother-of-pearl Vatican-stamped beads to make a total of
six. They are blessed. As we leave, I put them carefully
into the tobacco can.)

Out on the street, Frank turned on me and punched my
arm with the full fury of his 133 pounds. "You creepy bum!
I take you in to see the Pope—and you're plugging Crosby!"

Soon after I returned to Hollywood, I dropped in at the
Kraft Music Hall and presented the rosary beads to Bing. "I
want you to know the last hand that touched them was the
Pope's."

Bing shook his head. "Always kidding, huh? Everything's
a gag."

I just turned on my heel and walked away. Can't a comedian display a straight, honest sentiment? Bing sensed he had
misunderstood and later, in his own Crosbyan way, expressed
his thanks.

One base in Italy had an outdoor theater so large the GIs
called it Yankee Stadium. The show did not go well, and
there were razzberries because some couldn't hear us. Rows of
men climbed out of their seats and crowded around the
stage. I didn't like the sound of the crowd. Were they sore at
Frank or me for some reason? And no MP in sight. For the
finale, we four sang one chorus of a special lyric, and it
seemed to me the men down front were going to charge the
stage.

I yelled down to Saul, "The Star-Spangled Banner!" Saul
immediately hit it, and that froze everybody around the stage.
Before the end of the anthem, we jumped into our waiting
staff car and speeded away. Well, we'd beat another crisis,
I thought, but I was still seething. I muttered to Frank, in
the front seat, "Hell, you'd think they could put some ropes
around the stage!"

Frank turned to me. "You silly jerk, why didn't you think of
that before? You're the goddamned tour director!"

"Where the hell do you come off, calling me a jerk? It's you that sets them off!" I was yelling now. Frank screamed back. We were cursing each other for a riot that never happened.

Saul turned white, the girls hunched down into their seats. We rode in angry silence to our billet in a bombed-out hotel. Frank, in his grim, withdrawn mood, stalked right up to his room. Saul and I found the canteen in the cellar for some hot tea. How could we go on for three more weeks after the lousy names we'd called each other? I wanted to apologize, but I wasn't going to let Frank stomp all over me.

Into our gloom wandered a Navy lieutenant, handsome, beautifully tailored, right out of *Follow the Fleet*. Greg Bautzer, the esteemed Hollywood lawyer, slapped my back. "Phil! It's the greatest show ever. After all those dreary accordion players and the community singing we've been getting . . ."

"You kidding?" I said. "Didn't you see them ready to charge?"

"It was payday! They had a few drinks—they were enthusiastic. I just asked Frank who put this great show together, and he said it was you."

Typical Sinatra. He was burning, but to outsiders he still displayed his loyalty. I knew that, right now, I had to square things. But the conciliatory move had to be offhand; Frank hated thank-yous and sentimental gush. I grabbed Solly's shoes and mine, opened Frank's door, and threw them in to him. "Have these shined by the morning!" I ordered. "And you see that mud on the toes? Use some elbowgrease."

He looked up at me with the dark smile which is his and his alone. We were back in the groove again.

After V-Day in Europe, we were flown to Casablanca. For the rest of the way home, we were on our own. Frank found a *paysan* in a strategic position in flight operations, Sgt. Cuomo, who put us on alert, bags packed, for the first available plane. It carried fifty nurses, returning after three years in the China-Burma-India campaign. They were more intrigued by our two girls than by Sinatra: the nurses hadn't seen stateside lipstick in years. That night, over the Atlantic, as the moon lit up the cotton candy clouds under us, Frank sang as I'd never heard him sing before. It was a lovely moment that Zanuck, somehow, had overlooked in his musicals. We were suspended in a heavenly peace. The war was over; we and the nurses were going back to our unscarred homes. Surrounded by the silent, iridescent beauty filtering in through the windows, Frank sang for two hours. The songs became a lullaby as the weary nurses fell asleep on the floor and on the bucket seats. They had evidently lived together a long time in crowded tents and huts; whenever one turned over on her side, all fifty of them turned over, too.

My reunion with Jo-Carroll was happy and loving. And then, right back into the old rounds: the Legion fights, gambling, the nightclubs, the lots-of-laughs parties where I was always "on." Jo-Carroll was restless. She wanted a one-to-one relationship. With me, it was always one-to-fifty. Or three hundred.

Frank threw a New Year's party-show to end all New Year's shows, in his house at Taluca Lake. We put as much effort into it as a Broadway production. Music and lyrics by Sammy Cahn and Jule Styne. Richard Whorf, director and designer, painted a drop for us. Wives had to participate. Jo-Carroll, a reserved, almost shy woman, agreed to do a sock-it-to-'em number with me, written by Styne and Cahn. The title, "I'm the Wife of the Life of the Party," told the whole story of our relationship.

She appeared in a low-cut gown, looking like the Mona Lisa. The lyrics enumerated all my irritating habits, including the comedy routines I'd do at the drop of a chord. The last chorus threw a punch:

> . . . *he's a riot at every party*
> *In calm or rainy weather.*
> *He's the life of every party*
> *Except the one we have together!*
> *I'm the wife of the life of the party*

And he's boring the life out of me—
—GLAD TO SEE YAH!
He's boring the life out of me!"

Her song was the hit of the evening. Its obvious point
didn't trouble me at all. I was accustomed to ribbing; I prided
myself on being able to take it.

Performers, actors, can't be very objective about themselves.
They know their limits onstage, their vocal and emotional
ranges. They can take criticism of their performances but not of
themselves. If they looked too deeply into their own illusions,
they might destroy the confidence they need to build illusions
onstage. I've never known a performer who was rock-hard
secure inside. Not even Rags; he drank himself to death.

When I played on USO shows with Bing Crosby, he was
absolutely in charge. I was nominal manager and factotum,
but Bing, in his relaxed, jovial, pipe-puffing way, did what he
wanted. During the war, no matter what town you were going
to, there was only one train in the morning. You had to make
that 9:30 or else. I'd hustle Rags and Jimmy Van Heusen into
the station by 9:15. At 9:15 Bing was still shaving away, hum-
ming to himself. I'd call, "Bing, for godsakes!"

He'd sing, "Don't worry, Philly boy," continuing at his own
speed. And we always made that train. I never heard him
raise his voice to anyone.

I first met Bing in New York when he appeared with the
Rhythm Boys at the Paramount in Times Square. We renewed
old memories when I came out to Hollywood. And he was very
friendly. "How do you like it out here?"

"Great," I said. "But the afternoons bug me. All my friends
are working."

"You have to play golf," he said. "It's the only way." He
immediately called John Montague, one of the founders of
the California Country Club (it's all a big housing tract now)
to introduce me. I bought a set of old clubs and, always impatient, refused to take lessons. I'd play along by myself in

the late afternoon, when the fairways were empty. There's nothing lonelier than belonging to a club where you don't know anyone. I did meet the golf hustlers, but I knew enough not to play with them.

One afternoon I walked out to the first tee, to find Babe Didrickson Zaharias waiting to go out with a threesome. "Hello, Phil," she said. "Why don't you join us?"

I was flattered that the great Babe recognized me, but I protested I was just a rank beginner.

"You can only learn if you play with good golfers," she said graciously. So I went along. As I teed up, she said, "Let's make it interesting for yourself. I'll give you two shots to a hole . . ." and what sounded like "a two-two-two with an automatic press on the backside with a Texan and an Arizonan." I didn't know what in the world she was talking about, but it was a privilege to play with her. How much could I lose? After eighteen holes I paid her $186—with one of my best smiles. I was fuming. It wasn't the money. I just hated to be taken like a bumpkin.

When I came into the clubhouse, her husband, the mammoth wrestler George Zaharias, was sitting at a table for a cold drink. "I hear you played with the little lady," he said.

I admitted she was really a wonder. He agreed, "A little flower." I noticed a deck of cards on the table. "You play gin?" I asked.

"Why not? I have to wait for the little lady anyway."

Well, I am not a powerful gin player, but he was worse. I beat Zaharias for $200. After caddy tips, I came out even that day.

I soon became a guest at Bing's Rancho Santa Fe, where his wife, Dixie, rode herd over the four boys with a wire coat hanger. One wrong word at the table, pardner, and she'd tap the offender with that hanger. I was "on" at parties here with Rags and Jimmy Van Heusen, and I helped initiate Bing into comedy bits, which he loved to perform as a change from his crooning—which made all the money. Our friendship was rather close, I'd say, although nobody gets more than an arm's-length close to Bing. He is a private person. Going his way.

He'd been making contributions to the USO in the form of large checks. He wouldn't admit it, but he was a little afraid of working onstage, even with a mike, in front of a live audience. There was some subtle difference, in his mind, between entertaining a big live audience and amusing the unseen millions over the radio, even though he had an audience in the studio for the Kraft Music Hall.

Well, he became accustomed to working with me and Rags and Jimmy. We got him out of the house and into a USO tour. Now he was only interested in doing comedy. I begged him, "Bing, they came to hear you sing. Do a couple of songs, and then we'll do the bits."

Because I had a compulsion to be on time for engagements, and they were three guys who liked to relax and linger over their drinks, I was cast as the villain. I had the irritating job of rounding them up. Bing picked up Rags' pet name for me—Laddie Boy—and that became his joke. Laddie Boy, the shepherd.

Bing had the most admirable habits. I wished I could relax like he did. He'd rise early in the morning, take long walks, puffing on his pipe as he looked over the new town or its parks. We pulled into a small burg in Wyoming; I was still asleep when Bing went out for his stroll. A phone call from the town's one cop awoke me—get down to the Square. The Square was a small clump of grass, with a statue of the town founder in the middle and an iron fence around it. Bing had stretched out on the grass, his head on the base of the statue, to contemplate the fluffy clouds. When I got there, he was sitting up, on the defensive and a little perturbed while the townspeople gaped at him through the fence. As if he were in a zoo. The cop grumbled to me, "If that's Bing Crosby, what in hell's name is he doing *there?*"

Another town: the tracks were washed out, and we would be stuck there six hours. We four strolled into the center of town. The natives noticed Bing, turned for a double take, then shrugged him off. Ah, it couldn't be him. . . . Bing spotted a movie house playing *Whistling in the Dark*, with Red Skelton. Rags had a small part in it, and he was in one of the stills displayed in the lobby. Admission: twenty-five cents before noon. Rags insisted we should get in free, a common courtesy in the movie profession.

> *(At the ticket box: the manager in a frayed tuxedo. Only six people in the house.)*
> RAGS: *"We'd like to see this picture. Professional courtesy."*
> ME: *"This is Mr. Rags Ragland. That's his picture in the lobby."*
> MANAGER *(looking him over dubiously):* *"By George, it is him. (Shakes Rags' hand.) You can go in, Mr. Ragland. What do the other fellows do?"*
> ME *(pointing to Van Heusen):* *"He plays the piano. And I do comedy bits."*
> MANAGER *(indicating Bing):* *"What about this man?"*
> ME: *"I don't know. Never saw him before in my life."*
> MANAGER: *"You three can go in but he (pointing to Bing) will have to pay."*

Spokane, Washington: Bing graduated from Gonzaga University here, so it was like Homecoming Day. We raised $10 million in a bond drive that afternoon. As he sang "Sweet Leilani," a lost child started bawling in the audience. I lifted her up onstage, so the parents could see her, and then handed her to Bing. He continued singing—to the child—without missing a note. The little girl immediately stopped crying and gurgled at him happily. Bing had a way with women.

We'd been booked into a suite at the top of the top hotel. I discovered Bing had acrophobia, just as I did, although closed-in places didn't bother me. So we moved down to the third floor. Two women who owned a record company sent up a large jukebox, to play Crosby records for us. On our last day a call came from the lobby: "We're from the record store. We'd like to take the jukebox back, since you're leaving."

"Send 'em up," said Bing. Two very attractive girls in white linen dresses entered. Bing, stoned but you'd never know it, ever the gentleman, pressed a cool drink into their hands. And they came along to say goodbye at the station. It was a jolly farewell, drinks all around.

Bing convinced the girls to come along to Seattle with us. It was just a small hop. I read Bing's mind and nervously squeaked, "Bing, we don't have tickets. We don't have tickets for them. These are the war years and the conductors are very strict." Bing says, "Don't worry, Philly boy. Everything's in order." He sang me *and* the conductor into submission. Fade out . . .

Fade in . . . A day and a half later, as the train pulled out from Boise, Idaho, I noticed through the window the same two girls waiting at the track for the train to Spokane. The linen dresses were still immaculate.

Back in Hollywood, after the tour, Bing booked me on his Kraft Music Hall radio show. I was nervous because I am not a good sight reader and all the gags had to be read from the script. My introduction by Bing as we rehearsed it: ". . . And now a companion of mine on USO shows, a very funny man whom you're going to hear a lot from in the future . . . Phil Silvers!"

About five minutes to airtime, as my butterflies flapped around inside like buzzards, Bing called me into his dressing room and offered a drink.

"No, thanks," I said. "I don't drink."

"Okay. Good luck." No words of encouragement. No trying to relax me. I stood in the wings, waiting to go on but more nervous than before. Had he lost confidence in me?

Bing welcomed me to the network with this intro: ". . . a very funny man, with a great future—and he's very well thought of in Boise, Idaho . . ."

I laughed all the way to the mike, completely relaxed. That was Bing's way: never obvious, never pressing.

Bing was having dinner at the Brown Derby when his house at Taluca Lake burned down. It was crammed with all his old trophies and gold records for his hits and a collection of rare old records. Dixie was at home with the children; when the fire broke out, she put the safety of the children first and hurried them out of the house. It burned to the walls. Johnny Burke, a songwriter pal, brought the news to Bing at the Derby. "Before I tell you anything, Dixie is fine and the kids are safe. But Bing, your house just burned to the ground."

Bing just nodded. "Thanks, John."

"Well, come on," said Johnny. "Let's go!"

"Sit down, John. I haven't finished my coffee."

In 1946, Monte Proser, still producing shows for the Copacabana in New York, came up with a beautiful suggestion: Let's reunite me and Rags Ragland in an act at the Copa. A capital idea, I thought, because now that I was a newlywed *and* a gambler, I needed more money than before. Rags said yes, and disappeared, leaving the details of the act to me. We had worked out so many routines together at parties and Foy's and Ciro's that I knew this would be a breeze. And good old Saul Chaplin signed on to play for us. Rags and I made a date to fly to New York for a quick rehearsal.

Suddenly, at 11 P.M., I received a call from the Los Angeles airport—Mr. Ragland was ill. Somebody—I think it was Orson Welles—had an extra plane ticket to Mexico and invited Rags to keep him company. Rags was like that. He'd go off with anybody who promised fun.

I found Rags in terrible pain at the airport; his drinking had finally caught up with his liver. I persuaded him to come home with me, so Jo-Carroll and I could oversee some medical care. At that hour we couldn't find a doctor. My wife had some menstrual pills, the only help I could offer him. They relieved his pain a little. Next morning, Rags went home and called his doctor, who didn't seem to have a clue to the ailment or its relief. Rags lay in bed and begged me for those menstrual pills. I was very cautious and refused; I thought the doctor knew what he was doing. Frank Sinatra intervened with an important specialist, who immediately put Rags into Cedars of Lebanon hospital. This doctor told me that, frankly, with

Rags' kidney and liver destroyed, I could not expect a miracle. "He will not leave this hospital."

His neck hurt. As the nurse massaged it, his head jerked back and his eyes looked up to the heavens. The nurse blessed herself and began to cry. "Thank God, he is out of pain." Rags did not die—he lapsed into a coma. For seven days. His heart was so strong it would not quit. I watched my best friend die. And then I delivered the eulogy at his funeral. I hadn't cried at my father's funeral; this time I did.

Well, the show must go on—mainly because the Copa had an open spot and I needed the money. The club offered me what they would have paid both of us.

Help materialized out of thin air. During my *Yokel Boy* days, I was a member of Toots Shor's club. Here I met William J. McCormack, operator of tugs, barges and a string of other enterprises, and his son, Bill Jr. McCormack Senior wanted Bill to take over the business, but his heart wasn't in it; the son was an introverted, intellectual young man, not prissy, yet I couldn't tell a blue story in front of him.

When I came to New York to rehearse for the opening, I stopped at Toots' place for lunch. And there was Bill McCormack. He'd never seen a nightclub rehearsal so I brought him along. It was a rough afternoon. I had to work out new material with Saul Chaplin. The band backing me was Ernest Lecuana's Cubans; everything had to be translated for them, and their rhythm wasn't exactly mine. On top of that, when I opened my clarinet case, the instrument was cracked. A bandsman offered me his own clarinet. And one of the girls in the line, Julie Wilson, volunteered to work in a bit with me.

Emotionally drained and worried, I slumped back to the hotel. A package was waiting for me. A brand-new clarinet from Bill, with the note "Good luck, Señor."

It was a touching gesture, and totally unexpected from a man who was to become a priest. He reappeared, over the years, in other crises in my life. Always to steady me and offer a warm prayer.

The 8:30 supper show, not the official opening, was sort of a warmup. It was grim. I hadn't performed in a nightclub in years. I'd forgotten about the eating, the clatter of knives and dishes, and all the raucous yak-yak. I did not know how to cope with it. Saul and I sat, dejected, in the tiny dressing room whose walls leaned on me like a Dr. Caligari set. I offered to release Monte Proser from his contract. "Oh, no," he reassured me. "You'll be all right." But I saw he was as worried as I was.

The door opened and in walked Frank Sinatra. *Impossible.* He was shooting a picture at that moment in Hollywood.

"Well, when do we go on?" he said.

He'd walked off the set that afternoon and flown to New York to help me. Since he had played most of Rags' bits with me on tour and at parties, I quickly laid out the routine: "When I touch my tie, you come on. Then the interruption bit . . . And we go into 'Love That Boy' . . . and so on." We chased upstairs to the Copa Lounge, which had an unoccupied piano; Saul ran through the numbers with Frank and Julie Wilson. That was it.

When he strolled out at midnight, the surprise and delight of the audience exploded the room. We were on one hour and three-quarters, which was unforgivable. But who cared? It was a night in which sentiment washed away everything. When I came out for the bow with Frank, I knew I had to say something about Rags. I hadn't slept for five days, and when I'm exhausted I cry easily. I heard myself saying: "May I take a bow for Rags?"

And I ran off, my eyes brimming over. I sat down in the dressing room, lamenting my genius for ending a show on a dead note. No sound filtered through the plasterboard. At the end of a show, the room always rattled with calls for checks, chairs being moved, the rhumba band coming on. Silence. I peeped out at the house—*everybody* was tearful, even the waiters. It was a requiem for Rags.

The worst truth in that show-must-go-on cliché is: The show must go on and on and on . . . The 2:30 performance was coming up, and I was physically and emotionally exhausted. I gulped two drinks, to give myself an edge, and I disintegrated. I am the most flappable drinker in show business. My words thickened into potato soup, and a young comedian, Jackie Gleason, started to heckle me. Pleasant and funny, but still I was not in control of the stage. That was lucky, because every comedian in New York was there, helping me. Milton Berle came to my side to heckle Gleason. Joe E. Lewis joined in. Henny Youngman picked up a violin and went into his routine. Gleason turned a seltzer bottle on Berle who slipped to the floor, and they went into an artificial resuscitation bit. I thought Gleason was really throttling Berle—I knew they had a genuine feud about money—so I tried to pull Gleason away by his tie. With my other hand, I was calming Lecuana's Cubans, who didn't want to get their instruments wet and were preparing to abandon ship.

The audience howled with glee. After a while a nagging thought seeped through my glaze: How do I end this show? How can you stifle half a dozen comedians in an ad-libbing free-for-all? The ending came in the rumpled shape of B. S. Pully, the gruffest, dirtiest comic in town. He came on croaking, "When you're smiling . . ." as the tears ran down his Smokey the Bear face. He whispered to the gang, "Follow me." That pulled everybody together in a line, and we strutted off chorusing ". . . when you're smiling, the whole world smiles with you!" *

How do you top that? The show had to go on for four weeks. And the next night, the corpulent figure of Jackie Gleason showed up. "When do we go on? I want to do what Frank did."

"Great," I said. "But I can't pay you. I'm in here to pay off the bookies."

"Don't worry about it. How else can I get into the Copa, pal?"

He did all the bits I had done with Frank, and I must admit he was wildly funny. The show was held up every night until Jackie arrived for dinner—never with less than a party of twelve. The Copa, of course, picked up the check. He was

---

* "When You're Smiling," copyright 1928 by Mills Music Inc. Copyright renewed 1956. Used with permission.

soon booked into Ben Marden's Riviera in New Jersey, at
several thousand a week. But he still wanted to play my dinner
show. So the Great One hired a chauffeur and limousine to
ferry him in. He didn't miss one dinner.

About a week before I closed, the doorman announced, "Mr.
Rags Ragland."

It was like a kick in the stomach. In walked his son John.
"I've taken his nickname," he explained. He pulled out a gold
chain, on which hung a St. Christopher medal and on the
other side the six-point Star of David which Rags had worn. "I
know you'd like to have this."

I wear it today. I believe it has pulled me through some
tough times.

CHAPTER 9

The Steam-Fitted
Body of Bugsy Siegel

In the Hollywood of the 1940's, top-level racketeers were quite chic. Stars and producers liked to brag of their friendship with Benny Siegel. The moguls of the studios pulled strings to invite him to parties in their homes. These men had a great rapport with gangsters: They were self-made dictators who'd come up the hard way; they had the same relentless drive, the disdain for others' feelings and lives, the calculating minds for ruthless deals. The racketeers were well-entrenched in gambling, loan-sharking, movie unions. I don't think they bothered with prostitution because there were so many sweet young freelancers, looking for a break in films. The gangsters met in the Savoy Restaurant in the center of Beverly Hills. Upstairs was a convenient horse room. Siegel was vice-president for West Coast operations of the Jewish-Italian conglomerate known as The Syndicate.

Benny Siegel found me amusing. He adopted me—very much as Harry Cohn did—and for the same reason. I was the opposite of Benny. I may have sounded brash, but underneath I was a softy, and I never played tough. Some social climbers on the hoodlum circuit would absorb their mannerisms, talk out of the side of their mouth, slap men with the back of their hand. I was myself. And very careful. Years ago I had learned in Brownsville, where Siegel was a fearsome figure: Don't listen to their business. When they mentioned a specific deal, I'd jump up from the table and walk out, because when the pressure came, they might wonder who'd heard about that deal? That kid Silvers? Nice kid, but he's gotta go.

The hoodlums certainly did nothing for me. And all I ever did for Benny Siegel was give him gas-ration coupons so he could drive to Las Vegas. He would never break a minor law. He knew state and federal investigators kept a vigil on him.

Benny introduced me to the Hollywood Athletic Club steam room and handball courts. He always kept in shape. Strong, well-groomed, immaculately dressed and as handsome as a movie profile. He'd sit in that steam room for hours. In his Las Vegas hotel room, I'd watch him coldcream his face and put a sleeping mask over it. I'd never seen a man outside the theater do that.

Before he climbed into his bed, Benny took the folded wad of bills out of his pocket—it looked like several thousand dollars—and slipped most of them into the pillowcase under his head. The few other bills he stuffed loosely into his pants pocket. "Learn from this, Blinky. If a burglar comes into the room tonight, he should find *something*."

Anyone who called him Bugsy found it was a capital offense, punishable by maiming. My brother Harry joined the Hollywood A.C. for the steam—wherever I'd go, he'd come, too. And Harry, who was a fan of doctors, met Benny's doctor brother in New York. Back at the club, he told Siegel, "Bugsy, I bring regards from your brother."

Benny controlled himself by jamming his fists against his sides. "My name is Benjamin, or Mr. Siegel to you." That time, I think, Harry got a pass because he was my brother.

With all his ruthless drive and shrewdness, I'm convinced Benny could have been a success in any business. He had a vision of the potential riches of Las Vegas. Benny built the first deluxe splendiferous hotel, the Flamingo. His particular genius was mathematics: percentages, odds, instant multiplication and division. Betting the house limit bored him—he had to beat the limit, even in a courtesy play at a friend's casino. He gave me and three other friends $1,000 each, to be bet the way he bet. He usually bet against the dice. He won quickly, and he collected from each of us immediately. He then went back to the table—"to make room expenses." A Hollywood writer's wife had the dice. A little tipsy, giggling, betting one dollar at a time. She made nine straight passes and wiped out Benny.

Benny had a sense of the ridiculous, too. I recall him setting up one of the longest-running practical jokes in the history of Hollywood. The patsy was a stuttering furrier I'll call Sam Benton. He cultivated movie people by lending them fur coats for gala occasions. Sam worked hard to be one of the boys at the Savoy restaurant. The cast assembled for "The Big Gag of 1946" included:

Benny Siegel, deadpan, playing the movie version of a gangster.

Lou Clayton, of Clayton, Jackson and Durante, nightclub performer.

The original Nick the Greek, gambler, who would stand at a crap table for forty-eight hours.

Arturo DeCordova, a handsome Mexican leading man in films.

Two of the three Ritz Brothers, Harry and Jimmy, movie and nightclub performers.

Myself, also a gambler.

The plot: Benton knew nothing about golf. So phony bets were made on a never-never golf match between Clayton and DeCordova. Clayton, with a handicap, could really give a good game to any golfer in the country. DeCordova had never been on a golf course in his life. Siegel was betting on Clayton; the Ritz Brothers faction backed Arturo. The bets were up to $45,000 when Benton made his move. He called Harry Ritz into the men's room. "Can the Me-Me-Mexican really play?"

"Arturo? He's the champion of Mexico for godsakes!"

"I want $500 of the be-be-bet on him. But don't tell Benny I'm be-be-betting against him." And he gave a $500 check to Harry.

The arguments raged about the rules of the match. Arturo insisted on wearing a serape, and demanded photographers and the Mexican Chihuahua Band to accompany him while he played. Clayton objected. Benton, with a sure winner, begged Clayton, "Go ahead. Let him have photographers." The match was set for Thursday at Hillcrest.

Clayton got a genuine nightclub engagement, and had to ask for a postponement. Benny Siegel, playing a gangster, phoned Sam at 2 A.M. Wednesday:

"Lou Clayton slipped on his ass in the bathtub and got a bad headache. He wants a postponement, but the Mexican won't give him one."

"Wha-wha-why are ya calling me?"

"I know you got $500 on the Mexican. This was supposed to be a gentleman's game. Why don't you let him postpone?"

"Me?" cried Benton. He was scared now. "I swear I don't know nu-nu-nothing!"

"You don't, huh? Just don't come out at night," Siegel growled and hung up the phone.

Benton dressed in a frenzy, rushed over to DeCordova's apartment and woke him up. "Do-do-don't fool around with that cu-cu-crazy Siegel. Give him a postponement."

DeCordova absolutely refused. His personal friend, the Mexican ambassador, was coming to the match. The honor of his country was at stake. He'd fought the bull in Mexico—he'd fight Siegel with the same sword. To the death! Benton stayed all night, to make sure the actor did not fight Siegel.

The postponements and arguments went on for weeks. De-Cordova now wanted to play at night, under lanterns. He said the Mexican ambassador would throw out the first ball.

> *(The day of the payoff: we're all at the Savoy, raising the bets to $80,000. Enter a new face, J. Carrol Naish, the native New Yorker who played Indians and Italians and Mexicans; he knows nothing at all about our gag.)*
>
> SAM BENTON *(pulling him aside): "Isn't DeCordova a pa-pa-pal of yours?"*
>
> *(Naish nods vaguely.)*
>
> *"Can he pa-pa-play golf?"*
>
> *(Naish knows a patsy when he sees one.)*
>
> NAISH: *"Of course! I saw him win the championship in Paris!"*
>
> *(Where did he get that? Mental telepathy? It's just too absurd.)*
>
> SAM *(rushing back to the table): "Hey, Arturo, you never told us you won the ch-championship in Paris."*
>
> ARTURO: *"Oh, it was nothing."*

SAM: *"Who did you beat?"*
ARTURO: *" The Count of Monte Cristo!"*
(I collapse in laughter and fall off the chair. The joke is over.)

Benny Siegel got hooked up with legitimate businessmen for the first time in building the Flamingo Hotel. I think that's what killed him.

He made business trips to Las Vegas in my car, on my gas-ration coupons. In those days you drove for hours in the desert. Signs warned: LAST STOP FOR WATER. When we reached that point, Benny took over the wheel. "Move over, Blinky. Let me show you how I used to drive getaway." He jammed the accelerator pedal to the floor and we'd roar over that empty road, weaving in and out, as though he was avoiding the pillars of the elevated tracks in New York.

Finishing the hotel became an obsession, a chronic rage, because he could never admit defeat. The estimated costs doubled, then tripled. Benny began pressuring people for more money. He doubled the charges on the line that fed race results to the betting parlors, stifling many bookies. And then he tripled it. The Syndicate told him to back off—he was ruining their other operations. He kept pushing.

I saw him in the barbershop of the hotel before the opening. "Nothing but trouble," he announced. "Look at this." It was a check from one man for $500,000. "And I don't know if I should deposit this. Christ!"

Jimmy Durante was the opening attraction with a rip-roaring show. But Benny Siegel was cast all wrong as a front-of-the-house man in this plush hotel. He was angry. On opening night he even needed a shave. He was betting at his own tables, and his guests, giving him the usual courtesy play, won and won and won.

My opening night for *High Button Shoes* was in Philadelphia, September, 1947. As I got off the train, I saw the newspapers—BUGSY SIEGEL SLAIN. I had to stop and catch my breath. I was never sentimental about Benny's business—I'm sure some of his enemies were dredged up wearing concrete galoshes. And now some divine score had been evened up. But the pictures of the death hit me: The head shot open, his body wallowing in blood. What a dirty end for a fastidious man.

Since I have few athletic talents, I have always admired those who do. Particularly fighters. The hoodlums out of my youth in Brownsville were one kind—Barney Ross was the real thing. He won both the welterweight and middleweight titles.

I don't know how I met Barney. It must have happened during my years in burlesque. We found an instant understanding. Unlike most fighters, he was very verbal: a first-rate joke-teller and raconteur and an expert double-talker. He also played a surprisingly good jazz piano.

Barney was not a natural fighter; he made himself into one, on sheer guts, to support his family after his father was shot in a holdup of their little grocery in Chicago. He was shadowboxing one day at Grossinger's training camp when he saw me imitating him. "Hey, Phil. You want to box? Get in here."

"No, Barney. Don't embarrass me."

"I won't touch you. Swing at me."

Well, I have as many dreams of glorious conquest as the next man. I was in good shape, after running around the burlesque stage three hours a day. I was heavier. What if I hit him? . . .

I couldn't touch him. I couldn't even see him. All I did was swing, and in a minute and a half I was spitting cotton. Right there I gave up any thought of boxing.

Barney retired from the ring, after a terrible beating from Henry Armstrong, to open a restaurant in Chicago. When Pearl Harbor was attacked, Barney enlisted in the Marines. He was ordered to Camp Pendleton to serve as a physical training instructor. There he slugged an officer, for an anti-Semitic crack, he told me. The commanding officer, to avoid a court-martial, shipped him overseas quickly. To Guadalcanal. Barney went into battle with little combat training. He came out a Silver Star hero—and a dope addict, from morphine given to him in a hospital to relieve the pain of his wounds. I did not know of his addiction; neither did his wife. I accompanied him on a train to New York that year. He rambled on and on about opening a chain of candy stores and borrowed several hundred dollars from me to pay back "some gambling debts." It didn't occur to me that he was addicted because he also drank, and very few people on dope can drink, too.

After years of addiction, Barney walked into the office of the Brooklyn district attorney, told his grim story and asked to be admitted to the federal hospital for dope addicts at Lexington, Kentucky. The district attorney said: "This is a wise and brave thing you have done, Barney, and, as you must know, you are now technically under arrest. What can I do for you?"

Barney asked to be released on his own for the weekend. "I have some things to close out. I'll be at Grossinger's. I'll turn myself in to you on Monday." ·

That night, Friday, he came to the Copa to see me in the show. I didn't know where he was going—I ribbed him unmercifully about his loss to Henry Armstrong. Barney came backstage to my tiny dressing room to say goodbye. "I'm going South," he said vaguely.

The rest of the story came from Barney:

> (*Grossinger's Hotel, Sunday: Barney, in his room. He paces around, needs a shot desperately. Enter three men, obviously detectives.*)
>
> BARNEY: *"Yeh? What do you want?"*
>
> FIRST MAN: *"We're from the DA's office."*
>
> BARNEY (*bitterly*): *"Goddamn! A cop is always a cop. I gave him my word I would come in by myself Monday."*
>
> SECOND MAN: *"You'd better keep quiet, before you say something you'll be sorry for."*
>
> (*The First Man opens a small envelope. Three pellets of morphine.*)
>
> FIRST MAN: *"The DA figured you would need these . . . to carry you through the weekend."*

On the night of the Zale-Graziano fight, I remembered Barney's advice to bet on the underdog Zale, but I evaluated his

advice as that of a drug addict. So of course I bet on Rocky—
and blew $2,500.

Barney beat his addiction at the hospital with the same sheer
guts he'd used in the ring. Cold turkey. Then he got a job with
a publicity agency. I went along with him on personal appearances when I could. The public loved to shake the hand of
Barney Ross. Till the day of his death, he was still a champ.

My involvement in *High Button Shoes* began as haphaz-
ardly and chaotically as *Yokel Boy*. The character I played was
an afterthought. It all happened because in 1946 Jule Styne
lived on Elm Drive in Beverly Hills, across the street from
Stephen Longstreet. One day Jule picked up a copy of the
Saturday Review and read about his neighbor's novel, *The
Sisters Liked Them Handsome*, a charming, nostalgic picture
of life in the Longstreet family of New Brunswick, New Jersey,
around 1913. Jule walked over to Longstreet's and asked, "Is
there a musical in this?"

"I don't know," Longstreet said.

Sammy Cahn immediately began to write a treatment, following the novel closely. It didn't work. You can't put a novel
on stage and merely add music; the musical is a special medium that must be shaped for such purpose. The project got a
lift when Mrs. Longstreet thought of the title *High Button
Shoes*. I didn't think there was anything in it for me; I had
signed to do a weekly radio show that was moving from Hollywood to New York. One day, somebody—I don't remember
who—thought of switching the story to revolve around a minor
character, Harrison Floy, a flamboyant scamp with great
dreams. A Bilko in spats. And now I was sucked in.

I came to New York with my wife and worked in the radio
variety grandiosely titled "The Phil Silvers Show." Since my
comedy is mainly visual, not aural, there wasn't much Phil
Silvers in it. I took the musical to Monte Proser, who produced
the shows at the Copa. He was a little short on cash, so he
brought in Joe Kipness, at that time in the cloak and suit business. Joe is an exuberant, decent bull of a man, a Russian refu-

gee who started his career as a trucker in the garment district. He was dazzled by show business and just ached to be part of it. Joe put up most of the "seed" money. And then George Abbott came onto the scene. He and the other George, Kaufman, were the two most successful comedy directors and play doctors of the 1930's and 1940's. Starting with *Broadway* in 1926, Mr. Abbott—nobody called him George—participated as director and/or collaborator in an incredible string of hits: *Boy Meets Girl* by the Spewacks, *Room Service, Brother Rat, Three Men on a Horse, Pal Joey, Best Foot Forward, On the Town, The Boys from Syracuse* and others. Well, with Mr. Abbott involved, we had a guaranteed hit. The money flowed in and a faction grew, convinced that we didn't need Joe Kipness anymore. He looked like an uncouth slugger and he still mangled the English language. All he'd done was keep the show alive. The anti-Kipness faction held a meeting in Sardi's at Mr. Abbott's table. When I walked in, I spotted Joe sitting all alone. I sat down with Joe and that made it clear to the others: If you want me, you'll have to keep Joe. So Joe became co-producer with Monte Proser.

Now all we needed was a book. Mr. Abbott agreed to rewrite it, in return for a percentage of the show on top of his percentage as director. And now Stephen Longstreet felt he was no longer needed, and walked away from the show. As far as I know, he never saw the show until closing night of our second company in Los Angeles.

Mr. Abbott worked his magic on the book and Mr. Floy became the central character. He sold the Longstreets' property and eloped with Mama Longstreet's sister. The investors discovered the property was under water, and there was a grand chase in Atlantic City. We had two potential hit songs: "Papa, Won't You Dance With Me?" and "I Still Get Jealous."

We went into rehearsal—and the script was not funny. Floy was dull, and my mouth got drier with every line I said. All my life I'd wanted to work under the master, George Abbott; he was a millionaire with a record of hits two arms long. How could I tell him he was wrong?

In one scene, the townspeople I had conned into investing in mud flats cornered me at the head of a stairway in a living room. They were angry and hurt because I had bilked them out of their savings; they had me literally backed up against the wall—and all I could do was stare at them. Mr. Abbott had no lines to cover this crisis. In rehearsal I came up with a full-face grin, all teeth flashing, and a big amiable "Glad to see ya!"

It got a large laugh from the cast. Mr. Abbott walked up from the rear of the hall and said, "Phil, I don't want to restrict you, but—what's funny about that? It doesn't make sense."

Of course it didn't make sense. Mr. Floy was desperately using any irrelevancy to defuse his victims' wrath. Mr. Abbott cut it out.

There was more humor in rehearsal than in the script. Jerome Robbins' choreography for the Mack Sennett ballet was brilliantly inventive from the start: full of gusto, wit and nostalgia for those innocent years. The cops and I and the bathers chased each other in and out of doors and ended with a grand pileup on me, and on top of all, an American flag. In the midst of the chase, a gorilla came out of the bathhouse with his hand on my back—absolutely and hilariously irrelevant. For the gorilla, Jerry used a young man named Neil from the singing group.

In dress rehearsal the ballet fell apart, because the opening and closing of the doors consumed an extra beat that somehow Jerry had not thought of. Jerry stopped the rehearsal after Neil made a blunder, and vented his exasperation on him: Neil was standing with me behind a drop, steaming in his fur gorilla suit, with only slits for eyes in its giant head. As Jerry shouted on, the gorilla muttered to me: "One more word out of him and I'll claw him to death!"

When we opened in Philadelphia on September 15, 1947, the dancing and music were hits. The book was lame. *Variety* said: "Original story by Stephen Longstreet, on which libretto is flimsily based, gets lost much of the time, and still more of it will probably have to be thrown overboard. . . . Substitution of more spontaneous and funnier material, rather than cutting, is the need." And I took a personal beating from the critics. "Phil Silvers may be Hollywood's darling, but this show needs the energy of a Bobby Clark." (Bobby was, at that time, sixty years old.) I had stuck faithfully to what Mr. Abbott asked me to do; his lines kept the plot moving cleanly and inevitably. But, the critics asked, where were the laughs?

The reviews went right to my throat. An eminent Philadelphia specialist, Dr. Chevalier Jackson, told me that nodules had developed on my vocal cords. "It's not malignant, but there is only one cure—silence." I could play the show, but I had to rest in silence at all other times. I could only communicate by writing notes. I stewed while the music and production numbers rehearsed merrily every day, but nobody seemed to care about the dialogue. Mr. Abbott kept saying, "Don't worry, Phil, it'll be fine." Jule Styne would read over my notes and answer in shouts. I'd write furiously: *I am not deaf—I just can't talk.*

Monte Proser wanted me to step out; Joe Kipness was like a rock at my side. It took a powerful influence like George Solitaire, the leading New York ticket speculator, to convince Proser that I could carry the show when I recovered. The word on our show flew around New York—*High Button Shoes* is sick. The Forrest Theater we played in Philadelphia added about twenty-five points to my handicap. The builder somehow forgot to include dressing rooms. The Shuberts had corrected this by buying an office building next door and installing the dressing rooms there; we had to cross through an alleyway into the Forrest. It was an active role; with all that running around the stage and out in the alleyway, I was in a constant hot and cold sweat. Through all this, Jo-Carroll was phoning me in confusion and worry from New York. I'd asked her not to come on the road because I wanted to be free to concentrate on the show. I wouldn't let her share this problem with me. I supposed I was trying to protect her from it. I was wrong—it didn't help either of us. I was demoralized.

Despite all this, we sold out for the four weeks in Philadelphia. After my throat signaled all clear, I decided it was my turn at bat. I informed Mr. Abbott that I would be ad-libbing from now on, but always within the context of the story and the period. He gave me his blessing. And Jerry Robbins joined me in revising and changing the scenes.

Joey Faye, my old crony from burlesque, playing my sidekick, Mr. Pontdue, gave our scenes a great lift. My other accomplice was a boy eight years old, Donald Harris, the understudy to the juvenile lead. I had a great affection for Donny —he was the child I might have been if I hadn't gone into show business. He'd come in for a performance with a black eye, earned in a street argument. For matinees, his mother gave him a fifty-cent allowance; instead of buying food, he'd load up on mechanical gadgets. He devised a system to communicate with the stagehands in the fly loft by flashlights.

"Tonight, when I'm selling the lots at the picnic," I told Donny, "no matter what I do, you just stand in front of me." He turned into a perfect curious little pest; as I delivered my pitch, I was continually irritated by this little boy. To end the scene, I throw him across the stage. Now, audiences will bridle at a grown man picking on a kid, but somehow or other, they forgave me this audacity. To this day, my comedy borders on brashness, but, luckily for me, audiences have reacted, "This nut is more confused than the people he's confusing." Anyway, the scene evolved into controlled hysteria.

I pleaded with the producers to keep the show here another week or two—we were selling out—and I'd have time to develop improvements. No. They were worried about the competition of the Rodgers and Hammerstein musical *Allegro*. If we came into New York after this hot ticket, we might look like a cold turkey to the critics. Well, we did open a day after *Allegro*. The critics labeled it an elaborate sermon. We were the hit. "Glad to see ya!" became a catchword.

The critics rejoiced over the burlesque elements. Brooks Atkinson of the *Times:* "With Phil Silvers skipping through it like an old burlesque mountebank . . . *High Button Shoes* is an immensely likeable musical in a vein that was equally funny but much less splendid on the old Columbia wheel. . . .

"Phil Silvers is an uproarious comic. He has the speed, the drollery and the shell-game style of a honky-tonk buffoon. Fortunately he has the shifty assistance of Joey Faye, who also wears the school tie of the burlesque academies."

The august George Jean Nathan, in the New York *Journal-American:* ". . . funny business by Phil Silvers and Joey Faye, including an old burlesque skit which has been denounced as highly objectionable by various people in the audience as soon as they have been able to recover from their laughter at it."

Again, as in *Yokel Boy*, I was not satisfied. I kept changing and adjusting and adding to my role until by the fourth week we had what we should have had on opening night. We moved from the lonely Century, up near Central Park, to the Shubert, the hotspot of the theater district, and settled in for 727 performances. There was a Chicago company, and Eddie Foy was brilliant in the road version.

The man who, I believe, made more money out of the show than anybody was George Solitaire. He'd bought up all of Monte Proser's house seats at face value after Monte panicked, and so for many months, every celebrity coming to town had to sit in Solitaire's seats. At $50 a pair.

By opening night, not one line of my part remained from Stephen Longstreet's original script. Yet little releases from him kept appearing in the papers to the effect: . . . "Stephen Longstreet has contacted Danny Kaye with a view to playing the screen version of *High Button Shoes*." (It was never made into a movie.) To help Steve overcome his delusions of grandeur, I sent him a wire: "If I read any more press releases from you on who is going to do my role in the picture, I will play this show exactly as you wrote it." Walter Winchell used it in his column.

Joe Kipness went on to hits such as *La Plume de Ma Tante*, *Applause* and others, but the first success is the most delicious. He handed out gifts to the cast like an old-style maharajah. For Jerry Robbins, a large car; for me, a weekend at the Concord.

Joe drove me in his car, and in those days before the thruways, you climbed over and through the mountains. We came to a horseshoe turn, overlooking a beautiful wooded valley and a sparkling river. "Hey, wait a minute." He turned the car off the road. "Look at *that*," he sighed. "After all that fighting and screaming in the city, this is like poetry! It's God's beauty. . . . Let's sit here and bullshit a while."

Joe produced a high-toned drama by an Englishman. It bombed in New Haven. Joe sat in his hotel surrounded by three play doctors and asked, "Well, boys, what do you think?" They talked about a rewrite here and a cut there, and Joe was carried away. He sparked to the ideas; his eyes lit up like a marquee. In a corner of the room, the Englishman spoke up. "Let me remind you, Mr. Kipness, that we have a contract. The play you bought is the play that shall be done on Broadway. Not one word, not a comma, shall be changed."

Joe leaped up in all his fury. He couldn't hit anybody, so he slammed the table in frustration. "I'll be goddamned! This is the last time I ever do a play with *authors!*"

Early in the 1940's, I appeared on a radio show with Margaret Truman, when she was still a singer. She was a most charming, gracious woman, and I later took her to a film opening. In 1948 I was among the entertainers in a show raising money for Harry Truman's reelection. After the performance we lined up to greet the President. I stood behind Groucho Marx and Danny Kaye. My eye caught Harry's. His smile broadened, his eyes glowed and he exclaimed, *"Glad to see ya!"* He had my voice perfectly.

As *High Button Shoes* rolled on, a situation out of my past repeated itself, an eerie reminder of here we go again. Sylvester (Pat) Weaver, a high man on the NBC totem pole, had an idea for a television show titled, inevitably, "The Phil Silvers Variety Show." The time slot assigned for it was 8 to 8:30, exactly when I was putting on makeup and warming up for my stage appearance.

Weaver and Kipness came together for lunch one day. Pat wooed Joe so beguilingly that Joe agreed to hold our musical's curtain until 8:50. So that I could keep my TV makeup on, dash from NBC on 50th Street to the Shubert on 45th Street, and come running onstage breathless. It took me back twenty years, doubling with Morris and Campbell from the Palace up to the RKO Chester in the Bronx.

Who needed it? Harrison Floy kept me exhausted, rushing around the stage for two hours. My TV salary would be what a stagehand made with overtime. Weaver promised a top budget of $2,500 a week, and that included six writers. Among them were two brothers, Danny and Doc Simon; Doc later turned into Neil Simon, the most successful comedy writer since George S. Kaufman. They were very young then, on their first big show, and they argued with each other to be the first to read the jokes to me. I evaluated all the factors carefully, decided it was insane—and agreed to do it.

As soon as I signed, Mr. Lee Shubert, Pooh-Bah of the American theater, said, "Hold *what* curtain?" He owned our theater and rented only the four walls; *he* set the curtain time. Secretly, he hoped to move us into the large Broadway Theater, which happened to be standing vacant and far north. Lee insisted our curtain must remain at 8:40, and if we missed *one* curtain, our contract was void . . . and we'd be shipped to Siberia.

The TV show was arranged so that I never appeared in its finale. I'd run off at 8:25, run to a waiting elevator, drop down to the street, run to a waiting cab, run from the cab right onto the stage. It was a crazy running gag. If we hit one red traffic light or a traffic jam on Broadway, I'd miss the curtain at 8:40. Well, I made it. Lee Shubert was foiled, and Fred Allen called our show the most advanced step in variety comedy. I was lucky: It ran only thirteen weeks. And that's how I got my feet wet in TV.

South Pacific, with Ezio Pinza and Mary Martin, rehearsed in the Shubert during the day. I'd come into the theater early, pick up a few pieces of my mail and stand at the rear for hours, worshiping Pinza's voice. Director Josh Logan kept pounding away at his diction, after all his years as a star of the Metropolitan Opera. "They'll never understand you," Josh pleaded. "You've got to say the words."

Those sessions did nothing for my voice, but they did give me a nightclub and party bit: an observation of the great Pinza struggling to sing clear English. After a lot of practice I could fake his "Some Enchanted Evening." *High Button Shoes* raised my salary and my status when I returned to Hollywood. But it took "Some Enchanted Evening" to elevate my standing in Harry Cohn's house. After he heard Robert Merrill's magnificent operatic voice doing an imitation of Pinza, Cohn loudly announced, "That bum couldn't even touch Silvers doing Pinza!"

CHAPTER 10

Berle: "I Know Guys Just Like That!"

Metro doubled my previous salary for *Summer Stock* (1950), although the role was the same—Brother Confessor Blinky for Judy Garland, on and off the screen. Gloria DeHaven was her sister; Gene Kelly and Carleton Carpenter were the other men in the theatrical troupe, fighting to put on their show despite personal heartbreak, lack of funds and pernicious clichés.

Judy was unpredictable. She'd been scheduled for three previous pictures that year and she'd never showed up. For *Summer Stock* she would come in one day and miss two. Or three. Days when I wasn't on camera, I'd come in anyhow, trying to keep her spirits up. We both enjoyed the visits on the set of her daughter, Liza, who came with her father, Vincente Minnelli. Judy was going through uncontrollable inner torments which studio people analyzed as spoiled self-indulgence.

She was in her ballooning up—starving down cycle. She had two aunts who weighed a total of 600 pounds and, I believe, Judy kept seeing their obesity as her destiny. Her mother and the studio hounded her to reduce because a little plumpness goes a long way on film. On top of all the terrible pressures of growing from childhood to womanhood, she felt unattractive. She felt she'd rather be a sexpot in the chorus than the exciting star she really was. As she became a woman physically, she remained a child emotionally.

Shortly after her episode with Artie Shaw, she went off to Palm Springs with a writer. They had adjoining bungalows. On the way to the dining room, she stopped off for him, and found him kissing a man.

I tried to persuade Judy it was not *her* fault. Not some fatal defect in her appearance or womanhood. She could never win that writer away from his male love. No woman could. Yet Judy clung to this rejection as if it was a senior prom corsage.

Once I rebelled at my Big Brother role, after another of her laments about being unattractive and unloved. "Judy, why don't you go where you can win?" I said firmly. "You know I'm a man, too." And I kissed her warmly.

"All right!" she said, determined. And gave me a throbbing soul kiss. As if to say, "What do you want?" That brief moment was the end of our romantic aberration. It put each of us in a correct perspective—trusting friends.

Gene put me in the finale of *Summer Stock* for a reprise of a song-and-dance number, with him and Judy. As I came on the set, costumed and made up, everyone avoided my eye. When I walked over to talk to Judy, she broke into tears. Gene called me aside. "She's more upset than you will be when I tell you. Judy doesn't think you should be up front with us."

Always the star. I didn't blame her, really.

After *Summer Stock* I was bored and restless. The movies were Blinkying me into the ground. MCA assured me there was still a lot of money and fun out there in nightclubs. It was time to hit the road. Sammy Cahn helped with some delicious special material.

As I had done on tour with *High Button Shoes*, I asked Jo-Carroll to stay at home. I never carried an entourage with me, to wait in my dressing room, to socialize with after the show. I wanted to face the show alone. This was partly a protective cocoon I'd built around myself, so I could work all hours and at any time on my show. And partly, I guess, so Jo-Carroll would not stick her pretty nose into my coast-to-coast gambling. My brother Harry went along, as usual, to handle business and travel details. We were scheduled to break in the act in Las Vegas, then play the big clubs in major cities across America, closing in New York at the Copa.

The night before I opened at the Last Frontier, a young man on his honeymoon, betting five dollars at a time, had hit something like thirty-seven consecutive passes at the Desert Inn.

Gus Greenbaum, a high roller from Phoenix, made about $275,000 betting on him, and Zeppo Marx made $150,000. The boy made $750. I used the situation in my act. "What impressed me most," I told the audience, "was not the fact that he nearly bankrupted the casino. No, what I loved was the way the owners, the croupiers, everybody was rooting for this boy. He's here in the audience tonight—I'd like him to take a bow . . ."

And Sammy Cahn rose for the bow, swathed in bandages, his arm in a splint. It hit home. Every night of the two weeks, play stopped at the tables while the croupiers and dealers crowded around to savor this bit.

Brother Harry wrapped those bandages. On closing night, Sammy's wife came up with Jo-Carroll. Sammy, saving the surprise, excused himself as if going to the men's room and went behind a curtain for the wrapping. Harry packaged him in brand-new gauze. "Why the new bandages?" Sammy asked. "This is the last show."

"I want you to look nice for your wife."

After ten months on the road, by the time I reached the Copa the act was polished to a Tiffany gloss. I was booked for four weeks at $5,500 per week. This time, I was ready for anything the Copa could toss at me. Nightclubs will spend hundreds of thousands for crystal and velvet and gilt for the customers out front; their performers usually dress in a toilet. The Copa provided a small closet right next to the ladies' powder room. I rented a suite directly over the club, in the Hotel Fourteen, where the esteemed actress, Laurette Taylor, once lived. It had a view of Central Park and a tiny elevator that descended right into the kitchen of the Copa. From there, it was three steps and a hop into the spotlight. I could dress and make up leisurely at home, float down in the elevator to work; after each show, I came home in four minutes, showered, relaxed with a book or TV. The apartment gave me the greatest feeling of luxury since the Turkish baths in Philadelphia.

My appearance at the Copa led to another Phil Silvers TV show. This one lasted six days. Dean Martin and Jerry Lewis were demolishing Nielsen records on the "Colgate Comedy

Hour." They were scheduled every fourth week, but because of other engagements they had missed three shows. MCA, my agents—and theirs, was afraid it would lose the Colgate account. The agency asked the boys if they at least would do a guest spot.

Dean answered, "We can always put fifteen minutes together."

Great.

"Whose show do you want to do the spot on?"

"The Phil Silvers Show," Dean said.

What Phil Silvers Show? Well, Dean and Jerry were my pals. They had just decided to throw this little bonanza my way. The oil that makes show business seem to glide so smoothly is not money but friendship. I agreed to put together a Phil Silvers special—in six days, so they could fulfill their contract with Colgate. Next Sunday. Even though the boys could not rehearse with me because they were playing at the Chez Paris in Chicago. Again, it was a high dive into madness.

I rounded up four writers (one of them Joseph Stein, who didn't tell me he was going to write *Fiddler on the Roof*), a dance chorus and the music, all on Monday. Tuesday, as we rehearsed, I told Jerry Lewis by phone what I was preparing and where he and Dean fitted in. Wednesday night they opened at the Copa. Thursday they had a rough idea of what I was doing. Friday I had a rough idea of what they were doing. Saturday, none of us knew why we were doing it. Sunday, at eight, we had to go on the network, dead or alive.

It was a very live show: The Nielsen shot up to the stars. Everybody was happy. After the midnight show, Martin and Lewis popped in to my apartment to take a shower, then shot down to the basement for the 2:30 performance. I couldn't sleep. The tension of the past six days came up and met me. I put on my old bathrobe and slippers, dropped down into the kitchen and walked into the middle of their act. Loose and zany as the boys were, this stunned them as well as the audience. "Shh," I said, "would you keep it down a little? I'm trying to get some sleep upstairs." I walked back into the elevator and rode up to bed. Bedlam of laughter.

Dean used this as a running gag whenever Jerry got too rambunctious during the run. "Shh," he'd point upstairs. "He's trying to get some sleep."

The Copa was my last New York nightclub appearance. My kind of comedy requires complete audience concentration.

Sometimes, when I take time out to be grateful, I am grateful for three things, in the following order:

First, I don't have to go to school today.

Second, I don't have to fly today.

Third, I don't have to play the Copa.

My tour did one thing for our marriage: It drove the final nail into the coffin. Being left at home while her husband jaunts around the country makes a woman feel unwanted. Jo-Carroll and I separated amicably. No need for recrimination. We were clutching two different ways of life, and neither of us was about to change. Ours was not a Better Homes and Gardens marriage.

Jo-Carroll moved out of the house I'd bought and into an apartment. I remained in the house with her mother. The gossip columnists noted "Phil Silvers gets custody of his mother-in-law." The truth was, my weekly $5,500 had slipped into the pockets of the bookies as if they were magnetized. I offered Jo-Carroll the house plus a generous settlement. We were divorced in Los Angeles in 1950, and since then we've remained the best of friends. At the risk of sounding sickeningly saccharine, I deeply love her in the purest sense of the word.

Top Banana, like my two previous Broadway ventures, started with one story and ended with another. Either my kind of comedy attracts this frantic improvisation—or I am a sucker for chaos.

After I closed at the Copa, I sat around in my apartment at the hotel, wondering how I could have said yes to a musical I had no hope for. I was drawn into it because of an old Hollywood friend, Hy Kraft, who had written a successful comedy, *Cafe Crown,* in 1942. Now he had confected a musical called *Jest for Laughs,* and the title epitomized the problem of the book. It was cornball: A verbose tale of a great comedian who meets his wife in a department store, paralleling the story of Jack Benny, who met Mary under the roof of the May Company.

Johnny Mercer had agreed to write the music and lyrics. Johnny was a very accomplished and clever lyric writer, but this would be his first score for a show. The art of composing and the art of lyric-writing are two rare talents. Very few men in the American theater combined them successfully. I was a little doubtful on that score.

Musical books, even in raw, early drafts, seem to acquire a life of their own. *Jest for Laughs* found a producer, Paula Stone and her husband, Mike Sloane. Although Paula came from a theatrical family (she is the daughter of Fred Stone, one of the most engaging performers of the 1920's), both she and Mike were novice producers. The show attracted a director, Jack Donohue, primarily a dance director, who had staged many musicals for television; a warm man, with a great theatrical flair. I had an instant rapport with him, just as I had with Jerome Robbins in *High Button Shoes*.

Still, I kept asking myself, Jack, Hy Kraft, everybody—"Why are we doing this show?" What was the justification for producing this story at this time? There had been many stories about the tribulations of a comedian; did meeting his wife in a department store make it any more exciting for 1950? And once again, as in *HBS*, the answer was provided by the subplot: the manipulations of a television star. I suggested that we bring in the first musical to satirize the madness of week-to-week live television. In 1950 the tyrant of the tube was Milton Berle; on Tuesday night at eight, he had the whole country in his hand. I would do Uncle Miltie.

We were old friends—even his mother liked me. She always watched over Miltie carefully, and although he was three years older than I, she thought I was a good influence on him. "That's a nice boy," she told Miltie. "You can go out with Phil tonight, see a movie and have a sandwich." The first thing this nice boy did was show Miltie the nearest whorehouse.

I knew every flip gesture of Berle's, every ruthless smile.

Milton was, shall I say, an impatient man. He had to have his laughs, and he didn't care where or how he found them. We decided to project Berle into the burlesque background that was left over from the original story.

Now the show had a reason for being. Now we had an exciting character, Jerry Biffle. Hy Kraft agreed his script would need some revisions—which meant that it became an entirely different show. First to go was the title. I remembered that in the early burlesque era, before my time, the comics referred to themselves as First Banana, Second and Third Banana. The banana came from an ancient sketch popular with the Dutch-dialect comics.

> *(Three comics. One holds up two bananas.)*
> FIRST MAN: *"I have three bananas here, and I will give you one."*
> SECOND MAN: *"You only have two bananas."*
> FIRST MAN: *"I have three bananas. Look, I'll show you. (Holds up one banana in his right hand.) One banana have I. (Holds up one in his left hand.) Two bananas have I now. One banana and two bananas makes three bananas."*
> SECOND MAN: *"I only see two bananas. In your own words, I will show you, you are wrong. (He takes the bananas.) One banana have I. Two bananas have I. One banana and two bananas . . . by golly! he's right. (To Third Man) Would you like a banana? (Third Man nods.) Okay, one banana for you. A banana for me——"*
> FIRST MAN: *"How about me?"*
> SECOND MAN: *"You eat the third banana!"*
> BLACKOUT

"Top banana" was never used in burlesque, to my knowledge. Johnny Mercer thought it sounded better in his lyric than "first banana," and that is how the words entered the English lexicon.

To help the burlesque flavor, I surrounded myself with old cronies who knew that medium: Joey Faye, Herbie Faye, Jack Albertson.

In creating the role of Jerry Biffle, I used Berle's mannerisms and props. In rehearsals of his show, he would inject
himself into everybody's act. For our rehearsal scenes, my
costume was Basic Berle: a heavy bathrobe, with towel around
the neck—Berle could feel a draft in the middle of the Sahara
desert—a whistle to stop the action and, to top it off, for no
reason at all, a yachting cap.

Shortly before we went into rehearsal for *Top Banana*, I
had a golfing date with Milton. I knew he would inquire
about the show, and I would have to explain—before an
unfeeling friend revealed I was satirizing him.

> *(As we walk to the first hole):*
> BERLE: *"Say, what is this* Top Banana *you're doing?"*
> ME *(taking a deep breath):* "Milton, it's about a guy
> who's been 'on' all his life. His only goal is the laugh. It's
> got to come, no matter if it's at the expense of his mother,
> the President or himself. Everything to him is a comedy
> bit. If he has a girl, it's the girl bit. He tells his writers to
> take his girl home because he has to go to a club to watch
> another comic work. Always in action. He never listens to
> anyone's conversation—he's just thinking of what he'll say
> next. The poor guy never had a chance to develop in
> any other areas. He's been on the stage since he was five
> years old. His dedication—the laugh must come! So what
> chance does he have to develop a knowledge of politics or
> art? Or how to be generous? Getting the laugh is his
> whole life!"
> *(A pause.)*
> BERLE: "I'll be a sonovabitch. I know guys just like
> that!"

It never occurred to him that he was Jerry Biffle. Better
than that, he bought two backer's units in the show, and became our biggest booster.

The show went into rehearsal with an innocuous story line:
Jerry Biffle's Blendo Soap program shows tattletale gray

ratings. To enhance his appeal with women, he finds a Miss Blendo and convinces himself he is in love with her. Of course he does not know that she secretly loves the show's singer. The couple decide to elope. Jerry, who must have a hand in everybody's act, volunteers to help the singer elope with his own girl. And he goes on to greater heights of self-deception.

The simple story let us improvise two of the most hilarious scenes in rehearsal. They were so outrageous I don't believe any team of writers, working in a quiet hotel room under the stimulus of drugs and/or alcohol, could have invented them.

We hunted backers even during rehearsals. One such gentleman, a tycoon of the wicker basket industry, came to look us over. As I sang, I heard a dog howling melodiously in the lobby. And when I stopped—the dog stopped. The potential backer apologized. It was his airedale on a leash. The accompaniment of the dog intrigued me. "Will he sing when I sing?" I asked.

"I don't know," said the owner. "He sings with me." The businessman, who sang as a hobby, had discovered that if he hit a certain key, the dog would yowl along in a high, unearthly *ooooooooowwwww*. At our first audition, the dog, named Ted (Sport) Morgan, was flustered by the crowd onstage, and he refused to sing. When the owner sang *ooooooooooowwwwww*, Sport immediately joined in. After a while the dog was singing with me.

I integrated the dog into the show with another one of Berle's gimmicks. He always played up to children in his audience. Jerry Biffle would reach out to the animal lovers with this dog. Johnny Mercer wrote "A Dog Is a Man's Best Friend": ". . . when I'm blue and lonesome too, nobody understands me like my dog . . ." * As Jerry sang it, the dog would raise his nose to the heavens and yowl; Jerry became progressively more furious because the dog was upstaging him. For the tagline, Jerry roared, "If you want a pal that's quiet and peaceful—buy a *cat!*"

* Copyright 1951. Words and music by Johnny Mercer. By permission of Commander Publications.

To insure the dog's singing, we put the backer on the payroll as a stagehand. He'd wheel the dog out on a stand. If Sport neglected his cue, his owner, standing nearby, gave a discreet *oooooowwwww*. Sport and I developed a great palship; he'd stay overnight with me in my hotel, and immediately after "Man's Best Friend" I would feed him. This created an extra dividend: As we strolled off after the duet, Sport would lick my hands, signaling "let's go to dinner." The audience took this as the dog's love for Jerry. It created immediate audience empathy for egocentric Jerry Biffle. There had to be something good in him if a dog loved him.

In the elopement scene, we needed a reason why Jerry did not know he was helping his own girl into the arms of another man. Jerry held a ladder; out of a dark window, the girl dropped her travel bag, neatly knocking his glasses off. Without glasses, Jerry was blind. This gave Jack Donohue a happy inspiration to develop the scene. He recalled a hilarious act that had played thirty-five years in vaudeville—Walter Dare Wahl and his partner. It began as a straight hand-balancing act, with the partner on Walter's shoulders, but their hands became entangled and seemingly couldn't get loose. Suppose we used this in the elopement, too? Walter and his partner, Johnny Trama, would become entangled with Jerry Biffle— and there would be three pairs of hands groping for freedom. Walter was folded into the story as my masseur, whom I ordered to bring the ladder to the girl's house. Johnny was an innocent bystander who ended up on Walter's shoulders. It became seven minutes of unrelenting hysteria.

Walter, a gentle strongman, had been the light-heavyweight wrestling champion of the world from 1911 to 1916, and he was a Pole. His English was heavily accented and a maze of malaprops. He celebrated his wife's "thirty-fifth university." And he dabbled in the stock market until it dropped "a fracture."

Cary Grant came backstage one night to say hello. He'd started his performing career as a stilt walker with an acrobatic troupe under his real name, Archie Leach. Somewhere, in Walter Wahl's vaudeville tours, their acts crossed. That night, as usual, Walter came into my room to say goodnight. He turned to discover Cary, and his eyes lit up. "Archie! Archie Leach! What are you doing lately?"

At the start of tryouts, in Boston, the show was bumpy. Scenery did not move. Or it fell down.

In Philadelphia, by a careless lapse in booking, we opened on Yom Kippur, the most solemn night of the Hebrew calendar. The theater would have been three-quarters empty. The company manager papered the house with soldiers and sailors from the nearby defense installations. People in uniform are the most receptive, responsive audience. They're warmer than your own relatives.

I had a duet with Rose Marie, our comedienne, titled "A Word a Day." We filled in each other's educational gaps by defining long-tailed words, with the aid of a dictionary. Example:

> ROSE MARIE: *"What's a proselyte?"*
> ME *(singing): "Has to give the madame most of the dough."* *

In the Philadelphia opening, that little song stopped the show. Rose Marie's husband flew in from the West Coast and left completely dejected. He felt the show would run forever and their marriage would fall apart.

This song never stopped the show again. Not once, in the 350 performances in New York and hundreds on the road.

That is show business.

We were set to open in New York, November 1, 1951. The night before, a Sunday, I went to see Judy Garland at the Palace. After a visit to her dressing room, I left as thoroughly dejected as Rose Marie's husband. And for a similar reason: Her performance was extraordinary. She had come back to America after four triumphant months in Europe and the

* Copyright 1951. Words and music by Johnny Mercer. Used by permission of Commander Publications.

London Palladium. Her Sunday night show was dazzling, emotion-charged. There was by now a cult of Judy-worshippers. They screamed at every throb in her voice. Somehow, I felt my show was competing with hers. And how could I possibly measure up to her kind of mass hysteria? I felt I didn't even belong in the same city with Judy.

That triggered a tossing, sleepless night. I foresaw the details of all the accidents that could happen. The prop man would forget my water bag in the opening. He didn't forget it in four weeks in Boston, he didn't forget it in four weeks in Philadelphia—for our opening, I knew he would forget.

My own Nancey With the Laughing Face, age three.

Bruce Cabot, left, is the local villain, and Jack Benny and I
are the most cowardly gun-slingers in history, in a CBS
television special, "The Slowest Gun in the West," May, 1960.

As Hubie Cram in a dancing bit with chorus girls in
Do Re Mi, 1960.

Around the pool, 1962: From left, Nancey, Tracey, Candy, Evelyn, Cathy. Laury was on the way.

Reliving memories of *Yokel Boy* with Buddy Ebsen, on set of "Beverly Hillbillies."

June, 1970: Tracey, now thirteen and one-half, celebrates with Daddy at the Coconut Grove, Los Angeles; Liza Minnelli, now a star on her own, is the singer that night.

My first straight play, *How the Other Half Loves*, with
Sandy Dennis, 1971.

My five beauty queens, clockwise: Tracey, Cathy, Laury, Candy, Nancey.

As the conniving slave, Pseudolus, surrounded by the Roman courtesans in revival of *A Funny Thing Happened on the Way to the Forum,* 1972.

CHAPTER 11

Onstage Tonight—
and Every Night:
The Whammies

He didn't. That night my feet did not touch the stage. If I'd stopped running, the audience would have seen the holes in the show.

Berle was there with his mother, laughing it up. They were a wonderful team. Her laughter soared out over the audience. At the end of the intermission, Milton hustled the audience back into their seats, exclaiming, "Isn't it great?" Milton had to be in at the curtain call, too. He planned a surprise. As I took the last bow, holding Sport on a leash, Milton came dashing out onstage yelling, "I'll sue! I'll sue!"

It was a good gag, only the dog did not understand Milton's humor. All he saw was a strange man running toward me, screaming and threatening. Sport leaped for Milton's throat. Fortunately, I had a good grip on the leash. The whole bit got a good laugh. But Milton never did it again.

Top Banana became what the ticket brokers called "an audience show." It was also a critics' show. Brooks Atkinson again: ". . . Mr. Silvers is that tall, lean, toothy mountebank with a bald head and horn-rimmed glasses. After learning his trade the hard way, he took center of the stage in *High Button Shoes* in 1947.

"That was funny enough for most purposes. But in *Top Banana* Mr. Silvers is completely hilarious, throwing gags helter-skelter at high speed and running through some uproarious burlesque routines. . . . This column hopes he will husband his strength as frugally as possible. For this is a very funny show, and things being as they are at the moment, the country needs it sorely."

Richard Watts, New York *Post:* "The one man among the newer comics who seems worthy of the company of such surviving masters as Bobby Clark and Bert Lahr is Phil Silvers, and he has never been in better form than he is in *Top Banana.* . . . It has some of the funniest scenes in the recent history of the theater. . . . When Mr. Silvers and his colleagues get their hands madly entangled in an elopement, I found myself recognizably close to hysterics."

George Jean Nathan, chief justice of the critical bench: "The show, which is composed from first to last of the basic elements of old-time burlesque and of all the old gags and bits of business, has generated in [my colleagues] such unbounded mirth as they apparently have not experienced in many a season. They have swallowed everything from the venerable hand-tangling bit to the more venerable dumb magic act as if they were the true Beluga. . . .

"Such jocosities, when set down in print, obviously may not seem too killing; but when, in the famous burlesque tradition, they and the others in the catalogue are delivered with the intense gravity that accompanies a performance of Aeschylus, they roll you in the aisles." *

For a role that started out as a minor subplot, it turned out handsomely. Jerry Biffle won for me every award the theater offered a male star in a musical: Tony, Variety, Billboard, New York Drama Critics Circle, Donaldson, Sylvania. I think Berle felt he should have had some award, too.

My year with *Top Banana* turned into a year of grinding work, even more strenuous play, and a mysterious ailment that nearly drove me off the stage. Ray Bloch, the orchestra leader,

* From *The Theater in the Fifties,* by George Jean Nathan. Published by Alfred A. Knopf, 1953. Reprinted by permission of Mrs. George Jean Nathan.

conducted an all-night poker game in his office in the CBS building. The high-stake game provided good company: Clifford Odets, John Garfield, film director Martin Ritt, and Herman Levin, who later produced *My Fair Lady*. Food and drinks were served. Instead of a good, quiet dinner after the show, I ate pastrami sandwiches and killer-burgers. I was always too impatient to play poker well, but it was a pleasure to lose to such stimulating company.

I sat down at the table about eleven-thirty, and we broke up at about eleven the next morning. I'd totter home to the Hotel Fourteen and into bed for a stupefied sleep. The flushes I hadn't filled and the pots I'd been bluffed out of flickered into my dreams. I'd wake at 5 P.M., and that was my break-fast time. The only time I caught up with my body clock was on matinee days, Wednesday and Saturday, at the Winter Garden. After the first show, I'd shower. Dinner, sent from Lindy's across the street, would be waiting in my dressing room. I smoked a cigar in those days. This was followed by a bit of television, to put me fast asleep. At 7:45 Walter Wahl, who took his role of masseur literally, lifted me like a rag doll onto a massage table we used in the first scene. Then a re-laxing massage. I was a limber bundle of wires throughout the show.

Julie Garfield at this time was bedeviled with career and wife problems. One night he came to the game late, and his angers and frustration poured out in his game. He bet and raised erratically—his mind was not at the table. He left after 11:30 A.M. I awoke at my usual five o'clock, turned on the TV news while I shaved. I heard the middle of a sentence —"the actor was thirty-nine"—and I *knew* Julie was dead. His heart gave out that day, while he was visiting a girl friend in her apartment.

As the show and the poker sessions ran on and on, I became more and more tired. My brother Harry (the doctor buff) ar-ranged a physical examination. It didn't occur to me that what I probably needed was regular hours and meals. A noted consultant, as a favor to Harry, examined me after the Satur-day night show, then realized the tests were not a true picture: I'd just come off two shows—naturally I was exhausted. He gave me some pills and told me to come in Monday morning. The tests on Monday showed I was in good physical condition, but run-down, and he gave me more of the pills. I took them faithfully.

Monday night I came to the theater in a tuxedo because I wanted to catch Jackie Leonard's opening at the Riviera. As I applied my makeup, my body heated up as if I was sitting on a coal stove. My heart raced and my T-shirt was soaked. I thought it was the beginning of a heart attack. Then "places, please" and I went on for the opening scene. Jo-Carroll and a friend were out front; I played to her. I went through the lines, in Jerry Biffle's heavy robe and towel, and soon the heat built up so I could not stand it. My heart racing faster, I walked off quickly. "Get my doctor," I mumbled to the stage manager.

Jack Albertson and Walter were onstage. Jack, who was my understudy, had never learned the lines because he believed I was the most durable comic in the business. He walked off with an ad-lib to Walter that was totally unanswerable: "Take care of everything, Walter." Leaving Walter alone and help-less. The curtain came down and the management announced I was ill.

In my dressing room I gulped cold drinks while my dresser rubbed me with ice. My doctor, Lawrence Meyers, arrived quickly. I showed him the bottle of pills from the first doctor. The prescription called for three pills every hour, or one pill every three hours. Whatever it was, I had it reversed. And it was a powerful stimulant. Dr. Meyers was appalled: "The last thing you need is a stimulant." He gave me a sedative and drove me home. Jo-Carroll was standing outside the stage door. She had rushed backstage to learn what was wrong, and my ever-protective brother would not let her in—on the theory, I guess, that seeing her would disturb me.

Dr. Meyers, after several examinations, assured me my heart was stronger than the rest of me. There was nothing or-ganically wrong. Yet the heat and palpitations came flooding back. For three nights my doctor stood in the wings. Nothing helped. My mysterious hot spells returned every night. For an entire year. I would reach a peak—when I felt about to collapse—then, after a few minutes, I was in control and finished the performance. Herbie Faye, Walter and Jack watched me anxiously for that moment. I never walked off the stage.

My trouble could be psychosomatic, my doctor thought, and advised psychiatric treatment. My psychiatrist (let's call him Stein) was a dedicated man with the best of credentials—he had studied with Sigmund himself. After a few sessions, I felt I was in the hands of a Freudian Dr. Kronkite. He would interrupt our sessions to run out and repark his car on the street. He discussed the problems of parking in New York, on my time. I frankly thought this problem was boring. When it was my turn to talk, I caught him several times fast asleep. "Well," he explained with his most engaging smile, "I've heard your problems before." His solution to my problems was: "You must learn to relax."

I knew that. The problem was: how? For a temporary alleviation he gave me the inevitable red elixir. It was a calmer, all right. It took away my saliva. I found myself running dry onstage—I looked as if I was choking. We alleviated that by placing glasses of water in strategic spots around the stage.

The show closed after 350 performances, and we set out on a tour that would end in Los Angeles. My whammies came back every night. Dr. Stein had encouraged me to call or write, so I followed that instruction with long letters. He answered with clumsily typed notes. Their general theme: These things happen all the time—don't worry. I began to haunt bookstores and libraries on the road, to study psychiatry, Freud and the other masters so that I could understand what my penpal was writing. My mail-order treatment did not contribute much to my well-being. I stopped corresponding after I received an outrageous bill from the good doctor. He demanded $50 for every one of his letters to me. I returned them with a note: "These things happen all the time—don't worry."

Touring with a theatrical company is a way of life. New dancers, singers and pit musicians must be recruited because many don't want to leave the comforts of home and family.

The road requires an extra talent—survival. Experienced troupers acquire the art of sniffing out catastrophe before it happens. You have to be able to change direction, improvise instantly. On tour, only one thing is certain: If it is impossible for the conductor to fall into the orchestra pit and break a leg—he will do it.

Our theater in Toledo was a huge 1920 movie palace, decorated in Early Circus Wagon, with a pit platform that lifted the orchestra for the stage show. I scouted the house and knew it meant trouble. I didn't have time to warn the conductor, a new man making his debut here. He looked over the house, forgot that movie pits are thirty feet deep, stepped over the footlights and, of course, broke his leg. Our violinist took over.

We carried five key musicians with us: trumpet, saxophone, violin, piano and drum. The rest of the twenty-piece band was filled in with local players. Since no musical show had visited Toledo in years, the men did not depend on music to make a living. They were grocery clerks, students, teachers. The second sax was a copyboy on the Toledo *Blade*. They were all consistent—a half-tone off pitch. Opening night, I noticed the second sax was crouched so far down in his seat that he couldn't see his music.

> (*Orchestra leader and I meeting at intermission.*)
> ME: "*That sax doesn't even look at you. Why doesn't he straighten up?*"
> LEADER: "*He can't. He's moonlighting.*"
> ME: "*What's that got to do with it?*"
> LEADER: "*His managing editor was in the front row.*"

The chorus boys and girls who traveled with us were talented, amiable youngsters, most of whom happened to be homosexual. I spent most of my time with Walter. In his sweaty T-shirt, with a fat cigar in his mouth, he cooked up savory chops, steaks and chicken tandoori, something he'd picked up in the Far East.

One of the big comedy scenes in *Top Banana* was my

staging the Blendo commercial. In a manner typical of Berle, or Bilko, I was running everything. One line began with me looking at the girl, Judy Lynn, who played the part of Miss Blendo. I was supposed to say, "Listen, honey, do it this way." I was very tired this particular night and for some reason I turned to the sponsor's son-in-law, played by a six-foot-four virile actor named Brad Hatton, and said, "Listen, honey . . ."

I realized my mistake instantly and turned back to Judy, but I suddenly thought, what would our gay group think of my little slip, calling this big man "honey?" I imagined invisible voices: "Don't tell me Phil's alone all the time." "Now we know why we don't see him after the show."

I remembered the psychiatric books I had been reading. I turned to Brad and said, "I called you honey, right? You know, of course, that's a Freudian slip. You know, of course, about the debate between Freud and Spinoza."

Brad froze, as did the rest of the cast. None of this was in the show. They thought I had flipped out, but I had an inner glow from the top of my head to the tip of my toes. I felt I had come upon a hilarious comedy improvisation, and I also saw the blackout of it—all in my mind's eye in front of a packed house.

> ME: *"Freud maintained that there is an inner compulsion among all of us to rise and revolt, even though the situation is one of pleasanty—even though the one may be our best friend. But in order to maintain our own ego in the small sphere we live in, we must give forth with vengeance and revolt. Spinoza (no fool himself) denied all this, and they had this tremendous debate. They rented a big hall in Budapest—Loew's Budapest, I believe it was. Spinoza screamed, 'Freud, you are coo-coo!' The minute Spinoza yelled at him, Freud had him. Why yell at Freud? After all, they were the best of friends. He was rejecting knowledge!*
>
> *"A young man from the balcony kept yelling down, 'Freud, you're a fraud! Sex—it's all sex.' His name was*

> *Havelock Ellis. Freud ignored this amateur interruption.*
> *And there he stood, that giant of intellect, bearded before*
> *his time. He started to work over Spinoza. He told him*
> *of the Id Complex, the heriogienus sextion A, the*
> *heriogienus sextion B, the Ego, the Alter-Ego, the frustra-*
> *tions and the compulsions, and the manifestations therein.*
> *There he stood in the vast auditorium, in that sea of*
> *darkness, expounding his theories. (Loud)* Don't you know
> he finally convinced Spinoza! *With clear, cool calm*
> *thinking, and an intelligent approach, he finally convinced*
> *Spinoza. You know how?"*
>   HATTON: *"How?"*
>   ME: *"He hit him!"*

One of the loudest roars in the show. The kids backstage applauded with the audience, making it possibly the sweetest
moment of my career. I later wrote out the scene and we used
it all the way to the West Coast. In the smallest cities, it
received the laughter in the proper places and a long round of
applause, indicating that even twenty years ago, it was not
just the neurotics of New York and Hollywood who were on the
analyst's couch—they were on the couch in Dayton, too.

Crisis in Chicago. Brad Hatton took an emergency leave
to be with his sick wife. A young actor named Eddie, who
doubled as one of the assistant stage managers, tripled as
Brad's understudy. Now, Brad was a big, tough character;
Eddie was five-foot-six, slender and ever so wistful. He got the
understudy job because he was the only one who applied for
it. The Great Northern Theater was jammed, the performance
was rolling beautifully. The sponsor's son-in-law entered upstage, while my back was turned. I heard a tender voice
murmuring, "Jerry *Biffle!* Who the *hell* do you *think* you *are?"*

I turned to find Eddie enveloped in Brad's weskit, the
striped trousers flapping around his heels and the homburg at
a rakish angle over his eyes. Eddie was stoned with fright,
literally vibrating.

I bit my lip to keep from breaking up. I couldn't talk; I had
to turn away from him. And saw two men in the orchestra

fold over in their chairs. Their instruments fell to the floor with a resounding *bonggg!*—and rolled away. The audience was roaring, too, because Eddie was obviously a disaster area. I had to do something. I blew my rehearsal whistle. The two Fayes and Jack Albertson were up in their dressing room, playing poker in their shorts because they did not come onstage for fifteen minutes. The whistle was their cue. They ran onstage —one in pants, one in a robe, and Joey with a towel around his shorts. They looked at me: What scene are we in? All I could do was point at Eddie. They collapsed, and ran off, leaving me alone with Eddie. This set off another round of laughs, as he stood there, quivering. The show couldn't move on until I gave Eddie his cue, and I was afraid that if I stopped biting my lip, I would break up. To change the mood, I thought of the saddest moments of my life: my father's funeral, Rags' death in the hospital. After what felt like a week, I came through with the cue.

Near the end of the first act, Eddie struck again. I was in the middle of a rather touching soliloquy that gave Jerry Biffle some humanity. I was alone onstage, sitting on a TV camera: ". . . Who needs this? Every week I've got to come up with something new. . . . I see my mother only twice a year —once on her birthday and once on my birthday. And they're both on the same day. . . ." At that moment, I remembered Eddie wore a tailcoat in the second act. The vision of Eddie flapping around in those tails made me break up. I couldn't stop it—I sat there, guffawing. This time the stage manager, Freddie Hebert, thought I had really lost control, because there was nothing visible onstage to make me laugh. I couldn't finish the scene. Freddie ordered the curtain down, to end the act.

And every night, the same whammies. And insomnia. My sedative, a red medicine, began to look like a beautiful old Bordeaux.

A lovely interlude: Slapsy Maxey Rosenbloom was in Chicago; he had just closed as Big Jule in *Guys and Dolls*. We met for lunch at Gibby's, the show people's restaurant. Maxey's hobby was visiting. He'd visit every show in the cities he played, to be passed in as a member of the profession. As we left the restaurant, I walked by the table of a beautiful, chic girl, tall and thin as a model. I heard what must have been her voice, very British U: "Oh, I say. You are a dashing figure, Mister Floy!" Maxey and I were out on the sidewalk before the words soaked in. They were the maid's line in the first act of *High Button Shoes*. I walked back into Gibby's with Maxey. It was Audrey Hepburn.

> ME: *"Excuse me, Miss Hepburn. Was that addressed to me?"*
>
> MISS H. *(that radiant smile): "Yes. I played the maid in the London company." (She invites us to sit down.)*
>
> ME: *"Let me introduce one of the greatest boxers of our time. Former light-heavyweight champion, Maxey Rosenbloom."*
>
> MISS H.: *"What a pleasure. I've never met a pugilist."*
>
> MAXEY: *"You with a show in town?"*
>
> MISS H.: *"Oh yes. Gigi."*
>
> ME *(quickly, to Maxey): "A fine show. Adapted from the great French novelist Colette."*
>
> MAXEY: *"Yeh? What's it about?"*
>
> ME: *"Well, her grandmother was a courtesan, her mother was a courtesan, and they're teaching her to be a fine courtesan."*
>
> MAXEY *(shrugs): "I don't think I can make it."*
>
> ME: *"Let me put it this way, Max. Her grandmother was a hooker, her mother was a hooker, and she's in training to be a hooker."*
>
> MAXEY: *"I'll come to the matinee."*

Audrey and I became affectionate friends. Her current *amour* was a wealthy Canadian merchant who demanded she throw up her career for him. Audrey was a dedicated actress, not at all thrilled by the notion of hiding out in a mansion in

Toronto. She had just made a picture in Rome with Gregory Peck. Based on her description of the story and that glorious face of a lady out of the eighteenth century, I blurted out, "You know, Audrey, you're going to win the Academy Award."

She replied with indignant modesty, "Oh, *Phul!*" This was as close as she could make it to Phil. The Academy race was not the kind of contest I bet on. So, of course, she won the award, for *Roman Holiday.*

Ours was an easygoing, Blinky relationship. After our performances, we'd take in the all-night movies at the Wood Theater. Then a night lunch, and home to her hotel. She'd leave her morning call with the clerk, using the British colloquialism "knock me up at nine-thirty." She was not amused when I told her what that meant in American.

Since *Gigi* was also heading west, we occasionally met in the same city. If our time schedules were different, we'd leave notes on the best place to eat and what to see and do.

Salt Lake City: I sensed we lost the audience after the opening "If You Want to Be a Top Banana." The theater manager rushed into the wings to warn me, "They think you're ridiculing their religion."

I was stunned. "How could we?"

It was one line in the opening lyric, "This must be the place!" How could anyone have known this would offend the followers of Brigham Young because, when he first set eyes on the site of Salt Lake City, he said, "This is the place!" At intermission I ran from one dressing room to another, telling everyone who had lines in the song "Top Banana," "Do not say 'this must be the place.' Substitute anything that rhymes, whether it makes sense or not. 'You've got a funny face,' 'Set the pace,' 'Let's have a big race'—but do not say *this must be the place!*"

Denver: The management was ready for us with oxygen tanks. Because of the high altitude, I was breathless after the opening. Every moment I was out of a scene, I sat in the wings gulping oxygen.

Omaha: After I scouted the stage, I walked out in the afternoon sun for a stroll. In front of the theater, an elderly Jewish gentleman, a little frayed at the edges, possibly a sexton of a synagogue, surveyed the lobby photos. He recognized me.

MAN: *"You're the star from this show?"*
ME: *"Yes."*
MAN: *"It's a good show?"*
ME: *"Oh, sure. Lot of fun in it."*
MAN: *"Suppose I go in and see it?"*
ME: *"Go ahead."*
MAN: *"I mean, for free."*
ME: *"If you go in free, how are they going to pay the actors?"*
MAN: *"I won't take up any room. I'll stand in the back."*
(I know I am going to pass him in, but I want to hear the end of his scene.)
ME: *"They sell standing room, too."*
MAN: *"Tsk, tsk! They would let an old man stand—and even charge him for it? All right, I'll make you a proposition."*
ME: *"What?"*
MAN: *"Let me go in. And I'll give you my word of honor—if I don't like it, I'll walk right out!"*

San Francisco: The Geary Theater, across the street from the St. Francis Hotel, provided a Turkish bath on the eleventh floor. I booked a suite next to the bath. I awoke at eleven, called for my breakfast to be delivered at twelve, stumbled next door into the steamroom, shaved, had a rubdown and breezed back to my room for breakfast, a new man. On tour, the simple amenities are worth more than money.

The four weeks in Frisco were a sellout. Jack Benny, who had just closed in San Francisco in his own revue, called me from Los Angeles and said, "Phil, I've seen the show twice in New York and now I'm asking you to set aside four tickets for the Los Angeles opening. I want George Burns and Gracie to see it."

"You've got 'em," I said.

A few days later, Jack phoned again. "There's a certain pace in your show . . . I want my writers to see that." Six more seats. Before we left town, Jack had the entire second row.

Los Angeles: June 1, 1953, almost two years after we opened *Top Banana* in Philadelphia. I knew every gesture, every nuance of every note of everybody's part. Yet the opening night whammies hit me. Three decades as a professional performer and I was still jittery for the opening. Worse, I would be facing everybody in the movie business out there. The frustrations I'd felt in my first few years in Hollywood backed up inside me until I felt choked.

> *. . . I'd better walk out of the dressing room or I won't make it. The stage is not set yet. I wander around . . . My heart is racing; I go to the toilet four times, and I don't have to . . . The first scene is set now. Overture. That music is a bracer. Now my heart is racing at the Kentucky Derby, and I'm sweating. Yes, frightened . . . Is Benny in his seats? It really doesn't matter, but I have to do something. I look through the peephole in the curtain. Jack and Mary are on the aisle, and there he is laughing —at the overture! Each melody reminds him of scenes he has seen twice. I laugh my way onstage.*

Jack gave me a check for the tickets. I tore up that check. Getting him tickets was the best investment I ever made for an opening night appearance. If Jack reads this, he'll now know what happened to that check.

Shortly after we opened, our dog Sport created one of the wildest stretches of laughter I have ever heard. It was an accident no one could foresee or invent. Cary Grant came to see the show again, this time with his ex-wife, Betsy Drake. He sat in the second row on the aisle, and *Cary Grant is a star!* The whole audience was aware of his presence and where he was sitting.

Well, we got to the part of the show where the dog Sport came out for his number. Suddenly his voice changed. During thousands of miles across America he sang *ooooooowwwwww* in a high tenor. Now the *oooooowwwwww* turned into a high falsetto—a high, floating, ghostly tune as if he was keening for his dead Irish ancestors. The audience laughed the same way other audiences had laughed at that scene. Cary Grant, having seen the show before, detected the difference. His laughter soared over the rest of the audience's. The dog stopped in the middle of an *oooooowwwwww* and peered down at Cary Grant. It was as if he was actually saying, "What's so funny about this, buddy?" He then proceeded with his *ooooooowwwwww*.

Cary could not restrain himself. He howled louder. Again Sport looked down at him and his face seemed to say, "What's so funny about a dog singing soprano?" I thought Cary would disintegrate in his seat. All this time I was supposed to be playing straight to the dog, and the dog was upstaging me. I was lucky to contain myself until I got offstage, where I collapsed in hopeless hysteria.

Audrey Hepburn came back to Hollywood after the release of *Roman Holiday*, and she was the hottest thing in films since the May Irwin-John Rice kiss. At that time her representatives, MCA, were perpetuating a ritual that required the obeisance of their entire roster. The agency owned a large financial interest in an ice show; therefore, all their clients had to appear at the gala opening, to give the show a sendoff. The invitations for dinner before the show were handed out in a fixed, almost religious order. The lowest level, for peasants, was Chasen's. The next level was Romanoff's, for bishops and the lower angels. The summit, Mount Olympus, was dinner at the home of Jules Stein, president of MCA. From there you rode to the ice show in an omnibus, driven by Mr. Stein himself. I was only on the second level, a preflight candidate.

Since Audrey was not attached to anyone at the moment, the agency asked her to look over their list of the most eligible escorts for the opening: Clark Gable, Jimmy Stewart, other respectable swingers of Hollywood. Audrey picked Phul.

We sat in the front of the bus.

After she made *Sabrina Fair*, she fell in love with Mel Ferrer, an intense, cultivated man who opened her eyes to life. Audrey had been a sheltered, self-controlled girl. Now she flowered into a woman. Mel did everything right: He introduced her to the world of the arts, he picked the appropriate wine—not only the year but the side of the slope that faced the sun. Mel found a play for her and himself, *Ondine,* a poetic fantasy by Jean Giraudoux. He would play a dour knight; she, a water sprite. Almost perfect type casting. She called me for lunch before she left for New York to begin rehearsals. She was concerned about interrupting her film career.

In my firm Blinky voice, I said, "If you love him, Audrey, do it. You'll grow."

I was there for the opening. Audrey electrified that audience. Mel's performance was secondary. They shared star billing, so they took the curtain calls together, hand in hand. The audience was cheering Audrey; obviously they wanted to give her a solo ovation. Mel never let go of her hand—for which I admired him because the billing was equal.

During the run of *Ondine*, I received phone calls from her mother, her maid, MCA. Where was she? She was hiding out somewhere in New York with Mel. I had no idea where she was until she again phoned for a lunch meeting. Could I recommend a vocal coach? I did. And she talked about the handicaps of their relationship. "Why don't they leave me alone? I love Mel. We're going to be married."

"Why change?" I said. "You have the perfect arrangement for a dedicated actress. You're on top onstage—and he's on top offstage."

She gave me the "Oh, **Phul**!" look.

Top Banana ran for eight weeks in Los Angeles. Several weeks before we closed, I received an offer from an energetic promoter, Joe Justman, who operated a film production center.

"I haven't seen your show, but I don't have to see it to know it could be a big success on film. If we shoot it cheap—in 3-D— we can offer a $6 Broadway musical at movie prices." His gimmick: film the entire show, with the original cast, on stage, as if seen in front of an audience. All in two days. All in 3-D. "Bwana Devil" in this process had just made a fortune.

In spite of our box office and critical success, we had received no serious bidding for the movie rights. I do not know why, to this day. I was, as usual, hammered to a cross, repaying gambling debts. Joe Justman had very little money, too. But, most important, he had a studio to shoot the movie. I was to work on a token salary, in return for 25 percent of the profits. And the rest of the company would receive four weeks' salary. Harry Cohn said I was crazy, but he made no offer to produce the show at Columbia.

I should have turned off as soon as I heard Joe's "I don't have to see your show to know . . ." He did not know. The money he was supposed to promote was never raised. Our producer, Al Zugsmith, had made his reputation shooting thrifty Westerns. He assigned a director, Al Greene. Why, I don't know. Our project turned into a classic How to Murder a Picture farce.

I worked out a camera concept, to bring the movie audience into the stage show. During the overture, the camera, moving like a playgoer, picks up two tickets at the box office, strolls down the aisle, crosses into the center of the third row, looks over the program. Then the curtain rises. Well, the curtain couldn't rise because Justman's studio ceiling was too low. No overture. For a while I thought we'd have no music, either. Al Zugsmith brought in his conductor for the prerecording session: a flute player who specialized in background music for Westerns. He could not read our score. Coincidence leaped to our rescue. Hal Hastings, our original conductor, was in town to lead a show breaking in at the Civic Center . . . and he walked into our studio to say hello. The union gave him a special dispensation to take over. Otherwise we would never have finished the movie—which would have been no great loss.

There was so little money that the entire picture was shot in a day and a half. Al Greene just pointed the camera and let it roll. He didn't dare stop. In the final cut, you could see a stagehand walking behind a drop. The sound quivered and faded, and yet it managed to pick up every offcamera shoe squeak. The 3-D process was obsolete by the time the picture was released, so the 3-D film was projected on regular two-dimension machines. This left all sorts of strange vertical blurs. But the comedy was still there. Somewhere.

I made nothing out of the picture. At the last minute we needed "finish money." It came from Harry Popkin, a B-picture expert, who, of course, claimed most of the profits for his contribution. In a little maneuver beloved by Hollywood insiders, he took his entire family, including his brother-in-law, on a "promotion" tour of Europe and Israel, and charged it all to the picture.

I did what I could to promote the film, with personal appearances. I asked an exhibitors' convention in Philadelphia, since they knew more about film financing than I did: "I have a piece of the picture; if Mr. Popkin and his family do not have a good time on their tour—can he sue me?" And then I introduced Rita Gam, who was promoting another Popkin film, titled *The Thief*.

Top Banana is occasionally shown on the TV too-late shows, which add a little blur of their own. The young film buffs who stay up all night consider it a collector's item. With all its out-of-synch sound, inexplicable noises, scenes that seem to float under water, it's now avant-garde.

CHAPTER 12

The Preposterous Birth of Ernie Bilko

Sgt. Ernie Bilko first saw the light of night on the CBS network September 20, 1955, but the events that led to his conception began years before. He was hardly a gleam of passion and hope in his parents' eyes. Bilko was the rowdy child of accident and coincidence.

In October, 1953, while *Top Banana* was running in Los Angeles, I had a golf date with Jack Benny, which he canceled because of a cold. So I stopped in at his house. Jack looked sick and old (three days later he was thirty-five again). That day he was reflecting on his life, and he wished he had been able to spend more time on stage. "They're going to be after you for television," he warned. "That's the wave of the future. But it's a drain. Stay in the theater. It isn't the most fruitful in terms of money, but a performer has dignity on the stage. People *pay* to see you."

Jack meant what he said. It was heartwarming. But he was so wrong. Nobody pursued me with glittering TV packages. Nobody tried to seduce me with irresistible stage shows. My agent came up with one squeamish movie offer. "It's a lousy script, but Jack Donohue will be the director. . . ."

I went to work in *Lucky Me*, a squeaky musical with Eddie Foy, Nancy Walker and Doris Day. It made me a Blinky again—at a higher salary.

In 1954 the radio and TV correspondents in Washington produced another of their annual shows for the President and most of the capital bigwigs. Irving Mansfield, a producer for CBS, asked if I would MC part of the show. I would.

First, we were all cleared to make sure we had no leftist connections. The show was set in the ballroom of the Statler-

Hilton because there were no large mirrors; the Secret Service doesn't like to give anyone a view of the President it doesn't have. And all the telephones in the ballroom were disconnected, so that ringing the phone could not set off a bomb. I'm sure all these measures were justified, but they made me uptight. And when I'm tense, I become aggressive.

I walked onto the stage and looked over the audience: President Eisenhower, Vice President Nixon, the Cabinet, Congressmen and Senators, most of the Supreme Court. Everyone was there except John Foster Dulles, who was stuck in some weary negotiations in East Germany. Well, I'd come a long way from Brownsville, so I took a good look. About fifteen seconds—an eternity. Finally, I turned to Mr. Eisenhower: "My God, who's minding the store?"

Ike liked that. It was a knee-slapper. During my clarinet bit, in the middle of a good line, a phone rang. Three Secret Service men fell on it as if it were a grenade. I lost my audience right there. I looked off into the wings, as if getting the phone message. "What? Oh yes." Then, to the President: "It's long distance from a Mr. Dulles. He says he'll talk to *any-body!*" Mr. Eisenhower broke up. Another knee-slapper.

Hubbell Robinson Jr., CBS vice-president in charge of programming, was in the audience that night. A glint came into his eye. Three days later my agent reported that CBS wanted me to develop a half-hour situation comedy series. Recalling Benny's advice, I was not eager. I went in for a chat with Robinson, and told him I was tired of scripts that had little notes in the margin—"Phil will say a funny here." Only the writers didn't say what that funny thing was.

Robinson hooked me with two words: Nat Hiken. The most fertile TV comedy mind of the 1950's, Nat had spent seven years as a writer for Fred Allen's radio show. (Herman Wouk was another.) Nat had also written Berle's radio show, and Martha Raye's TV series. But he suffered from the Allen connection because the word around the studios was: Allen writes his own material. Shortly after we met—about four minutes—Nat told me this tale, which he swore, scout's honor, was true:

Nat piloted his own single-engine plane. Flying to Los Angeles, he ran into a snowstorm that forced him to land, without gas, on a desolate plain. His propeller was bent. A band of Indians, in old GI shirts, rode up on horses and invited him to take shelter in their village. Then they brought Nat to their chief.

> *(Enter the chief of the tribe, who does not speak English, and an interpreter.)*
> INTERPRETER: *"Chief wants to know what brings you here?"*
> NAT: *"A storm. I'm flying to Los Angeles."*
> INTERPRETER: *"Chief wants to know what is your work?"*
> NAT: *"I am a writer."*
> INTERPRETER: *"What newspaper?"*
> NAT: *"I write for radio. The Fred Allen show."*
> *(The stolid chief breaks into a gruff laugh.)*
> NAT: *"What's he laughing at?"*
> INTERPRETER: *"Chief says Fred Allen write his own material."*

Nat was a reserved, almost shy cherub in a rumpled suit. He cared little for material things. I had to pull him into Macy's to buy a suit.

We were put on a salaried retainer and all we had to do was come up with a TV format that was funny and durable. Comedy on television is a lot like comedy in burlesque. It's not how funny are you; it's how many weeks can you be funny? What will the twenty-third show be like? Does the format give you opportunities for variety in location, people and situations? It is not easy. And that is why so many TV pilots are shot down in blood and ulcers.

We went to work in Nat's office, a coldwater flat on West 48th Street that he sublet from a press agent, Jack Tirman. No air conditioner. A bleak bedroom with a view of a dirty red brick garage. The wallpaper, rug and drapes had different flower patterns—all peeling. Nat said he found this room stimulating. The first idea he came up with was: "I see you as a platoon sergeant in an American camp."

"*Oh, no!*" I groaned. "That's Abbott and Costello." All I could see was dumb drills, guys bumping into each other and their pants falling down.

Nat could not write a script unless he had a deadline, his back to the wall. And nice guy Hubbell Robinson did not even phone occasionally to ask what we did today. We took many long walks in Central Park. We went to baseball games, to talk over ideas. Jack Tirman introduced me to the press agents' late-late gin games, eight on a side. We were thinking hard.

About five months after we'd signed on, Robinson called to say hello, and I told him we had thirty-eight potential plots. Not one of them kept me awake: wise-guy brother-in-law, racetrack tout, manager of a minor league baseball team, peddler of phony stocks, larcenous theater agent, hotel bellboy, attendant in a Turkish bath. And a sergeant in business for himself.

I was stretched out on that corncob mattress in that miserable office when it hit me—why not a sergeant? He was the reincarnation of all my previous lives: the boy who was protected by Kid Posy, the press agent in *Yokel Boy*, Harrison Floy, Jerry Biffle. I was predestined to be Bilko. I would be a scamp again, this time protected by the uniform of the U.S. Army. And we would have a made-to-measure audience. The men in the army, men about to go in, men with dishonorable discharges, girls who had dated Army men, girls who wished they hadn't . . . I figured we could reach an audience of at least ten million.

Nat knocked out an outline of our ideas in one day. Hubbell Robinson said, "Go ahead," and I was in business for CBS. I sat in on the pilot script, but Nat wrote it. I would not give him a chance to switch his Fred Allen joke to me.

Since we were both sports fans, especially baseball, we used familiar names. Nat came up with Bilko, after a minor league player, Steve Bilko, who hit sixty-one homers. It also had the welcome connotation of a man bilking you. Paparelli, an umpire, became Pvt. Paparelli. Cpl. Barbello was the real name of Rocky Graziano. Rocky was our first casting director. He brought in Walter Cartier, a middleweight fighter who began as a stand-in and became a regular member of the platoon. Other ex-boxers we used: Lou Nova, once a heavyweight contender; Maxie Shapiro, a lightweight; Mike O'Dowd, a heavyweight. Jack Healy, who played occasional small parts, had been Graziano's manager. Sometimes I felt Rocky was using our show as a training camp.

From the beginning I wanted Buddy Hackett to be my assistant corporal. We'd met in the Catskills. Imprisoned inside that round, lumpy body was a very intelligent, angry young man. He knew more about medicine than my brother. He lived in a clothes-littered, dark little apartment, lairlike, so I called him The Bear. I knew I could bounce a lot of comedy off him. Two weeks before filming, The Bear came to me, acutely embarrassed. He had been offered a good part in Sidney Kingsley's stage comedy, *Lunatics and Lovers,* and he wanted his release. I didn't blame him: It was Broadway for sure versus a doubtful starter. I hesitated to tell Nat, but he heaved a sigh of relief. "Didn't you know you were throwing every line his way?" he asked me. "I am writing this show around *you.*"

Harvey Lembeck moved up to become my assistant, Cpl. Barbello. The other corporal, Henshaw, was played by tall, blond Allan Melvin, a wickedly witty young man. Maurice Gosfield came to us in an open casting call; we opened the doors wide and there he was. He claimed credits on 2,000 radio shows, 125 television appearances and three and a half years as a T/Sgt. with the 8th Armored Division. That didn't matter to me. We had to have him—the Slob of the Century. Nat had an instinct for unique faces; they created characters for him. Gosfield looked like a doberman pinscher, and that's what he became: Pvt. Duane (for a touch of class) Doberman. For added protection, I brought in my mentor from my early days in vaudeville, Herbie Faye, as Cpl. Fender.

Nat came up with the formal title of the series, "You'll Never Get Rich." The pilot script established the characters and setting. M/Sgt. Ernie Bilko, head of the motor pool at a mythical Fort Baxter, in Roseville, Kansas, was trimmed for the first time in the weekly card game by his buddies; he immediately concocted a beautiful, larcenous scheme to raise fresh money for the next game. The buddies were a platoon of malingerers, ragpickers, sharpies and enemies of any authority. Bilko was the eternal dreamer, the con man who dreamed up elaborate strategies to bamboozle the system. His high-flying plots collapsed because, like the hero of Greek tragedy, he had a fatal flaw: he was a softy. You had to like Bilko because inside everyone, even the straightest pillar of the community, there is a con man wiggling to sneak out.

Nat was not only head writer, he was director and producer. We rehearsed in the Nola studios, above Lindy's restaurant, and we filmed it in the DuMont studios on East 67th Street, before an audience sitting on wood bleachers. Three cameras were used; when one ran out of film, we worked with the other two. The story was shot in sequence, and we never stopped except for major scenery changes or a mechanical breakdown. We were not selling clarity, or arty close-ups; we were depending on speed to build a momentum of laughter. We were able to film the twenty-five-minute sequence in fifty minutes—an incredibly fast record for filmed comedy. I warmed up the audience before the show, and entertained during the scene changes.

Nat screened the pilot for Hubbell Robinson and the CBS brass that night; I went to my hotel to sleep. He awoke me at 12:30 A.M.: "They're in the skies now!" The final evaluation came from William Paley, head of CBS: "This is money in the bank. Take it off the rack and go ahead."

Translation: We'll get rich. Shoot the series, while we set up a sponsor and clear the time.

We made half a dozen episodes before the sponsor found us. It was a withdrawn, lonely feeling, to work in a vacuum without public notice. In television and the stage there's a morning-after reaction. Here we sweated and screamed and our captive audience roared and . . . nothing. Every Sunday I visited my mother in a nursing home in Brooklyn and told her I had a good job in TV. Five thousand a week and 50 percent of the profits. Well, Momma watched the tube religiously and never saw me. One visit, she opened a drawer in the bedside table and pulled out $100 in small bills. "Take it. You should eat while you're working in television."

Did we have a sponsor? When would we go on the air? These doubts frustrated me. Instead of buying into the show, I put my money into card games and benefits for bookies.

In the seventh week, an executive of the William Esty advertising agency, which had the Camel cigarette account, pulled a sneak attack. He somehow penetrated the CBS film storage vault, borrowed the pilot film and flew with it to Winston-Salem, North Carolina, headquarters of the R. J. Reynolds tobacco complex. A coup worthy of Bilko—and I never figured out how he managed it. It was love at first flight: Camels insisted CBS had to let them into this show. Later, the Amana refrigeration people became co-sponsors. We worked the cigarettes into the story line—someone was always stealing Bilko's packs of Camels. The Camels people liked the way I smoked on the tube: I really bit into the cigarette. I think they enjoyed that more than the show.

Well, great. Now we had a sponsor. When did we go on the air? So my mother could see I was working.

Into the DuMont studio one Friday strolled Harry Ommerle, Robinson's assistant. He was worried and determined to do his duty, like Gary Cooper waiting for the shootout in *High Noon*. After we'd finished the filming, Harry said apologetically, "You're going on at eight-thirty Tuesday."

Eight-thirty was the middle of NBC's blockbuster comedy hour. *I would be opposite Berle.* I had a hot flash in my stomach as if I'd swallowed a pack of Camels, already lit. Milton Berle owned Tuesday, eight to nine. He'd defended it six years against all comers. Now he was alternating weeks with Martha Raye and Bob Hope. CBS was sending us up against the strongest comedy bill in television.

It was all set, Ommerle said. The premiere would be September 20. Nat, who was always calm, looked seasick.

Berle phoned me:

> BERLE: *"Why did you let CBS do this to you?"*
> ME: *"It was a big secret. They never told me. I hate playing opposite you."*

> BERLE: *"And I hear you have a good show."* (*I know he is not gloating; he feels genuinely sorry for me.*)
> ME: *"Well, I'm a gambler, you know."*
> BERLE: *"Somebody's trying to destroy you."*

I watched the first episode at my hotel. And I was happy with it. I called CBS for the Nielsen rating. Our rating was 14.6. NBC's score was 23.6.

Second week: Bilko, 14.4, against NBC with Berle, 28.6.

We were sliding downhill.

I stopped calling. Then came the icing on the cake. CBS changed our time, beginning November 1, to eight to eight-thirty. That meant we had to break the NBC listeners' seven-year habit of tuning in at eight. If they hadn't switched to us in the middle of their favorite show, why should they switch at the beginning? I felt helpless. Maybe Berle was right.

The first week in December, Hubbell Robinson called me in for a conference in the CBS building. I had an unshakable chill: Camels wanted to cancel. I walked down a long aisle of open desks, girls typing away, and they glanced up, smiling. They knew something. I could feel the electricity.

Harry Ommerle caught me before I moved into Robinson's office. "I've been trying to reach you. Listen to this figure for November 29! 27.4 for you, 27.8 for Berle!" And then in December, we passed him.

Overnight—zoom! I believe the children found us. And in American homes, the children have first refusal on the tuner. Our share of the audience climbed with every show. Eventually we reached 23 million listeners. Bilko knocked Berle off the air. Milton phoned me: "You rat. You had to go on Tuesday?"

Milton was not bitter. The champ retired with a fantastic contract that paid him a large sum every year *not* to work on any other network. I think he was secretly relieved, after all those years of high tension.

After the first season's run, Nat and I won five Emmy awards. And most of the other prizes:

Sylvania Award for "Best Comedy Show on TV."

"Outstanding Contributions to the TV Film Industry" from the National TV Film Council.

"TV Man of the Year," named by 450 television editors in *Radio-TV Daily* annual poll.

"Best TV Performer" in poll of 7,000 newspaper and magazine writers taken by *TV Today* and *Motion Picture Daily*.

After all this, Jack Benny wired me: "You wouldn't listen to me!"

I waited a long time to answer him. In 1957, the Friars Club in Hollywood honored Jack as "Man of the Year" with a gala dinner. I was up to my elbows shooting Bilko, so I had to decline an invitation to the ceremonies. I sent Benny a wire:

"If I'd listened to you two years ago, I'd be at your dinner tonight."

A month after Bilko's premiere, my agent, Freddie Fields, found he had three tickets to the opening of the stage play *The Desk Set*. Two seats down front and one seat in row Q. When I joined him at the theater, he took the seat in Q and left me in the good seats with his date, Evelyn Patrick. And that's how my second wife entered my life.

Evelyn had won beauty prizes as Miss Vocal Speech, Miss Diction and Miss Florida, and she'd come up from Orlando to break into television. She had an electric quality and I had an affinity for beauty-contest winners. This was her first Broadway opening; she was a little awed by it all and very polite. "My parents love your Bilko show," she told me. As the final curtain fell, the critics rushed up the aisles. Evelyn, the Southern lady, was shocked. "How rude," she said. "Couldn't they wait a few minutes? Out of courtesy to the actors who've worked so hard?"

Her consideration touched me. Anybody who cared that much for performers deserved *my* consideration. We began dating. (That sounds so nineteenth-century now.) Evelyn was ambitious, feisty but unspoiled. She was still learning how to dress for New York: basic black dress and accentuated makeup. To her the city was romantic, Runyonesque. She had to see everything and go everywhere. She was a wide-eyed kid in a candy shop. And I was a romantic about women; she made me feel like a gallant.

Evelyn found her first break on a live quiz show, operated by Jan Murray. While she delivered the commercial, she'd brush her hand quickly across her right cheek as a signal to me: "I'll meet you right after the show." Then she moved up to become the Revlon girl on the "$64,000 Question," and she'd stop in to meet me at the Bilko rehearsals. She was warm and affectionate, yet I tried to stay objective. Evelyn was almost a rerun of Jo-Carroll Dennison. The career for which she fought so hard was a prelude, a way to make money to help support her mother and sister, before she achieved her real goal—marriage. Commendable, but not for me. I'd had my fill of marriage. I was not about to change my way of life for any beauty queen. More and more I hoarded my privacy, to come and go and be alone as I pleased.

On vacation from the Bilko show, I took most of the platoon to Las Vegas for an act at the Riviera. Evelyn had never seen Las Vegas, so I invited her to visit. The flight took eleven hours, and I waited up all night for the 9 A.M. arrival. She had never taken a transcontinental plane—I was afraid she'd come out in a wheelchair. She bounced down the gangway, fresh-faced under a giant picture hat, saying goodbye to the entire plane. "Edna, be sure to call Tom . . . And don't forget that recipe for me, Sarah . . ." For the first time I realized Evelyn was a woman who could cope.

She was not sleepy, so we ambled down to the swimming pool. "Gee, I'd love a soda," she said. I handed her four silver dollars, left from a hapless night at the casino, to buy a soda at the fountain on the other side of the pool . . . and I dozed off in the sun. I was awakened by the loudspeaker, paging "Mr. Silvers, please come to the casino. Miss Patrick wants to see you."

Miss Patrick was at the roulette table, surrounded by twenty-five-cent chips up to her eyeballs. She invested three dollars, after the soda, in her first plunge on the little ball. "What do I do now?" she asked.

"Cash in. How long can you be lucky?"

She raked in $425 in quarters.

Milton and Ruth Berle were visiting at the hotel; we arranged to go out with them after my second show. At the end of my performance, I drifted to the crap table. Evelyn hurried to push her luck at roulette. She lost everything she'd won, and continued coming back to me for twenty-dollar bills. I was losing heavily until suddenly I got a hot hand, and the money began flowing back to me. I was in a gambler's trance, oblivious of everything except the dots on the dice. A hand came up from behind and reached for my money.

"Can I have—?" Evelyn asked.

"Put it down!" I yelled. I didn't want to be interrupted in the middle of a streak. Evelyn was stunned. *"Nobody* talks to me that way!" And she went off to pack her bags. Ruth Berle followed her, trying to explain. She'd gone through the same thing with Milton. That outburst should have given Evelyn some clue to the gambler's uncontrollable fury, but she must have believed she could reform me. She unpacked. The gossip columns on both coasts promised early wedding bells for Bilko and Miss Revlon. The truth was, we decided to break it off. We were only lacerating each other.

Edward R. Murrow invited me to appear on his "Person-to-Person" show. In those days the guest took the cameras on a tour of his gardens or his collection of early French Impressionists. All I had was my small suite at the Delmonico: living room, bedroom, bath and a pullman kitchen. I took Ed on a mock tour of my apartment, bypassing the kitchen door. "The kitchen is behind this door," I told him. "I must go in there some day." I sat at a desk, behind pictures of my mother and father, and told about my beginnings. It was straight and sentimental and, I guess, it touched a great many hearts. Tallulah Bankhead phoned to compliment me—and I'd never met her.

I was hungry at the end of this show. I cleaned up and walked over to Toots Shor's for dinner. As I turned up 52nd Street I met Evelyn with two escorts. "A good show," she said. She'd seen it at "21" with a lawyer friend and her agent. We said a cheerful goodbye to each other; about fifteen minutes later, she sat down at my table in Shor's. We talked over my steak, then coffee, in the taxi to her apartment, and on and on.

> EVELYN (*curled up in her big wing chair*): *"You have to understand. It's you I love. You closed the door on me."*
> ME: *"I was trying to protect you. I'm not for you. I'm not meant to be married."*
> EVELYN: *"Do you love me?"*
> ME: *"I guess I do, in my fashion."*
> EVELYN: *"Then who are you to deny me my children?"*

That hit me like a slap. In a few weeks I decided I had made a horrible mistake with Evelyn. She was the best possible woman I could marry. Once I made up my mind, it had to be done quickly. We had wasted so many months. And it had to be done on Sunday, because we both worked. Again Freddie Fields came to my aid. He was familiar with the procedures—he had just married Polly Bergen—so he arranged the ceremony with a county clerk in New Haven, Connecticut. We were married October 21, 1956, exactly a year and three days after we'd met in Freddie's theater seats.

What if I had not walked up 52nd Street for dinner? What if Evelyn hadn't wanted to watch Ed Murrow at "21"? Wild coincidence.

We moved into my hotel until we could find larger quarters, and Evelyn, without my asking, abandoned her career with Revlon. Some months later, when Bilko switched from Tuesday to Friday nights, we found time for a proper honeymoon in Miami. There I had a strange, unhappy reunion with Sinatra. I hadn't seen him since I played on his show six years before. He now appeared in a series on ABC television on Friday night. Evelyn and I were able to catch his closing-night show in a Miami hotel. It was impossible to get a table, but a friend of mine, Bernard Frank, an attorney and ex-councilman whose home was in Miami Beach, took us in through the kitchen, and we caught Frank's show.

Frank introduced all his friends in the audience, but not me. I was sure he didn't see me. Then a wide-mouthed woman sitting next to us called out, "Here's Phil Silvers! Frank, here's

Phil!" Embarrassed, I tried to turn away. She persisted, and finally Frank introduced me, coolly and impersonally. I took a little bow, as the others had done, and sat. He looked down at me and murmured, "You had to go on Fridays, huh?"

As if I had personally arranged the network's time slot to challenge him. I did not hear from Frank again for sixteen years.

In the five years I was married to Jo-Carroll, we tried to have children and failed. We must have had an allergic set of genes. When Jo-Carroll remarried, she soon produced two handsome sons. Two months after I married Evelyn, she was pregnant. Our genes linked up as precisely as the Apollo spaceships. Every time I said, "Hello, honey" too loudly, I had another child.

During Evelyn's pregnancy, we watched Katharine Hepburn on the late show in *The Philadelphia Story*. She epitomized an ideal woman: resourceful, witty, loving. We decided to name our first girl after the character Miss Hepburn played—Tracey. (In the play it's spelled Tracy; the clerk who made out the birth certificate added the "e." To forestall him, we named our second baby Nancey.) Evelyn and I made another deal. If our children were boys, they would be raised in the Hebrew faith; if they were girls, Evelyn would decide their religious education. Evelyn delivered five beauty queens.

The first one was trouble. Neither of us had experience in this kind of production. Evelyn was in labor for twenty-two hours. We'd found an old-fashioned doctor who rejected the notion of inducing birth. I stayed up all night before Tracey arrived at 7:30 A.M., and that day, of course, I had to perform in a television special. Tracey was colicky, and I quivered with every burp. She cried so violently that I couldn't understand what kept her little body together. The doctor assured me the stomach contractions would end in three months. I didn't believe him.

Evelyn and I took the infant down to Miami with our nurse. When I was walking with Tracey one morning on the beach, out of the bright sun appeared an apparition: Joe

DiMaggio. I consider myself not just a sports fan but a knowledgeable one. And I guess Joe DiMaggio in baseball was my all-time favorite; on the field he had a dignity that was all his own. Joe immediately wanted to hold the baby. He pulled the blanket down to look at her face and I thought: If she cries now, at my hero, I'll sell her.

Tracey woke up with the happiest gurgle of laughter, and raised her little hands to his face. The colic disappeared for Joe DiMaggio. Time: exactly three months after birth, just as the doctor predicted.

Tracey is a ham, I'm afraid. When I appeared on "Person-to-Person" a second time, she was three and one-half. She wandered in between me and the camera, begging a drink from my bottle of Coke. Tracey topped that entrance by staring straight into the camera. Upstaging her own father.

When a situation comedy plays for over four years, all kinds of soon-to-be-famous people pass through. Most of the live shows were made in New York in those years, so we were a welcome paycheck for many young people trying to break into the theater. In one sequence in 1958, we employed the combined talents of Peggy Cass, Orson Bean and Alan Alda, age twenty-two.

I heard a young fellow delivering some very funny one-liners behind the scenery during a break. His real job was to hold two hinged sticks, the clapper, in front of the camera and announce "take one—two" before the scene started. He was Bill Dana, who invented José Jiminez.

Dick Cavett surprised me, when I sat in on his show recently, with a photograph of Dick answering the phone—for one line—on "You'll Never Get Rich." He'd started out as a TV writer, and when he went broke he tried his luck at acting. I looked closely at the photo and needled him: "That's very interesting, but who's that MP standing behind you?"

George Kennedy.

"My God," Dick said. "I was so scared I never looked up."

George has since starred in his own series, "Sarge," and won an Academy Award in his highly successful movie career.

When he came to us, he wasn't an actor. He was a captain in the regular Army, with a dozen years of seniority, assigned by the Defense Department as liaison officer for our show. He saw to it that our sets and costumes at least looked honest. Since he was on the set every day, and in uniform, I suggested he could cross over in front of the camera and make some extra money. Occasionally we gave him a line—and he became a member of the Screen Actors Guild.

In every interview George gives, in TV or any other medium, he never fails to mention "Phil Silvers started it all for me." And if I said this acknowledgment from him doesn't give me a warm glow, I'd be lying.

An elegant, rich-looking woman came into the office of our casting director, looking for a job. Her children were grown up, she said, and she wanted to try show business; she'd had some acting experience in college. Our young casting director was overwhelmed. "She looks like Grace Kelly." In 1956 a sequence came up calling for a cultivated WAC to teach culture to the Fort Baxter ruffians—finger painting, sculpture, modern dance—in order to divert them from gambling. It was two days of work, paying about $300. I told the casting director to find that lovely lady who looked like Grace Kelly. He tracked down Dina Merrill, on her yacht, *The New Yorker*. At her own expense, she chartered a plane and flew back to New York for a bit part that paid $300. When you're a determined young lady, I guess you can do these things. Being heiress to the Post cereal fortune helped a bit, too.

Dina reminded me that about twelve years before, I had been kind to her husband, who was in the Army. Flashback: the USO tour with Bing Crosby. We met a soldier in the bar car, and in those days civilians felt guilty if they didn't buy a soldier a drink. Bing and I kept picking up his tab, and he literally fought to grab it out of our hands. We won. The soldier was Stan Rumbough, on his way to Washington to marry Dina. His family was almost as rich as Dina's.

Pat Hingle played his first TV show with us—and rescued me from a booboo. He portrayed a soldier of Hungarian descent who'd gone AWOL, and I was deputized as an MP to bring him back. I had such a ball dancing in a wedding scene that

I forgot to answer my cue: the phone ringing with a call from Colonel Hall. Pat danced by and yelled, "The phone, Sarge! It must be for you!"

Thank you, Pat.

We found Fred Gwynne in an advertising agency. Our sequence was built around an eating contest, with Bilko backing a man who became a compulsive eater when he was unhappy. Nat liked to cast against type. Instead of a fat glutton, he looked through the casting directories for a gaunt, thin face —Fred Gwynne. Fred had abandoned acting for a steady job in advertising. We managed to spring him from the job for four days' work. He was so gaunt and so versatile we used him in another episode, satirizing the "$64,000 Question." He returned to his agency job. After the two episodes appeared, Fred went into orbit. First, on the stage in "Mrs. McThing." Then the Munster series, and "Car 54, Where Are You?" produced by Nat Hiken. In 1972 Fred played Abraham Lincoln in the Broadway drama, *The Lincoln Mask*. Fred eats very well now.

Dick Van Dyke made his first big impression in a sequence titled "Hillbilly Whiz," as a boy from the southern mountains who hit the bull's-eye on the firing range with rocks. Bilko switched his deadly accuracy to baseball, and connived to sell the boy to the New York Yankees for $125,000. I persuaded my pals on the Yanks, Yogi Berra, Whitey Ford and Gil McDougald, to make their TV debuts on this show.

Paul Ford made a comfortable living by selling insurance in Baltimore until he was about forty years old. Then he decided his destiny was the acting profession. He came to New York and made about eighty-five dollars a week in the stage drama *Command Decision*. He worked steadily in radio, but his rubbery face, with its helplessly quivering Jello jowels, was kept secret from America. When we hired him as Colonel Hall, he was playing, by coincidence, a colonel in *Teahouse of the August Moon* on Broadway. He continued to double in the play while he worked for us. After the first sequence was released, he'd receive a tremendous ovation at the rise of the curtain, throwing the entire scene onstage out of balance.

Paul fought a running battle with his lines. I learned to watch for the warning signal in the midst of filming: Two beads of perspiration broke out on the left side of his upper lip just before he went blank. I'd throw the line to him in the form of a question—"You mean to tell me . . . ?"—and Paul picked it up.

He had a peculiar talent with that wonderful basset-hound face of his. I have always felt I deserved some special award for working alongside Paul Ford without collapsing in laughter at everything he did.

Maurice Gosfield had played only bit parts in the theater. After a few weeks on our show he became a national celebrity. Offcamera, Dobie thought of himself as Cary Grant playing a short, plump man. The Beautiful People of New York invited him to their cocktail parties; he was the rage of the playboys on Fire Island. When we flew out of town for personal appearances, Dobie usually appeared at parties with an effervescent stewardess on his arm. I know there was never any romantic or sexual relationship, yet he attracted more pretty women than the obvious studs in our company.

He had no sense of professional discipline. He fogged out on lines, cues, rehearsal time—with the most outrageous explanations. If he missed an entrance, he'd say he tripped over a sheet of paper. He came late to a rehearsal once because "a priest short-hopped me for a cab!"

Dobie never disappointed us in one of his talents: slobbery. His tie was always stained and his pants drooped. When he sat down to a meal he felt surrounded by enemies who would snatch his food if he didn't gobble it up first. He clutched his fork and knife as if they were weapons.

I recall a sequence with Kay Kendall, at that time the wife of Rex Harrison, and one of the most beguiling, elegant comediennes since Carole Lombard. Came lunchtime, I stayed in the studio with a malted milk, to avoid that tired, logey feeling. Kay went out with the boys to a little Italian restaurant, which set up a long table for the company. Kay was the toast of the trattoria. The platoon put her at the head of the table; they drank to her eyes with red wine. Then her eyes dropped on Doberman.

On his fork, he'd speared two meatballs . . . the other hand squeezed a sausage and a chunk of bread . . . half a cannolli smeared his wrist . . . strands of spaghetti curled around his tie. At the same time he was swilling the red wine.

Kay, forever the British lady, stifled a gasp of shock, but her eyes popped open like monocles. Allan Melvin explained, "Remember, Kay, he's working without a net."

When I played the Riviera in Las Vegas with Dobie, Herbie Faye, Allan Melvin and others from the platoon, we wore regulation GI uniforms—no zippers. The boys ran a daily pool on how many of Doberman's fly buttons would be open.

In a spiffy Hawaiian shirt that couldn't quite cover the varicose veins on his stomach, Duane was inevitably drawn to the crap table. The heavy shooters stood five deep, bucking the house at $4,000 a roll. Dobie knew nothing about gambling. He sidled up to the table, pulled a tubercular silver dollar from his pocket with a *soigné* "I'm with you . . ." and pushed his hand through the crowd. As he dropped his dollar on the table—anywhere, since he couldn't see it—the dice rolled up against his pudgy hand. Seven. Wiping out all the numbers played. The gamblers and the house men berated Dobie for his clumsiness. He pulled himself up to his full 5-feet-3 and exclaimed, "Why, you run this casino like a *drugstore!*" And he withdrew his patronage forever.

As the television shows and appearances rolled on over the years, Dobie began to have delusions. He believed he was a comedian. He did not realize that the situations in which he worked, plus the sharp lines provided by Nat and the other writers, made him funny. Ed Sullivan asked him and Joe E. Ross (Sergeant Ritzik), who had been a stand-up comedian in small clubs, to appear on his show. Their sketch was painful. Not a laugh. Monday, Ross eased himself into the rehearsal hall, embarrassed. He received an enthusiastic phone call from Doberman: "Baby, we're the talk of the town!"

After the Bilko series, he appeared in sketches on several shows. But only once; he was never called back. Then the engagements petered out. Most performers have gorgeous fantasies to keep themselves going. Gosfield never accepted the realities of his appearance. And talent.

CHAPTER 13

The Bilko Murder
Case, or The
Sergeant Sevens Out

Nat's instinct for far-out faces stimulated his invention, but it also created heartburn. Not every face is an actor.

As we entered the CBS building on Madison Avenue, a little boy—his name, ZIPPY, embroidered on his sweater—skated out of the elevator. I looked again. It was a chimpanzee, with his trainer.

"Wouldn't it be funny," Nat asked, "if a chimpanzee is drafted by mistake?"

"Ah, come on," I said. "It's got to be plausible."

Nat made it work in "The Trial of Harry Speakup," my favorite sequence and, I think, the most hilarious of them all. It was so wild and we adjusted so well to the chimp that actors, writers, directors asked, "How could you do it?"

We were told that the chimp might appear on cue—and he might not. He had never been trained to act; he was a skater and bike rider. We had to rehearse without him because he was like a little boy: He would rather play than work. His playmate was Doberman. As soon as the animal saw him, he felt an instant understanding, and leaped into his arms. So we wrote Dobie out of the sequence, and had him stand off-camera, as a come-on for the chimp.

The situation: An eager-beaver captain devised a technique to cut the time of Army induction in half. The platoon became an assembly line. A young man appeared at the train platform for induction, with the chimp, planning to turn the animal over to his brother. (A chimpanzee will die without companionship or affection.) The brother didn't show up. The draftee, in panic, stuffed the chimp into his duffle bag. When the chimp climbed out of the bag, the assembly line inducted him. The harried WAC, typing his dossier, couldn't hear his name; she called out, "Harry, speak up!" The chimp nodded agreeably, and that became his name. For the psychological test, the monkey leaped onto the doctor's desk and spun around on his skates (this was a lucky accident) while the psychologist mouthed all the clichés: ". . . rejected by mother . . . violence under control . . ." And the chimp placed fourth highest in the intelligence test. After Harry was sworn in, a visiting general congratulated him. Then all hell broke loose.

The dossier proved Harry Speakup was officially inducted into the U.S. Army. How could he be removed without revealing the awful fact that he was a chimpanzee?

Solution: a court-martial, because Harry had bitten a sergeant. And Bilko was assigned as defense attorney, so that both men could be booted out of the service.

Before we started filming, I was apprehensive, on guard. Animals can make a monkey out of any actor. Their reactions are not predictable; they have hidden likes and dislikes. And in this show we couldn't stop the cameras except for major errors, like the chimp urinating on me. To complicate matters, I discovered Zippy had a peculiar vice. Sport, the airedale, loved showers; Zippy had an obsessive passion for telephones. Before the show, he picked up the phone in the reception room, and when the receptionist took it to make a call—he bit her. He was really angry about it; she'd taken away his teddy bear. We had to have the girl inoculated against rabies. And Zippy was a ham of the old school: When he heard laughter, he'd repeat or stretch whatever he was doing.

The climax was the court-martial, with the chimp sitting at the table beside Bilko, his counsel. I found that a soft *tsk-tsk-tsk* made the animal lean toward me, as if consulting. So Bilko ad-libbed, "Don't worry, I'll bring that up."

The prop men, in changing the previous scene, had left a telephone on a stand near the courtroom. In the middle of Bilko's impassioned plea to the panel, the chimp spotted the phone. He left his seat and picked up the receiver. This received an immediate laugh, and I had to have a line to explain it.

"I plead for adjournment," I ad-libbed. "My client is calling for a new attorney!"

"The Trial of Harry Speakup" is to my mind the funniest half-hour situation comedy ever done on television. This episode has been repeated over the air more than any single comedy show I can recall.

Another episode called for a man who looked like Doberman. Dobie was chosen, by computer error, as the All-American GI, whose face would appear on recruiting posters. Nobody had a heart to tell those sad sheep eyes that he was a mistake. The Army called on Gen. Iron Guts McGinty, their toughest officer, to do the job. Since the general looked exactly like Dobie, he said, "Nice looking soldier—should be on all the posters."

Our demon casting director found Duane's double in Staten Island: Sailor Jim Williams, a professional strongman who worked in carnivals, pulling army tanks with his teeth. He was delighted to make his debut on television—but he garbled the one line. Throughout rehearsals, it was, "Him a nice soldier, he be ah—eh . . ." or "It's nice for a soldier to look like me." He tried hard, muttering, "Can't understand it—forty years in show business!" As the audience was being seated, Sailor Jim asked me if Mr. Hiken would mind his suggestion. "When I come through the door, when I'm gonna say the line, suppose I come through pulling a tank with my teeth?" In his panic, he clung to the one thing he was sure of—physical strength. When we shot the scene in front of the audience, he delivered his line perfectly.

The Bilko Biggest Pain Award for nonactors could be given to Mike Todd, the whirlwind who had recently produced *Around the World in 80 Days* and married Elizabeth Taylor. He was more unpredictable than the chimp. Bilko's grand design: Persuade Todd (playing Todd) to pay for a round-the-world-in-80-hours tour, presumably to promote Todd's picture. I knew Mike from the racetracks. He had his own obsession, slightly different from Zippy's—phonophilia. If he was separated from a telephone for more than five minutes, his pulse faded out and he saw zeros in front of his eyes.

I explained we had a tight schedule. "I'll be there," he promised. He appeared at the first rehearsals with an entourage. We couldn't get a line out of him; he was on the phone, transferring Belgian francs from Zurich to London, or hiring a cavalry regiment for a picture in Yugoslavia.

Finally, I put my foot down. "Mike, you've got to rehearse."

"Your troubles are over. I gotta fly back to L.A. tonight!"

Our crew built an office set in three hours, and we set up the cameras that night, before his departure. Still he wouldn't rehearse. He clowned on every line. I lost my temper—just the way producer Todd did on his own films. "Godammit, Mike! You're in this business yourself. You know you're costing us overtime!" And I cursed him out, in front of the stagehands and Liz, who was sitting behind a camera on a campstool. He then played Mike Todd as if he'd been doing it for years.

One happy result: Next day, Nat and I realized we'd produced an excellent sequence without an audience. After we got over the shock, we had the same reaction: Who needs an audience? For three years we'd struggled through the weekly hassle of the warm-ups, nonstop filming in sequence, tension and turmoil because we didn't want to look silly in front of an audience. From then on we shot each scene separately, including the closeups, out of sequence. It was much easier. And we could swear at each other as much as we wanted.

Every week the filmed episode was taken to an Army installation near New York by one of the enterprising men from the platoon, Tige Andrews or Mickey Freeman. (I called little Mickey "But Sarge" because, if he didn't speak in the episode that week, he'd manage to toss in a, "But, Sarge . . ." Speaking one line raised his salary and rerun rate.) A sound man suspended microphones over the GI audience and, as the film rolled, recorded their laughter. It was genuine, not the canned laugh tracks used at the time, and the response was very much the same as an audience seeing it live.

When the foundation of a show is right, anything you do

is right and nothing can stop the momentum. I was on top of the television world—everything was going my way. Evelyn, of course, tried to tout me off gambling, but . . .

Bilko made me an international celebrity. What affection, what recognition a half hour on American TV can arouse. The BBC also telecast it for the British Isles. I had spent thirty-five years in vaudeville, burlesque, twenty movies, nightclubs and two hit stage musicals. *Really?* Who knew it? When I walked up Broadway now it was, "Hello, Sarge! . . . Hey, Bilko—sign my book!"

I'm ambivalent about fans. They're euphoria and affection and, God knows, if they ever stop asking for autographs, I'll be out of business. But they can invade your life. Since Bilko was brassy and bouncing, they assumed I had a tough hide. They grabbed me, they poked. They yanked my tie and clutched my arm. When Evelyn was on my arm, they grabbed at her, too. I couldn't escape: The horn-rim goggles and gleaming pate were beyond camouflage. To say I didn't enjoy this recognition would be denying the very impulse that made me want to be an actor. But I do have a sense of dignity and sometimes they went too far.

Last year I was walking up Fifth Avenue, across from Central Park. A soberly-dressed couple, walking downtown, planted themselves in my way. The little white-haired husband cried out, "Blimey, it's Bilko!" in impeccable Cockney—fifteen years after Bilko went off the air in England. The woman quickly took hold of my arm, and as I continued uptown, the man uncorked the lens of a 16-mm. movie camera. Walking backwards, he recorded The Missus and Bilko out for a stroll. And not one cent for residuals.

I managed to keep my perspective. Helped by a fan I met early in the Bilko run.

(On the sidewalk, East 48th Street: I'm walking west when a tight-collared, ramrod-stiff gentleman—a lawyer? a retired colonel?—approaches me.)
GENTLEMAN: *"I beg your pardon, Mr. Silvers. I just*

*wanted to thank you for the moments of pleasure you
have given me."*

ME: *"Thank you very much."*

GENTLEMAN: *"Your timing has such finesse, it's a delight
to watch."*

ME: *"Thank you again. (Now I'm curious.) You watch
the Bilko show?"*

GENTLEMAN: *"What?"*

ME: *"The Army comedy. On TV."*

GENTLEMAN: *"No, I don't have much patience for TV
anymore."*

ME: *"Possibly you saw me on the stage. Top Banana?"*

GENTLEMAN: *"I'm afraid stage shows are much too
expensive."*

ME *(it's a long shot, but I have to know):* *"Perhaps you
were a burlesque fan?"*

GENTLEMAN: *"Good heavens! Were you in burlesque?"*

ME: *"I'd really like to know, sir. Where did I entertain
you?"*

GENTLEMAN *(delighted):* *"On 'Leave It to the Girls.' "*

ME *(baffled):* *"What's that?"*

GENTLEMAN: *"You were on the panel with Maggie
McNellis."*

ME *(still blank):* *"Where?"*

GENTLEMAN: *"Don't you remember? Channel five.
Sponsored by Ex-Lax."*

Bilko brought me friends I never knew I had. Long-lost
street pals from Brooklyn, lost relatives. And somebody I've
never seen, whose name I'll never know.

In the middle 1950's, black soldiers were finally being integrated into the U.S. Army. So we had black soldiers on our
show. P. Jay Sidney was a regular, Private Palmer. Billie Allen
played a WAC. Terry Carter, Bill Gunn and others appeared
frequently. Nat and I heard a few little murmurs from the
agency people: Winston-Salem is down in North Carolina,
you know . . . those dark faces cloud up the show. We ignored them. Our platoon had to look genuine, otherwise the
audience would never believe the farce comedy.

This had a feedback a dozen years later. I was playing in *How the Other Half Loves* on Broadway, and my agent took me to dinner after a performance.

> *(Sidewalk, midtown: Shortly before midnight.)*
> AGENT: *"Let me give you a lift."*
> ME: *"No, I like to walk after a show. Walk off the tenseness."*
> AGENT: *"You've been away a long time. Nobody walks in New York now."*
> ME: *"Ah, come on . . ."*
> *(I walk up Park Avenue to 82nd, cross to Madison, down to 79th, and turn back toward Park. As I walk downtown, something cold and hard is pushed into my neck.)*
> A VOICE *(soft, a drawl but edgy):* *"You make a move, you're dead."*
> ME *(petrified; the most perilous moment of my life; trying to keep my voice calm):* *"Yes, yes, but please don't get panicky. I have five children. My money's in my right-hand pocket. Take it. And my watch. I won't say a word."*
> *(Long pause.)*
> A VOICE: *"You Bilko?"*
> ME *(exhaling):* *"Yes, I'm Phil Silvers."*
> THE VOICE: *"You're all right. Other pigs bastards. You were good to my people. Give me five minutes. Don't move."*
> *(He disappears. I wait and then hail a cab. When I get to my suite, I retch for three minutes.)*

I think I recognized the voice. It was a black extra we had once hired. I'm no do-gooder, but I certainly got paid off that night.

The BBC telecast Bilko two years after we were seen in the U.S. Coming only about a dozen years after the American armies had landed in England to prepare the invasion of Europe, Bilko was received as the Second Coming. In Ireland

and Scotland, too. He must have represented what the British liked to believe were real Americans—brash. Soon, over 75 percent of my fan mail arrived with United Kingdom stamps. In our fourth year the BBC decided it was time to invite me over, for a bit on their variety show and a formal interview.

It was a splendid vacation.

I went with Evelyn to London by way of Rome and Paris. While she shopped, I wandered around the Via Veneto—where I walked face-on into Robert Alda. He'd starred in the movie, *The Gershwin Story,* and *Guys and Dolls* on stage, and he was now married to an Italian countess. When I knew him at the Gaiety burlesque, he was the "tit serenader." He sang "A Pretty Girl Is Like a Melody" while the showgirls paraded into position to expose their charms.

My mind flicked back a quarter of a century to a night on which Bob introduced a beautiful stripper, a former Ziegfeld girl who had taken the name Charmaine:

"Mr. Harold Minsky proudly presents the lovely charms of the inimitable, delicious Char . . . maine! . . ."

As she paraded out slowly, an entranced voice called from the audience, "If that's chow mein, I'll eat it."

Coming off the plane in London, I was surprised by the full media reception: BBC television and radio, newspapers, magazine writers. Bilko Arrives! Evelyn later had a solo interview. I am an Anglophile. Not only is the country green and clean, it's so small that whatever they have is beautifully manicured. And the people are, in one word, civilized. I suppose my love dates from my early years of knocking around the stage, admiring the diction and polish of the British actors. Evelyn covered Regent Street and Harrod's; I did the rest of the town. Particularly Hyde Park, for the best histrionics in the world. Those speakers are performers: what a flow of improvisation; how they can color and embroider the language—all protected by a bored bobby. The black Marxist demanding freedom for Northern Ireland; the pinched little Irish radical, demanding freedom for sex, to do whatever to whomever he wished. The

Arab demanding the destruction of Israel and "all Zionist Jews." I couldn't believe it. This was a little too civilized. I pressed into the middle of the crowd, and I sensed they were with him. A nervous hum, waiting for an explosion. A bulky man moved closer to me, and on the other side a Trench Coat jostled me. After years of playing in firetraps, I have a habit of looking for an exit whenever I enter a crowded room, a hall, a racetrack. I figured this exit would be to slug the Trench Coat and cross fast to the bobby. The Trench Coat nudged me: "We don't want anything to happen to Bilko here, do we?" And like two sheep dogs, he and his partner opened a way out of the crowd. They were London detectives . . . "And would you mind an autograph for the kiddies?"

I had to see a cricket match. My escort from the BBC reluctantly took me to an England-India encounter at Lord's, the most important match of the year. British reticence is at its best in cricket; I could barely hear the discreet "ahhhs" and "well-played" from the gentlemen around me. We sat in a section reserved for Lord's Taverners, an esteemed society for the encouragement of the game. Directly behind me, in the broadcasting booth, the BBC's equivalent of Mel Allen relayed the high points, but in one long murmur, like a slow tobacco auctioneer. My escort whispered a crawling commentary; I managed to grasp the fundamentals in half an hour. It's based on the aristocratic principle: Work hard, play fair, play the game and play it for weeks—you have a lifetime to kill.

The BBC announcer joined us with a patronizing, "How is Bilko enjoying this dull game?"

I suggested he was dulling it considerably. "Here's how an American announcer would do it." And I called the game into his ear: "Krishna is at bat. He's up to forty-two runs. Good God! *There goes a sixer!* . . ."

I was putting BBC on—but they put me on. The announcer said, "Would you care to do that for us?" Fair enough.

I was introduced as a "well-known sergeant-major, who will describe the match, as if broadcast by an American announcer."

The venerable Lord's Taverners turned on the broadcasting

booth as if someone was desecrating religion. Then they saw it was me and everyone relaxed. "Oh well, it's Bilko. We all know he's balmy." And indignation turned to smiles.

I am an inveterate walker, and as I strolled the streets of London, cabbies and various other people yelled to me, "Loved you on the telly," "First time we enjoyed the cricket match," "Jolly good, Bilko."

On the afternoon of my departure, a delegation of Lord's Taverners called at our hotel to induct me into their society. I received a tie with the Taverners' colors, and signed their registration book. This indeed was an honor. I took the liberty of thumbing through the pages of the book and saw among the historic names Sir Winston Churchill. It was a treasured book to the Lord's Taverners, of which I am still a member.

When I received word that my old friend William McCormack, Jr., was studying for the priesthood, it was no surprise to me. I guess he always knew he was heading that way. Although he was heir to millions of dollars, the only expression of his wealth was giving a yearly dinner in the upstairs room of Toots Shor's for the New York Rangers hockey team—who, as I recall, never finished better than fifth or sixth place. I corresponded with him in upper New York State when he was studying for the priesthood and sent him two or three cans of film of Bilko episodes, which he and the others enjoyed.

Bill invited me to the seminary for his ordination, a high moment in a young priest's life. As a matter of fact, it cost me half a day's shooting of a Bilko episode to attend the ceremony. But I wouldn't have missed it for the world. Bill did what you're supposed to do perfectly, it seemed to me, but there was an old bishop watching every move. I smiled to myself. "Well, now you know what it was like for me at the Copa opening night."

After the ordination, the young priest changed into his clerical garment and people lined up at the rail to receive the first blessing of the new priest. This is considered good luck. The crowd held back, to permit his mother and father to be the first two at the rail. Then the long procession began. I got in line too. I knelt at the rail, and when Bill recognized me, his eyes moistened up. He held my hand and said, "Phil, you came. I'll pray for you."

I said, "Never mind me. Pray for the Rangers. They're on a losing streak again."

He managed to keep from breaking up in front of the bishop.

I was instrumental in putting together a pilot television show for a new young comic who I thought was great. His name— Alan King. We were in rehearsal prior to shooting. I called Father Bill and asked him if he would like to see the actual shooting.

"Very interesting," he said. "When?"

"I'll call you back and give you the exact time."

The rest of this episode was related to me by Father Bill. The phone rang five minutes later. He lifted the receiver with positive assurance that it was me calling. He said, "Father Bill here, rockin' and rollin', swingin' and swayin'. Lay it on me, Phil baby."

A voice at the other end said: "This is Cardinal Spellman." Bill knew *that* voice. "I want to see you in my office as soon as possible."

Father Bill told me he flew his car from City Island to 451 Madison Avenue in ten minutes.

The cardinal had merely called a group of young priests in, to inform them of a tour he wanted them to make in the Far East. After the other priests left, Bill lingered behind and said, "Your Eminence, I believe I have to explain my behavior on the phone." He then revealed he'd been expecting a call from me. The cardinal smiled. "Yes, that Bilko is naughty, isn't he?"

The priest visited my home many times and was, of course, always addressed as Father Bill. This confused my little girls, who called him Daddy.

Several years later he was assigned as assistant to Cardinal Spellman. As a matter of fact, he had the desk immediately outside the cardinal's office. On my way to Belmont racetrack, I stopped in to say hello, but he wasn't at his desk. One of the young ladies said, "He'll be right back." When he returned, he found a strange man sitting in his chair, his face covered with the Racing Form. There was a slight gasp. I pulled the papers down from my face and said, "Well, you're in touch with the Main Man. Who's going to win the first race?"

The Bilko show was hard, grinding work. A new script every week with three days of rehearsal; Thursday, setting the camera shots; Friday morning, a runthrough; and then the filming.

In the first year, a friend of Nat's, a young writer, died of a heart attack. Nat said, "They're not going to kill me." At the end of that season he turned over the head writing position to his assistant, Billy Friedberg. We had about four pairs of writers, among them A. J. Russell, Sidney Zelinka, Danny and Doc (Neil) Simon, and Aaron Ruben, who later became our director. Nat still okayed their outlines, and reworked, cut and polished their scripts. In 1957 Nat relinquished the producer's job and sold his interest in the show to CBS.

Early in 1959, CBS canceled the show without telling me first; at the height of our ratings. The corporation had two good—for them—reasons. Both of them were money. Most situation comedies had four or five regulars, with occasional guests. Our basic cast started with twenty-two actors, most of them under contract. Hollywood production costs were zooming up, up. Each half hour cost as much as half of a feature movie. The other, most important reason: CBS wanted to cash in its chips—144 episodes—while Bilko was still hot. They sold our earliest series to NBC for daytime viewing for $2 million. In addition to the British Isles, Bilko eventually played Australia, Argentina and France, where I became known as Pepe le Bilko. Bilko died on CBS September 11, 1959, exactly four years from our debut.

My brother Harry died in August. We'd had our arguments; I often resented him, trying to smother my freedom like a father. Still, we had been close, propping each other up in our troubles. His death came as a blow. I heard of his seizure after

I came home at midnight from the press agents' gin game. I hurried over to the hospital to find my three older brothers huddled in a corridor. A young doctor told us, "Your brother has gone. Would you like to say farewell?" But when we got to his room it was like a 1940 B movie horror. Harry was not dead. He was sitting up in bed, his eyes glazed, while two interns applied electric shocks to keep him alive. A nurse wiped the sweat off his brow. The terrible thing was his stare—straight at me. Reproaching me, I thought, for playing cards while he was dying, and now I was just standing there, unable to help him. Once again I was overwhelmed by guilt. He died a few minutes later.

I relived this moment many times in the following years. Doctors assured me the best of modern science could not have helped Harry, and he could not have seen me—he was drowning in his own edema. Yet his face haunted me a long time. I had watched Rags die, and now my brother. I was emotionally bankrupt. I broke down and wept at his funeral.

The Bilko series was the top of my career. I felt I'd now come to a break in my life. A hiatus. Time to rethink and regroup. I was only forty-eight. Where could I go from here?

I plunged into several hour-long TV specials. "Just Polly and Me," music and fun with Polly Bergen, wife of Freddie Fields and my favorite woman—next to Evelyn. "The Slowest Gun in the West;" I was the spineless sheriff of Primrose, Arizona, outfumbling the one man in the West who was yellower than I—Chicken Finsterwald, alias Jack Benny. Nat Hiken created "Summer in New York," a delightful musical variety with the two Carols: Haney and Lawrence. These specials were a little ahead of their time, and each displayed the special comic inventiveness of their creator, Nat Hiken. Still, I felt flat, unused. I was yearning for a stage show.

Three friends came up with a project. Larry Gelbart and Burt Shevelove were writing a musical, with music and lyrics by Steve Sondheim, based on characters and situations out of the 2,000-year-old Roman comedies by Plautus. Old Plautus understood a farce situation; some of his gimmicks were used by Shakespeare and Minsky's circuit. Still, I thought, the musical version was too precious, too artsy. It was to be called *A Funny Thing Happened on the Way to the Forum.*

I didn't want to hurt my friends' feelings with a rejection, so I quickly got involved in a musical by Garson Kanin.

CHAPTER 14

Swimming Pools and Deep Waters

Do Re Mi originated in a short story by Garson Kanin, who
interested me in it. Jule Styne was composer; Betty Comden
and Adolph Green were lyricists. This was top drawer. At one
of our meetings at Garson's home, David Merrick arrived and
said, "I don't know what this show is all about, but I've got to
be part of it." There was some friction between the people involved and Merrick because of an earlier unhappy experience,
but cool heads prevailed. We decided, since Merrick was always in action on Broadway, we would get the best theater
and the best rates from the stagehands. He became our producer.

At our rehearsals, far back in the house, sat one of the great
ladies of the theater, Garson Kanin's wife, Ruth Gordon. While
she had nothing to do with the show, I am sure they conferred
constantly.

The rehearsals became more like a civil war than theater.
Jule Styne would order costumes, and Comden and Green
would infringe on Garson's directions to the actors. It was a
lovely show and one of my favorite roles, but the formation of
it was full of tension and anger. At many rehearsals, while I
waited to make my entrance, one of the civil wars would
break out and there I'd stand—the star in the wings waiting to
get on. I evolved a little gimmick to relieve the tension. I would
lean out the proscenium making the OK sign with my fore-
finger and thumb, and yell to Miss Gordon sitting far in the
back, "Going well, isn't it?"—the exact words I used years later
when I wired congratulations on her winning an Academy
Award for best supporting actress.

Opening night in Boston was a disaster. The Colonial Theater, an old lady of a theater and full of tradition, still used sandbags for counterweights. You can imagine how confident it made me feel to have sand dripping on me, wondering when the whole sandbag was coming down. The second-act curtain went up but not all the way—about two-thirds.

None of this was conducive to a relaxed and enjoyable evening in the theater. The critics were understanding, however; they saw its potential. We had a rousing, swinging pop score; one of the songs, "Make Someone Happy," is now a standard. The dancing was fluid and exciting, and Nancy Walker and I did some of the best work we'd ever done in the theater.

Jule Styne and Comden and Green injected a last-minute soliloquy for me to do about two minutes before the final curtain. It was called "All of My Life." I reviewed the stupid values that I thought were important: knowing the mob, front-row table at the Copacabana, etc. It was my first foray into something deeply dramatic. Every night that I did it, I broke into tears, all planned theatrically. There must have been something very right about it because it stunned the audience. We were never greeted at the finale bows by hordes of theatergoers running for their last-minute bus or train to Scarsdale. They sat in their seats.

I managed to create the same emotional collapse during the entire run and subsequent road tour. I would start preparing about the beginning of the second act. I'd think of a sick child, my brother's look as he was dying, other grim things I had stored up like a reservoir, so that when I came to the breakdown, I would call on these subconscious memories. Maybe Lee Strasberg was right—maybe I *am* a Method actor.

We opened in New York the day after Christmas, 1960, to mainly happy reviews. Walter Kerr, in the *Herald Tribune*, made it a personal valentine: ". . . To watch Mr. Silvers make for the portals like a drum majorette who has lately taken to marijuana is—quite simply—to live again.

"There's a lot of Ed Wynn in him, and a bit of Harold Lloyd, and a bit of Leon Errol, and a bit of Bugs Bunny (his cheeks chock-full of the most flavorsome nuts), plus a whole lot of the Mr. Silvers who is the only man left alive who can do all this, and, if you don't mind my saying so—hooray."

We seemed to be set for a long run, even surpassing "Top Banana."

I came home to a surprise party: Nancey and Tracey in their party dresses, champagne in a cooler, and our doctor proudly displaying X rays. Evelyn was carrying twins. They'd caused her pains beyond the ordinary call of duty.

The doctor cautioned her to stay in bed, be a queen bee, to help the babies reach normal weight. She cooperated. Except for occasional nights when I was working, she stepped out to another apartment in our building, to play low-stake poker with Comden and Green and Sydney Chaplin. Friday night, after one of those games, the intense labor pains arrived. Evelyn's mother, who had come up from Florida for the occasion, helped Evelyn dress. And in the midst of my calling the doctor, and checking a car and driver, which I had standing by to rush Evelyn to the hospital, Mrs. Patrick asked me if her hat looked right.

I reached the theater for the matinee with no sleep at all. The chorus kids had hung up little doll twins on my dressing room door, sprigs of flowers, cheery notes. We were a happy company, and this was a manifestation of it. However, I called the stage manager and said, "I have a peculiar weakness. When I haven't slept, I'm very susceptible to tears. I cry at Wallace Beery pictures. I know the kids in the show love me and want to express their happiness to me. Please tell everyone to stay away from me or I'll break down in tears. At the end of the matinee we'll have a ball." The whole company adhered to this, but there's always that one guy you never figure on.

In the finale, after we had all lined up for our bows, I would nod to the orchestra leader, get a key note from the trombonist and reprise the beginning of the last thirty-two bars of our hit song, "Make Someone Happy." I got as far as the first five words when our juvenile lead, John Reardon, sneaked offstage, put on a doctor's white coat, came back on and deposited two rubber dolls in my arms. That took care of that finale. I collapsed in tears. Happy tears. Curtain.

It was a wonderful, happy, tear-filled day. After the matinee there were hordes of ladies waiting, waving and shouting lovely things to me. I guess there's something about a man who's just had twins that reaches women. I don't know why, I didn't do anything different.

I hurried over to see Evelyn, and she was crying. Our first-born twin, Cathy, who came a minute and a half before Candy, had a nose like Pinocchio. I told Evelyn we'd just have to love her more, and when she grew up, she could have the nose straightened. The doctor straightened us out. It was only a bruise; the second baby was in such a hurry to be born she kicked Cathy. In a few days she had a beautiful thumbnail nose.

I'd met Mrs. Joseph P. Kennedy, mother of the President, at a small dinner party given by Ed Sullivan. She told me Jack became a Bilko fan after he underwent operations in 1955 to correct a spinal injury he received in the war. He would watch on a portable TV set as he lay on his stomach.

So I looked forward to meeting the President after he decided, on a moment's notice, to see *Do Re Mi*. The President arrived at the theater just before the overture, I was told, with Pierre Salinger, Arthur M. Schlesinger Jr., and others. He excused himself and went to the men's room. There was one man in there, a cousin of my publicity agent.

> COUSIN: *"I'm standing there, at the urinal, and next to me is the President of the United States. I thought I'd flip. When I looked at him, a little bewildered, he smiled at me, as if to say, 'Yes, it's me.' Then I said, 'Mr. President, my daughter won't believe this. May I have your autograph?'*
>
> *"And President Kennedy said, 'Don't you think we'd better wait till we're both finished?' "*

At intermission I was told the President was coming backstage to meet the cast. My dresser and I quickly tidied up the place. Then I heard that a group of priests from the audience

had converged on him in the lobby, for greetings and auto-
graphs. The President leaned over to Salinger and whispered,
"I wish they wouldn't do this now. I give them my business on
Sunday."

Then the intermission buzzer rang, and that's how I never
met President Kennedy.

My children discovered the theater was a magical place.
When Tracey was about four, she came to the *Do Re Mi* rehearsals with me. She sat silent and enthralled, her white-
gloved hands folded in her lap. Garson Kanin at one moment
discussed a line with Ruth in the last row. Tracey turned
around and said, severely, "Sssh. Quiet, please."

Nancey, about two and one-half, came in occasionally with
Evelyn for a quick look from the rear of the St. James. Then
Evelyn decided it was time to accustom the child to a complete show. The only vacant seats for that performance were in
a box.

My first entrance came in the middle of a crowded nightclub. I was pushed around, looking for my wife and a good
table. As I peered into the half-dark for Nancy Walker, a bright
voice piped up from out front, "Daddy, there's a seat up here!"
That was the end of little Nancey's debut as part of the audience.

About eight months after we opened, my barber, clipping
away in the dressing room, remarked, "I hear the show's
moving to 54th Street."

Nobody had told me, and my contract specified that the
show could not be moved to a theater with a small seating
capacity. The 54th Street Theater was far out of the theater
district. A jinx house. David Merrick was playing musical
chairs, just as Lee Shubert had tried with *High Button Shoes*.
David wanted to move us out of the St. James, a prime location,
to bring in another of his shows.

I couldn't stop him. The renegotiated contract permitted
him to move us in return for a hefty increase in my percentage

for the six weeks on the road—15 percent of the gross. This deal massaged Merrick's ego and mine, but it did not help the show. Business dropped off steadily after we moved to 54th Street. We closed January 13, 1962, after 400 performances, enough to label it a hit. It could have run on and on.

Freddie Fields had made arrangements for another television series that I would control completely: 100 percent of the ownership. That was irresistible. Since the series had to be made on the West Coast, we packed up our entire household and moved to a rented home in Beverly Hills, until I could find one to buy. A house was very important to me: I was fifty years old and I'd never owned one.

The series was titled, inescapably, "The New Phil Silvers Show," and it was the old Bilko in civilian clothes. I was Harry Grafton, foreman of the maintenance section of a factory, who is surrounded by a group of con men, malcontents and malingerers. Like Bilko fighting the Pentagon, Grafton conspired against the factory owner. We had some of the best writers— A. J. Russell and Danny Simon, among others—and an experienced producer-director, Rod Amateau. I felt very confident.

While the scripts and pilot were being written, I went to work on *40 Pounds of Trouble*, with Tony Curtis. It was a rather witless remake of the charming Damon Runyon fable, *Little Miss Marker,* which introduced Shirley Temple. Tony played the manager of a Nevada gambling club who finds himself custodian of a little girl. I played a Runyon type. Much of it was shot at Harrah's Club at Lake Tahoe.

The only memorable scene I remember on location was subbing for Danny Kaye at Bill Harrah's casino. The room was jammed, and Kaye suddenly took ill. The management asked me to step in, with about 15 minutes notice. I borrowed a shirt and tie from a local fireman, a clarinet from the band, and went on for an hour. It was one of those evenings when I was in full control; I could do no wrong. Bill Harrah is notoriously generous to his performers—he once gave Jack Benny a Rolls. He gave me a pair of golf shoes, from which I got blisters.

Then I signed on with Stanley Kramer for *It's a Mad, Mad, Mad, Mad World*. This started as fun and games. Stanley had rounded up every comedian who could stand on two feet: Jerry Lewis, Sid Caesar, Terry-Thomas, Ben Blue, Edward Everett Horton, Buddy Hackett, Jack Benny, Ethel Merman, Jonathan Winters, Mickey Rooney. We filmed in Palm Springs in July, so there would be no traffic, and the reason there was no traffic was the 110-degree heat. Only mad dogs and comedians go out in that midday sun. The clowning off-camera was madder than the scenes on. Jonathan Winters was never himself: One day he was an African explorer, next day he was a German colonel. He's the greatest improvisationist I've ever seen. Mickey Rooney was in a tree, doing *Bridge on the River Kwai*. Everybody was doing bits. Except Sid Caesar: He sat in the shade and watched the show.

We moved to Long Beach for a street scene in which a group of us ran into a loft building, led by a double for Spencer Tracy. His health was fading; except for closeups, a man in a rubber mask appeared for Tracy in action scenes. The run was about forty yards. I ran ten yards when I felt an excruciating pain in my groin. I dropped to the street. Merman started to cry because it looked like a heart attack. Buddy Hackett's immediate diagnosis was, "Pulled muscle. Terrible pain, but not serious."

The doctors at Long Beach Hospital agreed. They could not understand, though, why my blood pressure read like my income tax. When my personal physician, Dr. Clarence Agress, tested me, the pressure was normal. As a result of that report by the hospital, I could not get insurance for the television series. If a stranger takes my pressure, it shoots up into the stratosphere; if Dr. Agress measures it, I have the numbers of a twenty-five-year-old. My normal neuroticism.

Life in Hollywood had pleasures that escaped me when I was there before. The children were growing up, and there were clean sidewalks and grass on which to walk with them. The grass *is* greener in Beverly Hills—they use a mulch of old twenty-dollar bills. I had time and a pool in which to play with the children. For an unreconstructed bachelor like me, they became a joy.

The kids were not impressed by Daddy's appearance on the Bilko reruns in the afternoons. To them, the title of the show was "Daddy and the Dirty Men." Their attention span for Bilko was about two minutes. Of course, when they met Milton Berle, they leaped to the moon. They spared me the shame of asking for his autograph because they were too young to know what that was.

To amuse the little darlings, I drew cartoons. "Make me a mommy," Nancey ordered, and I came up with a circle, two eyes and a scrawl of hair. For "make me a daddy," I drew the same circle and heavy glasses. I walked to school with Tracey, Nancey and the twins so that Tracey could meet her new teacher in kindergarten. The eighth-graders, dashing out for lunch, gathered around me for autographs. *They* knew me. Now my children were thrilled. Daddy was somebody. As I signed the notebooks, Nancey nudged Tracey, with a little tinge of pride: "Look—he's making them a mommy."

Art Linkletter booked Nancey on his TV show, just when her front teeth had been pulled out because of an infection. Nothing bothered her.

> ART: *"And what is your name?"*
> NANCY: *"Nanthy Thilvers."*
> ART: *"Oh—Silvers. What's your daddy's name?"*
> NANCY: *"Thergeant Bilko, thilly."*
> ART: *"Where is your mother? Is she with you?"*
> NANCY: *"Oh, no. (Looking grim.) She's thick again."*
> ART: *"You mean sick? (Quickly, afraid he's hit a bad note.) I'm sorry to hear that."*
> NANCY (*shrugging casually*): *"Ith the thame old thing."*
> ART (*bewildered*): *"What same old thing?"*
> NANCY: *"She's got a baby in her bunny."*

Six months later, I drove her to the dentist, up Santa Monica Boulevard. Tourists waved to me as they passed by. "Look,

Daddy," Nancey said. "They all saw me on the Linkletter Show."

Already a ham at the age of five.

The baby in the bunny was our fifth, Laury, who was born on the day Nancey had her birthday party. Nancey did not mind one more sister, but she did object to her having the same birthday. "It's not fair—I got here first!"

Shortly after that, Evelyn suffered internal bleeding and had to be rushed back to the hospital. Cathy, one of the twins, was two and one-half and talked like a Dutch comedian because she picked up most of her English from our nurse, Anna, who had a German accent. When Cathy saw the ambulance, she demanded to know, "Vy iss here de krankenwagen?"

The doctor informed us that Evelyn's ailment was simply too many children—five in seven years. She and I agreed that we had both been overbearing. Luckily, we did not have to explain this to Cathy.

Our nurse made the same formal announcement every week: "I take the day off." Now, Evelyn and I were very careful in our choice of what our children should see on television, especially the days following the assassination of President Kennedy. On the afternoon that Lee Harvey Oswald was shot in full view of millions of television viewers, our youngest twin, Cathy, slipped unnoticed into the room where we were watching. She saw the shooting. She was unable to comprehend what was actually happening, but instinctively she knew it was something horrible. From the lips of a two-and-one-half-year-old child came the most astute observation of the time we were living in: "De whole vorld iss shtupid. I take the day off." Exit.

The children changed me. For one thing, they made a swimmer out of me. Ever since my father had thrown me into the water at the Turkish bath in Brownsville, I had a morbid fear of water. And I never had a chance to overcome it. My childhood exercise was milking the audience for applause. When I played Las Vegas in the heat of the summer, I used to hang around the pool. If no one was looking, I'd climb down the ladder into the water, dunk my head, and climb out again. I never dived.

Well, Evelyn, a native of Florida, had luxuriated in water all her life. She brought in a swimming teacher, Mrs. Fenney, an ample contemporary of Gertrude Ederle, and the children soon turned into fish. Evelyn established one rule, which we all had to take a blood oath to obey. Nobody goes into the pool alone. The penalty: barred from the water for a month.

I awoke one night with a tremor: What if Evelyn was not at the pool and one of the children was in trouble? I couldn't even dive in.

When I was gambling and I lost, I never told myself you'll have another chance tomorrow. Maybe your bad luck will warm up. No, I had to get even that night. Well, the entire house was asleep. I turned on the pool lights and paced around the water. I had to do it *now*.

I stood at the diving board for what seemed like an eternity, but I finally dived in.

I plunged in again. Exhilarated, I pushed off for the other end of the pool. Splashing, thrashing, but I was moving. And I made it. That was for Tracey. I took some deep breaths and set out for the other end. For Nancey. And two more, for the twins. And Laury . . .

I completed five lengths.

Evelyn was delighted, and barred me for a month.

"The New Phil Silvers Show" opened on the CBS network September 28, 1963. After a few weeks it was clear that I owned 100 percent of a sinking ship. Some episodes were as colorful and electric as the best of the Bilkos. Still, in television if you don't make your ratings in the first eight weeks, you're doomed. Harry Grafton had a fundamental flaw: The audience was not rooting for him. Bilko was an underdog—Grafton was not. In a small factory, the real underdog is the *owner*. He's the one who has to cope with union rules and strikes, laziness, absenteeism, defective workmanship, theft, rising taxes and falling sales. This never occurred to us. We received resentful letters from workingmen: "Why the hell is Grafton horsing around? He's got a good job." "If he doesn't shape up, all the guys will be out of work."

James T. Aubrey, production chief of CBS, came out to Hollywood with his entourage to see if Grafton could be repaired. We tried desperately. We agreed Harry would have a family—his widowed sister and her two children—and gradually he would be eased out of the factory into a family sitcom. Aubrey renewed the series for another thirteen weeks. There was no hope. Grafton and his pals were thrown out of work on June 27, 1964.

The musical shows I played had been hammered and shined into hits through reworking. Almost recycling. You can't do that with movies or television; once the audience sees your show, it's out of your hands. And if the beginning premise is wrong, the most brilliant show doctors in America cannot save you.

All the while I was building a nest for the family. We bought a house in Beverly Hills, a block away from an excellent public school. I didn't want my children to grow up with the disadvantages of private schools. We knocked down some walls and added extensions, and by the time we finished the nest had cost $375,000. I didn't care. I was happy. At last, I owned a home.

Shortly after that, my real troubles began: a slow slide downhill to emotional and financial depression. A blue-gray period. I had achieved everything I wanted out of life: a lovely wife and children, a home, professional success from which I had a sense of pride and a large income. My troubles started, of course, in a small way.

I have the usual shakes on opening night, but as soon as I am onstage or in front of a camera, nothing can panic me. What unsettles me is physical disability, because then I can't perform. If I can't perform, I'm dead. I have no other way to make a living. This shock hit me after another birthday party. This time Nancey was a guest. It featured a clown in a dusty Pierrot costume. When I arrived to drive Nancey home, the party was still swinging, so I helped the clown blow up balloons.

Next day, Saturday, I took our nurse, Anna, to a movie and

had a drink of cold water from the theater fountain. When we came home, Evelyn was still out, and her mother was in bed with a temperature. I felt feverish myself, and kept away from the children. I went to bed as soon as I could, because I'd promised to do a song routine Sunday for the Screen Writers Guild show. It had been written for the occasion: "The Fiddler and the Nun," in which I, as Tevye, debated Polly Bergen, playing the Nun from *Sound of Music*, on the question of who had the biggest hold on show business. It was an engaging bit of satire, and I wanted to be in good shape for it.

I awoke Sunday morning with a raging fever. And my mother-in-law seemed to be seething with pneumonia. I managed to reach Dr. Agress on the golf course. He examined Mrs. Patrick first, then ordered an ambulance and oxygen for her. He took one look at me and had an instant and correct hunch —thank God for me, Father Bill. "Where have you been?" I told him about the party, blowing the balloons, drinking the water at the movie theater. He thought it was a bacterial infection, and switched the ambulance order—now it was for me. Mrs. Patrick would stay home under an oxygen tent, with day and night nurses.

By now my fever was up to 106, and I blacked out in the ambulance. As I was wheeled into the Cedars of Lebanon Hospital, I saw a visitor who looked like Liz Taylor walking by. I wasn't sure, because I was floating in and out of consciousness. "Hi ya, Liz," I mumbled. She answered, "Hi ya." I must have looked like a bum, with two day's growth of beard. Then, a doubletake, and she recognized me. She ran alongside the stretcher: "Phil, what happened?"

"Get away, Liz. Don't come near me!" One of the few times a man ever brushed off Elizabeth Taylor.

The hospital tests showed I had salmonella paratyphoid. It's a rare thing, and could have been fatal. Evelyn went through a wretched week: me in the hospital and her mother home with double pneumonia, while the house was quarantined.

After my fever cooled off, Dr. Agress said, "It's a shame you never got to perform that number. Brilliant."

"What number?"

"Tevye and the Nun. You did the whole routine in your delirium on the way to the hospital."

Another shock was waiting for me, on the golf course months later.

> *(Approaching the seventeenth green, Hillcrest.)*
> Dr. Agress: *"I suggest you play it a little to the left of the pin."*
> Me: *"Where's the pin?"*
> Dr. Agress: *"Cut the clowning. Don't you see the flag?"*
> Me: *"No. Must be the camouflage in the background."*
> Dr. Agress: *"Phil, it's only ninety yards."*
> Me: *"I can't see it."*

He immediately phoned from the clubhouse to an eye specialist and made an appointment for me the next day. With Dr. Robert Hare, head of eye surgery at St. John's, who has perfect eyesight and great compassion for people with eye problems, a dear man and later a close friend. He told me I was forming a cataract in the left eye. "After it develops, we'll operate. Nothing to be alarmed about. You'll have to wear a contact lens afterward." He thought it would be months before the cataract was operable.

Mel Frank was setting up the film production of *A Funny Thing Happened on the Way to the Forum.* In Spain. Zero Mostel was to repeat his Broadway role. Would I play Lycus, the procurer? I consulted with my eye specialist, who assured me the cataract was a long way from maturity, and I flew to Madrid.

The project started off badly enough. As soon as I unpacked my bags in the Palace Hotel (actors can't stay at the Ritz because of some heinous crime committed by Errol Flynn) I received a phone invitation to lunch from our director, Richard

Lester. Good. I ordered some tea, which arrived cold. Since I don't know Spanish, I picked a word from the Pan Am language booklet. The closest I got to "hot" was "steam" (*vapor*). The waiter nodded, and I went into my shower. When I came out to dress, there was no tea and all my suits had disappeared. The assistant manager explained the waiter had carried my clothes off to be steamed. He lent me an undersized suit, considerably bent. And that's what I wore for my first meeting with my director.

This kind of thing is hard to explain, even to an Englishman. Actually, Lester was born and raised in Philadelphia, but after zooming to success in England, he had a teddibly Old Boy accent. He's a brilliant director of the camera: It swings, it sways, it grinds like Georgia Sothern. Dick is also a very charming man. He persuaded me that I could not wear my glasses—my trademark, which I now needed just to see the camera—because they had not been invented in the time of Plautus. Of course, Stephen Sondheim's music hadn't been invented, either. Two weeks into the shooting, I was blind in the left eye. Literally. The cataract closed off my vision. It created irritation and anxieties. I bumped into furniture and felt like an idiot when I missed my marks for the camera. I phoned my doctor in California. He assured me that in his forty years of practice he had not heard of a cataract developing that quickly. He encouraged me to hang on, and the minute I came home he would operate.

A retired American Army colonel kept me from disintegrating. His wartime back injury and my eye gave us a common bond, and he introduced me to the steam bath at an American airbase near Madrid. The soothing *vapor* made me feel at home.

There was an elaborate dinner to honor Jack Benny, at which my pulsations broke out again, as if I was on the road with *Top Banana*. I looked for a way to ease myself out without disturbing the party. Just then an aristocratic Spanish woman, sitting next to me, confessed she was pregnant and needed fresh air. We teamed up for a strange kind of invalids' balancing act, supporting each other out to the terrace. The sultry Spanish air improved her—not me. She instructed her chauffeur to drive me to an American doctor. Sure enough, my blood pressure was flying high. The good doctor hadn't talked to an American in months, so we had to have some drinks. Then my pressure went back to normal.

Evelyn came for a visit. I wanted it to be a carefree vacation for her, so I said nothing about my blindness. The pulsations continued. She found a highly-recommended Spanish physician who arrived half-soused. I was alone and the gentleman's English was as numb as my Spanish. He made a short visual examination: pointing to my mouth, he commanded, "Breathe!" I gathered he was telling me, "Let me smell your breath and I'll tell you what's wrong." He couldn't smell my fever, and I certainly didn't want to smell his breath, so we had a few drinks. He forgot all about my troubles.

Madrileno social life starts about midnight; that's when I had to be asleep, to be alive for the next day's shooting. You're swept up in the flamenco and the sangria, and one couple always had to go on to the *tasca* that has the best *tapas* in town. So Evelyn spent a lot of her late nights with English and American friends of the colonel.

The filming didn't help my state of mind either. Dick Lester was so busy shooting chariot races and richly colored backgrounds that he found little time for the musical numbers. Jack Gilford and I worked out the staging for "Everybody Ought to Have a Maid." Dick shot it in several takes, then went back to his chariot races.

With one eye out of commission, I could not judge depth or distance accurately. I stumbled through an acrobatic sequence, where I was photographed swinging on a rope from the ledge of a porch forty feet high and falling into a pool. Actually, a stunt man swung on the rope; I appeared at the beginning and end of the stunt in matchup shots. I dropped into the pool from a height of two feet. The matching shot for the start of the swing required me to swing out a few feet from the porch— which was still forty feet up. I asked Evelyn, who was on the set, not to watch me, but she couldn't resist. I did it perfectly. Then the camera and crews swung over to another scene. I stood up on the ledge, frozen—a rerun of the acrophobia that seized me in the ferris wheel sequence in *My Gal Sal*. I could not bring myself to come down the narrow escape ladder. Evelyn stared up at me, puzzled, then frightened.

One man in the entire company saw, and understood, my torture. Bob Simmons, a tough British ex-commando, the second unit director who staged the stunts. He was the daredevil in *Guns of Navarone* who leaped off a cliff 180 feet into the sea. Bob climbed up the ladder and talked quietly to me, for what must have been fifteen minutes, to relax me and give me confidence. It was a calm, earnest recital of the strange fears that overcame even the most experienced stunt artists. They all froze at the least expected moment, he said. He was going to walk down the ladder, one step below me, so that his arms would protect me from falling. I closed my eyes and did it. Then I broke out into welts, exactly like the ones that hit me after the ferris wheel rescue.

My series of shocks was caused by tension, neuroses, childish fears and a genuine loss of vision, all completely logical and adding up to as much sense as the "one-banana, two-banana" bit. One fear fed another, and I could not break the cycle.

After a day of inner debate, I decided, what the hell, we'd been married for seven years and had five children together . . . it was time to break through the protective cocoon I had wrapped around Evelyn. She had to share my troubles as well as my joys.

I sat with her on the edge of the bed and said, "Look."

She looked into my eye and, for the first time, saw the pearly film covering the pupil. She lay back on the bed and cried. She understood now, she said. She knew what I had gone through. Shortly after that, she had to return to Beverly Hills because of the children. I had hoped she would stay longer. I was there alone for four more weeks.

CHAPTER 15

The Tunnel at
the End of the Tunnel

I came home in time for Christmas. I wanted to be gay and congenial, for the sake of the family and the holiday season, but every time a door closed, it sounded like a pistol shot.

The removal of the cataract was not painful. After five days in the hospital, I came back home to convalesce. I adjusted quickly to inserting and wearing the contact lens. It was a little devil to handle; it slipped out of my hand and clung to my clothes like a sandspur. The lens in the left eye balanced my vision. I now had depth perception. This good news was balanced by a cataract developing in the other eye. It would be operated on when it matured at some unspecified time—here we go again, I thought.

The lens should have relieved some of my tensions, yet it was still an infirmity. I hesitated to drive at night. And, since much of my comedy is physical, I was always afraid that I'd lose my lens in the middle of a scene. This feeling of helplessness, of moving around on a visual crutch, depressed me. I felt old age had crept up on me at fifty-four. My throbbing, flashes and sweating returned. The healthy cries and laughter of the children bored through my head like a dentist's drill. I had all the crotchets of a granddaddy: irritable, withdrawn yet garrulous. I was certainly a poor companion for my family. Huddling in my homespun cocoon, I even turned down television and film offers.

My personal physician suggested psychiatric treatment. Obviously, much of my hurt was self-inflicted. All right. I certainly needed help. A psychiatrist worked with me for a while, and then had to go off to Europe to deliver a professional paper. He turned me over to No. 2, whom I met with every day, several times a day. I had confidence in him—he was head of the psychiatric department of a large hospital.

He tried to give me insight into the heavy load of guilt I'd been shouldering all my life—irrational, uncalled-for guilt: that sex is furtive, and nice girls must be put on a pedestal, a complex which gummed up my youth . . . The feeling that I wasn't handsome enough to be worthy of beautiful women . . . Why hadn't I done more to keep my father alive? And my brother? . . . My feverish gambling, which now became a way of proving that I had all the zip and daring of those days before my depression. My losses only made me feel I was undermining my family's future . . . All these stabs of conscience grew out of each other and fed on each other.

Guilt is a complex phenomenon. It lurks in the back of everyone's head. Primitive man, the doctor told me, must have watched a flood wash away his hut and felt sure it was *his* fault. Many people rid themselves of guilt through religion: confession, absolution, the belief that evil is God's retribution, beyond your control. But I was never able to believe divine authority, handed down by priests and rabbis. I never accepted anybody's authority. The psychiatrist tried to make me realize that every disaster was not my fault . . . that pleasures are not sinful . . . that I could say *no!* and my children would still love me. He told me if I could just get *angry*, I might be able to vent my guilt. People like Harry Cohn exploded into cursing furies with as little guilt as brushing teeth. He lashed his underlings and went home to a good sleep. I couldn't do it.

To make life harder for myself, I took to telling my troubles to every friend I could back into a corner. After a while, I ran out of corners. I was pleading for help, I guess. Hoping that someone, somewhere, would come up with the Perry Mason clue, the magic word that would solve my case. I made my scream louder: I talked of suicide. Psychiatrists assured me that a man who talks about suicide seldom goes through with it. The people who threaten to jump from bridges and hotel ledges want attention, some cop to tell their troubles to. I didn't jump off a bridge—I merely burned them behind me. The word filtered around Hollywood: Silvers has "problems." Then it was magnified to "Silvers is a risk." He might finish a picture; then again, he might not. I was destroying my own career. And my gambling was another form of self-destruction. I could no longer smile at my own folly. Everything looked grimmer, heavier, harder than it ever looked before.

My marriage hit a low point one Sunday. Some friends stopped in and I was loquacious. Evelyn reproached me for talking so much about myself. I felt I had to get out of the house. I hopped into my car and drove off to see a friend and his wife. When I came home, my suitcases were standing in the driveway, packed with my clothes. Evelyn had a distant look in her eye. She had made up her mind.

"I've made a reservation at the Beverly Hills Hotel," she said. "That's where you'll stay."

I was stunned. "Why? What have I done?"

"I can't have you talking like that in front of the children." She had sent the children out, to visit with friends, to spare them this confrontation. She was determined to have me leave right then and there.

If only I could have said *no!* Or an angry *never.* Throw the bags into the house. Break a lamp. Do something irrational but vehement, to release my outrage. No, I was paralyzed by guilt. Somehow, the separation became entirely my fault.

I docilely picked up my bags and moved into the hotel, where all my self-reproach mushroomed in the dark, lonely nights. In all the years I'd been a bachelor, I was self-sufficient. I enjoyed being alone. Now, after nine years of marriage, I could not bear to be alone in that room.

Two months later, Evelyn suggested I might as well come home. I tried to be more outgoing, more aware of Evelyn's needs. And the children's. I played along with the game of Keeping the Trouble from the Children. More self-deluding nonsense. You can't keep anything from children; they *sense* tensions and unhappiness. Even through the walls.

In desperation, I switched to psychiatrist No. 3. He and my personal physician agreed that I needed intensive psychiatric treatment. They recommended Las Encinas, a hospital on a large wooded estate in Pasadena. It was known for its therapy facilities, in the secluded atmosphere of a vacation resort.

My doctor drove me there in his car, to introduce me to the staff and make my entrance easier. It was dark when we arrived in Pasadena, and my doctor lost his way. I took this as an unfavorable omen.

I moved into a pleasant little cottage, with a small living room, bedroom, kitchen and bath. Surrounded by trees, with not another cottage in sight, it reminded me of what the Catskills must have been before the social directors took over. The male nurse searched my clothes for possibly dangerous weapons—knife, razor blade, nail file. And then a sedative put me to sleep.

My therapist and constant companion, whom I called Robby, was so conscientious and warm-hearted that he had picked up some of his patients' problems. He was deeply troubled. There were moments when I had to assure him tomorrow would be a better day.

The head psychiatrist at Las Encinas, my No. 4, worked diligently with me. I also developed a rapport with a doctor who checked my physical status. He had five daughters, too, a sympathetic bond anywhere in the world. No. 4 played golf in doctors' tournaments. One of my modest achievements, which gave me a great lift, was correcting his swing. He said I took eight strokes off his game. He invited me to his house several times for dinner. Since the staff was strictly segregated from the patients, this friendliness indicated the doctor believed my mind was operating on all cylinders. He kept urging me, "Don't identify with the extreme cases you see here. Consider this episode as a rest period." I tried to see it that way, but my anxieties didn't.

I said good morning every day to an elderly gentleman who might have been the model for Mr. Magoo. Quite senile, he had to be helped on his walks by an orderly. After a few weeks, he suddenly spoke to me. "Sergeant Bilko, are you on duty here?"

Slight gasp from his orderly, who said to me, "This is a small miracle. Those are the first words I've heard him say in three months."

Somehow the vision of Sergeant Bilko had broken through the terrible wall he put around himself. He was a member of a wealthy family, and occasionally his mind recalled an important business deal. Then he would borrow two dollars from me for "the streetcar to the Bank of Los Angeles." His therapist returned the loan next day.

When you're confined in an institution—fed, housed, exercised, carefully watched—it's like being a baby again. After a while, if the routine changes, you behave like one. The physician came to my cabin every other day for my examination. I would practice on a little putting green nearby that had its own problem: elephant grass. One day he did not appear. I putted and stewed and walked and stewed. *I wanted my visit.* Finally, I marched into the doctor's office and exploded right in front of his other patient: "Why did you let me down?"

He said he had come by my cabin and I wasn't in. He took my temperature, assured me I was in good shape, and I left. I felt great: I had straightened out my doctor. In my euphoria, I walked out the rear of the building, missed the last step and slammed onto the concrete pavement right on my face and my eye. Fortunately, not the left eye. I lay there, blood streaming from my lip, and I smiled. I didn't feel guilty after this fall—it wasn't my fault. It was just bad luck. I could accept it.

I knew enough not to move until a doctor examined me. The paths behind the offices were deserted. After a while a woman in a white uniform walked by. I called to her for help. She recoiled from me. I must have looked like a violent case, with blood all over my shirt. She was not a nurse but a kitchen worker, and I suppose they had rules not to touch patients. Again I flared up. "Now you listen to me! You go in there and tell the doctor a patient is hurt!" She did.

My doctor ran out with his black tool bag. I had wrenched my leg and my split lip needed some stitching. But I felt elated all day. I had demonstrated the power of positive anger.

One day all my anxieties hit me at once. I couldn't sit. I couldn't stand. My whole body was an exposed nerve. I called the head doctor and broke into tears; I said, "Help! I can't handle it this day."

"All right, Phil, just relax." He called the dispensary and a nurse brought over a small container of liquid. It was greenish, and to this day I don't know what it was. The doctor said, "This will get you through the day, but don't ask for it again if you can possibly help."

It did help. Peace and contentment were my companions the rest of that day.

Some time later, I was urged by Freddie Fields to make an appearance at the SHARE show, one of the most lavish "in" benefits in Hollywood, patronized by top echelons of the movie industry. I had entertained at the last three shows. Freddie wanted me to be seen, to prove that I had not completely disintegrated. My psychiatrist let me leave Las Encinas for the occasion. Since I was in no mood to perform, I took a table as a guest, with Freddie and Polly Bergen, Evelyn, her mother and stepfather.

As I dressed for the night, fright poured over me like wet concrete. I'd be meeting old cronies, people I'd worked for and men who knew me at the top of my form. I begged my psychiatrist to give me some of the magic potion; he said I did not need it. Well, I wanted to have it in my pocket. Liquid security. The psychiatrist presented me with a *pint* of it. "Take a little if you need it. If you take it all, it could kill you."

It was a good bet. A little drastic, maybe, but smart. He was betting that I was strong enough to beat that bottle.

At the show I smiled at everybody, I applauded everything. I was the perfect benefit audience. Next morning I presented the bottle to my doctor. I had not touched a drop.

I lost track of time at Las Encinas. One day my psychiatrist told me I could leave. "You don't belong here. The best cure for you is work." I felt I had accomplished nothing here.

When I came home—surprise! Evelyn told me she wanted a divorce.

On what grounds? I could not pin it down. Some of it, of

course, was my gambling obsession. But most of it was her feeling that our personalities were hopelessly mismatched.

I packed my bags and moved into an apartment in Los Angeles. I sat on the edge of my bed and tried to analyze my position. After four psychiatrists and two months in a hospital, I was back where I'd started. Nowhere.

Except that now, I was all alone.

The divorce proceedings were a blur of lawyers' voices. Ed Traubner, my business manager and friend of forty years, urged me to reject some of the arrangements in the settlement. He pleaded with me, "This is an extremely unfavorable set of terms." But he couldn't persuade me. I was tired of all those voices. The divorce was granted for incompatibility.

It had one wonderful, almost magical, effect—I gave up heavy gambling. What Evelyn had not been able to do while married, she accomplished by divorce. I was gratefully indebted to her.

Shep Fields, Freddie's brother, who also works in the CMA agency, is a very close friend. He planned to drive to Las Vegas to look over an act, and I wanted to go along, to take me out of myself.

He refused. "You'll get lost in the casinos there."

I promised I'd only gamble what I had in my pocket— about $400.

"No. They'll carry you on credit."

That was one cause of my indifference to losing. I always paid my debts, so casinos and bookies were happy to extend credit. Now I had a heavy drain on my earnings: an immense settlement, five children and two households to support. I told Shep, "I promise you I won't ask for credit."

"Is your promise good anymore?"

Good question. Could I gamble on myself, quit while I was ahead? "I promise, Shep."

I went into a casino that night with my $400. I experienced a peculiar sensation: My hand trembled when I dropped money on the crap table. And my palms sweated. I was afraid of what could happen to me if I kept on gambling. And if you're afraid, you can't really gamble. I could not wait to rid myself of the money, so that I could get the hell out of there. Fear can be an enlightening and cleansing emotion. I know now that, like the alcoholic for whom there is no such thing as just one drink, for me there is no such thing as a little bet.

The doctors' prescription for my troubles was work. But work did not come very often. I made some television appearances and a few movies. My irrepressible urge to blab my troubles made even my friends worry I would not show up on cue. I did. I was still a professional. I performed as well as ever. The rest of the time, I sat in a corner of the set, like a wounded animal. Or I holed up in my dressing room, brooding. Shep Fields kept me company on these stints, or he'd send a man from the agency.

Between jobs, I spent my afternoons at the Friars Club; it became a cocoon for me. Evenings I retreated to my apartment, sitting up late to watch television. I didn't want to see people, and I didn't want anybody to see me. I was faithfully following the classic pattern of withdrawal. The days dissolved into months, the months quick-cut to years. My life became a montage of drifting on a blue-gray sea of depression.

A Guide for the Married Man reunites me with Gene Kelly as director. For me, it's a long way from 1950 and *Summer Stock* at MGM. Making movies is not fun anymore. This is an independent production, and aside from the stars, Walter Matthau and Robert Morse, the important performers are working on a "cameo" deal: $10,000 for two days' work. This is a gimmick to get a lot of star names on the marquee at wholesale rates: Jack Benny, Art Carney, Sid Caesar, Terry-Thomas, Polly Bergen, Joey Bishop. But if your scene runs one minute after midnight of the second day, the producer must pay you another $10,000. So there's the inevitable rush—let's get it in the can, we'll fix it later. Despite this, the picture is mostly a hilarious string of farce sequences. I finish my dubbing—handicapped because there is no film to which I can match my words—at exactly two minutes before midnight.

Kraft Music Hall: these shows are made in New York. I meet Jo-Carroll on the street, near the Plaza. A warm, joyous reunion. She's the wife of Russell Stoneham, a producer for CBS. She takes me home to meet her two boys. What a happy family. Jo-Carroll is lovelier than when I met her eighteen years ago, and I'm happy she is so happy. She and Russell are a great comfort during my stay.

The pool in my apartment house is my therapy. I'm no Mark Spitz. I thrash around, I kick up a spray like a sidewheel steamboat. It's exercise and ultimately relaxing, because I end up exhausted.

The gambler in me needs a specific goal, a race. I wager I can swim twelve lengths. The pool is almost Olympic length; I have to time myself so that when I feel almost exhausted, I'm near the shallow end, where I can stand up if I have to.

I even dive off the high board. I can't swim with a contact lens—it slips out in the water. This isn't much of a handicap, since I don't want to see how high I am anyhow. There is no guard at the pool when I go in. It's deserted. So my twelve lengths is another test, and an accomplishment. I can beat the water—why can't I overcome my other fears?

Another Kraft: with Joe Frazier, the heavyweight champ. Joe displays his speed and instant reflexes. It's the time of the daily bomb scares in New York; we receive a phone warning at the rehearsal. Before I can find the elevator, the champ is five blocks up the street.

La Scala restaurant, Los Angeles: Buddy Ebsen in makeup. He's making a pilot film for a series about a hillbilly family living in a mansion in Beverly Hills. From what he tells me, I frankly think this idea is good for a one-shot.

Six years later, Paul Henning, his producer, asks me to play a small part, as a fast-talking con man who sells the

Staten Island ferry to the hillbillies. What's my fee? I'm so indebted to Buddy for his open-handed support in *Yokel Boy*, I'm happy to do it at minimum scale. My agent later raises the price—"Hillbillies" is not a charity case— and I make seven episodes. It's like the old days: fun again, and working with Buddy.

I promised my daughters when they reached thirteen they would have a night on the town. Tracey is a tall thirteen now, and oh, so cool. Evelyn puts her into a glamour gown, with an upswept hairdo, and Tracey is ready to slink onto the cover of Vogue. I arrange for a center-front table at the Coconut Grove, to catch Liza Minnelli.

The house is crowded with show people, from whom I get those wondering glances . . . "if he finds them any younger, he'll have to bring his own Pablum . . ." I don't know why, but very few people connect me with five daughters.

Near the end of Liza's act—a rocking, socking explosion of tremendous talent—she introduces me in a little speech: "He was there, always near me, when I was a child. He was my Uncle Phil." She leans over the platform and kisses me.

Now, for the first time, Tracey is impressed. A little.

We take a cab home, driven by a moonlighting hot-dog vendor who needs directions. Tracey takes over. "Please stay in your lane—we're not in a big hurry." She kisses me good-night on the doorstep, and warns me to go straight home. As soon as I enter my apartment, she phones: "I just wanted to see that you got home all right."

Seems to me I was diapering her only ten minutes ago.

Buona Sera, Mrs. Campbell: Mel Frank liked my work in *Forum* and now he wants me to be the father of three sons. It's a clever, warm comedy, shot in a village near Rome. Telly Savalas, Peter Lawford and I are in an Air Force platoon in wartime. We are all intimate with Gina Lollobrigida— at different times—and she gives birth to a girl after we leave.

The platoon holds a reunion in the village, and the three of us desperately want to know whose child it is. We never find out.

Lino, the virile husky assigned to drive me from Rome to the filming in the village, attaches himself as my companion. He informs me that he'd had a worse depression than mine and in time it disappeared. He assures me, so will mine. Everybody's a psychiatrist.

I use some of my paternal experience in the last scene of the film. My wife (Shelley Winters) laments as we pack: "I always wanted a little girl. With me, you have three boys. With her, a little girl!"

I persuade the producer to let me add: "I didn't do anything different."

When I come back from Italy, I'm jittery. I can't sit down; it's like sitting on broken glass. I'm frightened to be alone. I put myself into Cedars-Sinai Hospital for psychiatric treatment. The doctors allow me to go out for the day whenever I wish, with a therapist. He accompanies me to the beach, or a movie.

My psychiatrist (this is No. 1 again) tells me there's nothing really wrong with me. My anxieties will all go away —someday. But when? When?

Three patients, whom I've come to know, commit suicide. That shakes me up, but still I know that's not a good exit for me. How could I do an encore?

I'm not working, my expenses are adding up and I'm bugged by the knowledge that I can't see very well with both eyes now. Everything I do seems futile and wasteful, but I don't know which way to turn. I move back to my apartment.

Shep Fields says, "You've got to work." He ships me off to a nightclub in Sydney, Australia. Why Australia? Well, 1968 is the 200th anniversary of Capt. James Cook's sighting of its east coast. It is June, and I insist on a hotel with a swimming pool. My accompanist and straight man is Leo DeLyon, whom I worked with before in clubs. A gentleman and a polished musician.

The night before we leave, we see the film *Airport*. Van Heflin is the mad bomber who plants one on a plane to collect insurance. That triples my tremors about flying: Australia is a 7,000-mile hop. As we walk to the plane, I quip to Leo, "If Van Heflin is on this plane, I'm getting off!"

I put my coat up on the overhead rack, and I see, sitting directly in front of me, Van Heflin. Leo turns pale. Am I also afflicted with *future* vision? Van confesses he hates flying, too.

I discover a few miscalculations in Sydney.

(1) It is June all right, but that is their winter. I dive into the pool once and freeze.

(2) Queen Elizabeth and Prince Philip are my opposition. They're in Sydney to represent the Commonwealth, and they're a hard act to beat. Everybody is out watching them. One night, I count twenty-four people in the club. At the only other club, Tony Bennett with a twenty-piece orchestra draws only eighteen people.

The operators of the room, an Irishman and a Chinese named Wong, are remarkably unconcerned. Neither one can blame the other. In his last booking, Mr. Wong lost face because he hired Marie MacDonald, the film sexpot, at $5,000 a week, on the assumption he was getting Jeanette MacDonald. And he didn't understand why she couldn't sing "The Italian Street Song."

The young man assigned to drive me from the hotel to the club soon confesses he is terrified to be alone. Is there some secret international underground that brings us all together?

Sydney is not a particularly swinging city even on its 200th birthday. Still, I can't fall asleep. I long for the magic potion of Las Encinas. Mr. Wong refers me to a Chinese doctor, who turns me over to an Australian. This gentleman produces another elixir that brings sweet rest. And he assures me I am not in a state of permanent depression. He believes it comes and goes in periods of five to seven years. And someday I will wake up, as if from a bad dream.

This is what my doctor in Los Angeles told me.

Well, it's now five years since the cataract set me off on this downer. The doctors seem so sure of my recovery—why doesn't my body wise up?

In Los Angeles again: I really don't want to work. I don't want to leave my apartment. Larry Gelbart, co-author of the book of *Forum*, drags me out for his television pilot, "Bel-Air Patrol." The community of Bel-Air near Beverly Hills operates a patrol service of retired policemen. I'm one of the men in the car: all the maids adore me, I live like a king, lunch at the richest houses. It's a funny format that opens the screen to many adventures, and the pilot is as good as Bilko.

The networks pronounce it dead on arrival.

The Boatniks: a Disney production with Robert Morse and Mickey Shaughnessy, made in Newport, 1970. I'm the head hoodlum in a jewelry heist. To escape a roadblock, we rent a boat, hide the jewels in a basket of chicken and head for Mexico.

I head straight for my motel and stay there. Buddy Ebsen, who has a house and boat here, Bobby and Mickey do their best to pull me out of my cocoon. One night I have a relapse: I am my old self again. Bobby steers me to a cocktail bar that features a pianist who played for Martha Raye. He's clever and quick, and almost subconsciously I slip into comedy bits. I do about an hour of bright, witty material. The bar becomes jammed. Bobby Morse is elated at my sudden change in attitude. I'm told the bar was jammed for the next three nights, waiting for me. But I never returned to it.

The escape scene in the boat demands two of my weakest talents—swimming and eyesight. We shoot it in the mammoth Disney tank in California. The Coast Guard boat, officered by Bobby Morse, rams us. Trying to rescue me with a life preserver, he circles the basket of chicken holding the jewels. I have to dive down under the water to rescue the basket. The director won't use a double because he likes the close-up of my panic reaction. And he wants to continue it under water.

I go down, fully clothed, and lose my contact lens. I'm practically blind. Under water, my frantic thrashing looks like one of those giant octopus battles.

"Great!" the director sings out. "Your panic is hilarious." I wasn't acting.

I return to acting in *How the Other Half Loves,* my first Broadway show in ten years. (Where have I been?) And my first show ever without music.

I've run into Robert Morley at the West Coast tracks— we're fellow punters, as he puts it—and he is now a big hit in this play in London. When Michael Myerberg acquires the American rights, Morley insists I'm the only choice. The role is written for a distracted and stuffy English businessman. After a prolonged gasp, director Gene Saks agrees. Sandy Dennis will co-star.

The play demands great precision. The single set serves as two different rooms. One is my living room in Scarsdale; the other is the living room of my employee, who is carrying on an affair with my wife. The action takes place in both rooms, sometimes simultaneously and unrelated, and the characters must be careful not to confuse them. The Americanization loses something. Class distinctions are still important to the English; the upperclass businessman has a drawing room. In Scarsdale, that's a living room, and my employee has one, too. There is not much contrast. The simultaneous action of the two households confuses the audience a bit.

Excellent notices in Washington: "Jolly good fun" . . . "It surely will repeat its London success . . ." I am elated. Now, at last, I can carry a show without song and dance.

The New York critics find it "grimly frantic . . . singularly heavy-handed." Clive Barnes salutes "the remarkable Mr. Silvers . . . his performance has style, pace and assurance." That's not enough. Audiences are sparse.

How the Other Half Loves closes after 107 performances. I know it's one of the best performances I've ever given—and the play is not a success. I've never had such a short run on the stage in my life. Anyhow, my depression is a success. It's running longer than Herbert Hoover's.

CHAPTER 16

". . . And the Winner Is—"

The Ahmanson Theater complex in Los Angeles had already booked its second play for the 1971 season, *The Caine Mutiny*. Now it was looking for an opener. A young agent at CMA, Frank Levy, had a happy notion: Why not revive *A Funny Thing Happened on the Way to the Forum* with the man whom the authors wanted from the beginning?

I was hooked right away. Burt Shevelove, co-author of the book, agreed to direct. And Nancy Walker, my wife in *Do Re Mi*, signed on as Domina, the pre-Women's Lib wife of the philandering Senex. Steve Sondheim wrote two new songs for her.

I was hooked all right, but years of pulsations, hot sweats and depression had made me apprehensive. I had been away from musicals since *Do Re Mi*—a lifetime ago. I'd played this kind of rowdy part before, and yet the butterflies of opening night hit me as I walked into the first cast meeting. In the first reading, everyone is cautious, feeling out the part, feeling out the other actors. Nobody wants to *give* too much, because he doesn't want to be caught wrong from the start by the director.

These people were different. They greeted me as if we'd been on the road since Wilmington. They were mostly young, they were right for the parts and they were enthusiastic. Smiles of delight lighted up the circle as we read. We were in understanding, creative hands. After all, the director was one of the co-authors. There was a heady perfume of success in that hall. What could I possibly worry about? I felt a sense of joy, refreshment. It was an exciting romp, in which I could use all my skills. This was my real medium. I could expand on the musical stage. I could be bigger than myself. *Better.*

I went home with the production dancing around in my mind. Complete. And in color. The phone rang, and I picked it up instantly. I caught myself—my God, what was I doing? For so many years, the ring of a phone literally made me wince. It was the messenger of bad news, and I dreaded answering it. Now I picked it up like a box of chocolates. It was a good friend from New York; we chatted about the weather here and the weather there. I felt relaxed that night. Easy sleep, and no hard-edged, troubled tossing. I was almost happy.

I immersed myself in the show, and for several weeks didn't want to believe too much had changed. I didn't want to push my luck. Maybe what I experienced was a freak of climate. Or vitamins. But as the days passed, the grass did look greener, and the sky was clearer, smog and all. I looked forward to receiving phone calls. I wondered why people didn't call more often. I enjoyed lunch with people. I enjoyed people without lunch. I was revived, renewed. I had crawled out of the mud. It gave me a real sense of power. I could beat any curve my brain or body could throw against me.

It was seven years since my depression began. My lead collar had melted away, as my doctors had predicted. I was free at last.

Steve went to work with me on the lyrics. A very meticulous man, he demanded I sing every syllable at twice the speed of the original production. He explained, "It was always you I had in mind when I wrote these numbers. Then you turned down the show. Now that I got you, I want it done the way I always hoped it would be done."

The language of the show maintained the flavor of Plautus, 200 years B.C. It required intense concentration and preciseness. (There were no anachronisms, as there were in the movie version. Only one line remained intact from Plautus: Miles Gloriosus, glorious ham of a warrior, proclaiming, "I am a parade!")

The previews rolled along beautifully. The happy company

stayed happy, a rare occurrence in musicals. To help me get "up" for my first entrance to deliver the prologue, the men stood offstage left and ad-libbed the muffled noise of a crowd scene—"Go get 'em . . . hubba-hubba . . . wurra-wurra . . ." I backed onto the stage, quieting them, discovered to my surprise the audience out front, and went into the welcoming speech.

I had some trouble with the rough-and-tumble business. My right eye was still building up the cataract. I could not see on that side. Sometimes I fell over a prop bench, receiving a big unwanted laugh from the audience. At the end of the prologue, I leaped onto the back of the three Proteans, to be carried off. Marc Breaux, my favorite choreographer, was their leader. I had to land on a certain spot on his back, below his neck, so that he could grab me. Otherwise I'd fall into the orchestra pit.

The authors were delighted; at last, their show was being performed the way they had written it.

Opening night: my usual premonitions of disaster.

I once asked Ethel Merman her secret—she plays the best opening night of any musical comedy performer. She never had any doubts, she told me. "If any of them out there could do what I'm doing, they'd be up here doing it." Somehow, that never helped me.

My premonitions this time were more than fulfilled. Four—count 'em—four disasters, pyramiding one on top of the other. All in the first act.

When I came on for the prologue, I was rocked by a thunder wave of welcoming applause. It startled me. Goof 1: *I forgot the prologue.* My mouth went dry, as if I'd swallowed alum. The opening lines were: "Playgoers, I bid you welcome. The theater is a temple, and we are here to worship the gods of comedy and tragedy . . ." After 200 years, I blurted out, "Welcome, playgoers! The theater is a—a—church? . . ."

Standing at the back of the auditorium, Burt Shevelove turned to Steve and sighed. "If a nice Jewish boy like Phil Silvers can't remember 'temple'—we're in for a rough evening!"

Goof 2: When I called "Raise up the curtain!" the curtain

was designed to drop instead, into a long trough with a cover. This night, the curtain did not drop all the way. One of the Proteans kicked it into the trough. Then the cover fell—clamping his foot like a bear trap. I stalled and repeated while his partners pried the heavy cover open and dragged him off. Our tempo slowed badly.

Goof 3: Larry Blyden, Domina's prissy, precise slave clerk, came on for an important scene in which I had to steal his recipe book of potions. It was my passport to freedom. Larry patted his tunic, where the book is hidden, and turned green. He'd forgotten it. I stumbled offstage, to the prop table, bumping around in the dark. After some long minutes, I ran back with a shamefully limp ad-lib: "Oh, those stupid Roman stage-hands!" And the situation was confused, because now, how could I steal it from him? Confusion on stage is not funny unless it's wildly funny, like a man losing his pants. I lost the audience right there. It took about ten minutes to bring them back into the play. And then—

Goof 4: Marc Breaux, now playing a Roman soldier, marched in to announce the impending arrival of Miles Gloriosus. "He is but half a league away, and he bids you honor *this!*" "This" was a marriage contract. But Marc did not have the scroll in his hand. Marc is a gentle man; he looked at me grief-stricken, and I thought he would disembowel himself with his sword. Larry Blyden, offstage, saw the crisis. He raced to the prop table and slipped the scroll to me. That created further confusion. Some of the audience began to think they were attending an Azusa High School production.

I had been a ferocious gambler; my whole way of life was based on the certainty that I'd win some and lose some. But this string of blunders was beyond the laws of probability. It was not fair.

We gained ground in the second act, but the reviews were so-so. The second night was perfect, of course; unfortunately, the word of mouth had scared off half the audience. I always believed a show could be improved after the opening. We kept the faith and worked like demons. In the third week, Dan Sullivan, the all-important critic from the Los Angeles *Times*, returned for another look. His review this time brought in the customers. We slowly built to capacity audiences.

Now was the time to plan to extend the run, play San Francisco and other West Coast cities. Larry Blyden called a meeting of the cast, to explore means of raising money for a tour. Nothing came of it. After the show closed, he flew down to Houston, his home town, to raise money for a tour that would end in New York. His budget was comparatively low for a musical, $175,000—new shows were opening in New York for $750,000 and a million—but we had no movie or subsidiary rights to offer investors. Freddie Fields was so determined to have me play this show that he waived his agency commission. Greater love hath no man. I agreed to work for half price. Backers reneged on their promises, and after a great, long hassle, Larry put the road show together. He got $40,000 from the cast and, I think, $12 from a newsboy.

By now some of the cast had moved into other shows, and Nancy Walker did not want to tour.

We opened in Chicago at the end of February in the worst possible theater, the McVickers, a big old carbarn that had been showing porno movies. Our manager put up signs outside the theater:

LIVE!   LIVE!

NOT A MOTION PICTURE!

Again we built up from a slow start. The road show of *High Button Shoes* played Chicago for a year. I felt *Forum* could have stayed six months. But the producers had already rented the Lunt-Fontanne Theater in New York. We had to come in. Five previews were scheduled, starting Tuesday. That night a closing notice was posted backstage, "a legal formality." Wednesday, the producers were so short of cash they decided to open Thursday, instead of next Tuesday. I was "up" for the opening, without my jitters, because in my mind this night was scheduled as a preview.

The opening scene played at breakneck speed. We were great. The response was great. Then the battens of the scenery broke; they hooked onto the asbestos curtain and swayed back and forth. It could have been a disaster, but I was ready this time. I surveyed the holocaust, then turned to the audience with a look that belongs only to me, and said, "Rome wasn't built in a day."

The scenery was fixed and everyone turned in an almost perfect performance. I pranced through it. I was Top Banana in a Roman toga.

The result made up for all our struggles and disasters. Clive Barnes of the *Times* said: "Mr. Silvers is a total delight. There is a new light that has brightened up Broadway." Doug Watt, *Daily News*: "Phil Silvers is absolutely perfect. How could we have let him go?" Hobe Morrison, *Variety*: "Silvers is at his superb best." Richard Watts, New York *Post*: "Silvers, one of the season's greatest joys." Walter Kerr, *New York Times*: "Phil Silvers is a national treasure."

They are the greatest set of reviews since *My Fair Lady*.

My warmest valentine came from the Kanins. Garson and Ruth had a country home, where they arose at 6 A.M. for a brisk two-mile hike. The night our show opened, Garson could not sleep. He told me: "I fell asleep around five and missed my walk. Then I felt this dear woman, who is supposed to love me so much, shaking me out of my sleep. It was six-thirty. 'Get up! Get up!' I thought we were on fire. Ruth cried, 'Read this, read this!' It was the Barnes review. I didn't need any more sleep."

I heard, from a usually well-informed leak, that David Merrick postponed his opening of *Sugar* so he wouldn't have to compete with us for awards. The change in our opening night was a bit of serendipity: It made us eligible for the 1972 Tony Awards, the American theater's supreme accolade. They have an emotional hold on everyone on the stage because they are decided by your peers. After I was nominated for best actor in a musical, I instinctively knew I would win. This is no conceit. I just knew. I wanted the man who got me there to share this joy with me. I flew him in from California. My date for the evening was Shep Fields.

Larry Blyden was named best supporting actor in a musical. This sent me off on a cloud of exhilaration which I find difficult to describe. He had worked so hard getting us there, and now he won his own Tony.

When Gwen Verdon announced, "And the winner is—Phil Silvers," I bounced on that stage with the exuberance of an elated panther. I went into a hysterical, happy routine, forgetting it was a coast-to-coast broadcast, limited to a certain time. I naturally was thrilled, but actually I went ape because of Larry's award.

I also swept all the other awards that year. The Top Banana returns.

Offstage, my life remained quiet. I lived alone in my favorite suite, high up in Delmonico's Hotel. I had lunch and dinner dates with a few friends. I enjoyed sitting at an outdoor café across from the Plaza, watching the people-zoo parade by. And all those lovely girls in their summer dresses. I no longer winced when I thought of my broken marriages, and I did not speculate on whether I would or would not marry again. I walked in Central Park, I lolled around in a Turkish bath, I stopped in at the Friars Club to play pinochle. I was serenely alive, savoring the best of each day.

I could sense, by the electricity crackling between stage and audience, that the customers were enjoying the show, even if the orchestra floor was only half full. Summertime, in the theater, the livin' is not easy. The temperature hung in the nineties for weeks, and stage shows languished and expired. Some weeks we lost money; some we broke even. For once, I was not hanging by my thumbs. If we could hold out until August, I knew our business would build until 1973. It was probably the best year of my life, and I looked forward to the fall.

I never expected it to be *my* fall.

In the weeks to come, I tried to piece together and rearrange the sequence of events of that wretched weekend. What did I do wrong? What could I have done differently that might have saved me?

I wasn't eating regularly or wisely. But then, for most of my life, my meals were catch-as-catch-can, except occasionally when I was married. On the road, the show came first. If it was an eight-thirty curtain, I did not have dinner at a conventional seven o'clock. I ate at five, to give myself time to digest the meal, so I wouldn't feel heavy and sluggish. The *Forum* curtain went up at seven-thirty; my dinner hour was four o'clock. If I did not have a late lunch with friends, or I stayed too long at the Friars, I'd gulp a malted milk or a pastrami sandwich before I walked into the theater at six. That delicious, lethal deli food is an occupational hazard.

After my show, about ten-thirty, I liked a small supper. Pseudolus was an energy-burning role; I was onstage for most of the show. Well, room service at my hotel closed at ten-thirty. I'm a loner, but I hate to eat alone. Unless I met friends, it was again a hurried sandwich or omelette before a book and bedtime. One thing I did have: enough sleep. Ever since I put on long pants, I've never slept more than six hours anyhow.

Friday and Saturday, July 28–29: After the shows, I stayed up with friends who had troubles. Marital . . . family . . . a wife had just died. Now that I was out of my gloom, I wanted to show others the light. I was a missionary. We talked into the late, late hours.

Sunday, July 30: Could not sleep late. Dinner at friends' house. Everything askew: They did not have their regular kitchen help, so they sent out for a Chinese dinner. Spicy. So exhausted I could hardly sit up at the table.

Monday, July 31: Awoke early, tired and restless. Called several friends for lunch. Everybody was out. Suddenly the room began to revolve like a carnival funhouse. I threw myself on the bed. I was soaking wet, as if I'd just showered. I tried to stand up—and couldn't. This was worse than my old whammies. I phoned the hotel's bell captain. He came up in two minutes, took a quick look and phoned my personal physician. He was out. His nurse said she would come right over. I

phoned my agency. Everybody was out, except one agent—
Irving Squires—on a long-distance line. Otherwise he would
have been out, too.

Squires walked in my door together with the nurse, a most
attractive, take-charge woman, Alice Hogan. Both agreed I
must go into the hospital. As they helped me into a cab, a
hippie on a motorcycle yelled, "Hey, Phil Silvers! What kind
of act is that?"

St. Clare's Hospital emergency room took a cardiogram.
The physician filling in for my doctor arrived, an excessively
cheerful man. My cardiogram was inconclusive. I was put into
the intensive care unit and given intravenous injections. Three
doctors consulted, and could not decide what ailed me. Next
day, the room began to revolve again. And the ceiling fell in.

It was a stroke. A minor one, they assured me, but major
enough to close *Forum*. My brain was not permanently af-
fected, and I was not paralyzed. But I temporarily lost control
of my arms and legs. The intravenous injections, given to me as
a general precaution, had reduced the severity of the stroke.
If I had been onstage, or alone in the street, it could have been
my final curtain.

Why me? Why now, after I was back on top of my career?
My physicians had no answer. My body had been accumulat-
ing more than the usual quota of hurts and shocks in the seven
years of my downslide. It was again blind bad luck. Some accidents had come up in my favor; this one, the big one, was
against me.

My hard-working friends in *Forum* were out of work. This
time I did not lash myself with guilt. I had not chosen this
stroke; I could not have prevented it. *It was not my fault.* It's
a peculiar business when the livelihood of twenty-five people
hangs on the health of one man.

After a few weeks the hospital promoted me into therapy
to exercise my limbs, to regain control. They gave me a four-
legged walker, weights, an exercise program to work on. I
would not do it. I told the therapists I was trying, but I wasn't.
I resented lifting weights, hobbling around.

My nurses, doctors, friends who came to visit were puzzled,

then exasperated. How could a man who had worked on the stage for fifty years—and comedy requires application and self-control—not use that discipline to make himself walk again? It seemed so outrageously perverse to them.

I had been struck down by dumb chance, and I felt that only good luck could cure me now. No benign power was watching over me, equalizing the good and the bad. There was no fair system of probability Up There. I believed I had no control over my future. Why try to make choices? I lost my will.

My therapist, a most genial, enthusiastic soul, handed the list of exercises to me and said, "Starting tomorrow, someone else will see what he can do with you."

An instant stab: she'd let me down. I respected her, and I did not know what inner sore spots a new therapist might rub. I pleaded with her to stick with me.

"You're a waste of time," she said abruptly. "You'll never do what I ask you to do."

That day I started to exercise. My will toughened up, with a little help from my friends—including both my former wives. Calls, cards, notes, gifts from people I hadn't heard from in years. A giant red balloon arrived with the message: "I know this will give you a lift." And next day, a wire: ". . . we're all praying for you . . . Positive you'll be fine in good time. Love, Frank Sinatra."

We hadn't talked since Miami, sixteen years ago.

Notes from other long-lost pals. Bing Crosby. George Kennedy. People from *Yokel Boy* and burlesque. And visits from Father Bill—now Monsignor William J. McCormack. St. Clare's is a Catholic hospital, and one of the priests who made the rounds evidently told him of me. Bill was still hip—only his title had changed. "Let me lay a little prayer on you," he said —and implored the Hebrew prophets to rescue me. He visited four times, and lit up each day.

Some time later: a buzz of voices in the hall. A nurse hurried in to straighten out my bed. And me. Terence Cardinal Cooke was visiting the hospital and planned to stop in. We had never met, so I guessed the monsignor had told him I was breaking in a new act in Room 311. I received the cardinal with the respect due a Prince of the Church.

> *(Inside Room 311: The TV set is turned off. The cardinal enters, a man of dignity with humor.)*
> ME: *"All the priests stop in here to ask my advice. Somehow, there hasn't been a single rabbi."*
> *(Slight gasp from the nurses. The cardinal laughs.)*
> HIS EMINENCE: *"I could hardly leave the hospital without saying hello to Sergeant Bilko."*
> ME: *"I wish I was Bilko right now. You know the rates in this very Catholic hotel?"*
> HIS EMINENCE: *"You don't have to pay them."*
> ME: *"Can I quote you to the room clerk?"*
> *(The cardinal smiles, and gives me his blessing.)*

I needed all the help I could get.

I left the hospital after five weeks, walking with a cane, and returned to my apartment in Los Angeles. I could hobble a few steps without the stick, but I needed it for balance.

I had my regimen, my list of exercises. My doctors had no idea of when I might throw away my cane. Only one thing was certain: I had to do it myself. Walk, walk, walk.

It was September now: Sometimes the air was crisp, often it was as clinging wet as summer. Los Angeles is not a city for walking, like London or New York. Few interesting shop windows to inspect, no neighborhoods varying from block to block, no people strolling. In my area, anybody walking around after dark is suspect. After a while the police cars let me walk.

I lifted weights and walked the sidewalks for months, hoping I would not run into a friend who knew me when. . . . I was always an active, light-on-my-feet man, so I felt embarrassed when anyone saw my infirmity. After I met someone who wished me well, I retreated to my apartment and holed up for the rest of the day.

And one day—just the way my depression had disappeared —my stiffness was gone. I was walking with the cane, and the next moment I didn't need it. I strolled several blocks, swinging that cane as jauntily as the early Charlie Chaplin. Occasionally I slipped in a bit of soft-shoe routine.

I was standing on my own two feet again.

I have beat my depression and my cane. Nothing much can put me down now. I know, when I am in front of an audience, doing my best, nothing can stop me. I *exist* onstage. I have no intention of retiring; I have too much within me to give in entertainment. The pain I've endured, the waste I've made of years in my life, have made me a more serious, deeper comedian. Acting, in comedy or tragedy, requires understanding human emotions. I feel much more now than I did even two years ago.

It's all so clear to me now. I've gone back to people—I don't see how I can withdraw into my cocoon again. I am available to my children again. They have been through some bewildering and unhappy years, and I can talk to them on an adult level now. I am gambling on them. And work.

Goodbye, Blinky.

So long, Bilko.

I want to hear that line again: ". . . and the winner is—"

Copy 1.   B
                 Silvers
Silvers, Phil
   The laugh is on me.

                 7.95